PRAJA PARISHAD
A Saga of Sacrifices

PRAJA PARISHAD
A Saga of Sacrifices

Prof. Kul Bhushan Mohtra

PRABHAT
PAPERBACKS

Published by
PRABHAT PAPERBACKS
An imprint of Prabhat Prakashan Pvt. Ltd.
4/19 Asaf Ali Road,
New Delhi-110002 (INDIA)
e-mail: prabhatbooks@gmail.com

ISBN 978-93-95386-47-0
PRAJA PARISHAD: A Saga of Sacrifices
by Prof. Kul Bhushan Mohtra

Edition
2023

Price
₹ 500.00 (Rupees Five Hundred only)

Printed at
R-Tech Offset Printers, Delhi

Unyielding Dogra

The Praja Parishad in Jammu & Kashmir was formed to keep the spirit of democracy alive. While many buckled under various kinds of pressures, Pt. Prem Nath Dogra stood like a rock. He faced all sufferings and difficult situations with stoicism and determination despite his age.

Many observers are of the view:

'Pt. Prem Nath Dogra was the Praja Parishad or in other words, the Parishad and service to the society was Panditji. For him, India was the real mother—Bharat Mata'.

This book is therefore, dedicated to this great soul, whose mission was unity and integrity of India with equal rights for all, irrespective of religious faith and gender, as also region.

It was a long-cherished desire of many to bring out such a book that can be a torchbearer for those who believe in serving the country and mankind.

My New Task

To strengthen the operations of Bharatiya Janata Party in Jammu & Kashmir, various departments were announced with their heads in-charge earlier this year, i.e. 2017.

It was an honour for me to be entrusted with the task of heading the newly created wing of library and documentation. I have been associated with the Bharatiya Janata Party for the past two decades now. As I have contributed mostly in the industrial sector, this department was not only new, but a challenging one as well.

I strongly feel that the Praja Parishad, a patriotic movement, should be known to one and all. All the activites of the party and the contributions of its workers really deserve recognition by each and every citizen of the country. It is, therefore, with great pride I took up this task and did all possible research, starting from the end of the autocracy in our state, the sad communal Partition of India in 1947, and the emergence of the new dispensation which was called Lok Shahi in J&K.

This whole transformation in the state involved a long chain of events, starting with the Praja Parishad, which later got merged with the Bharatiya Jana Sangh (BJS) and now incarnated as the Bharatiya Janata Party (BJP).

It is essential to go back to our history to know about the series of events that happened and the long-drawn out movement to bring our state on par with other states of the country–a movement that frustrated the designs of separatists and semi-separatists.

The Great Movement

The enormity of the struggle to remove the barriers between J&K and the rest of India can be understood by the situation wherein as many as 16 people were shot dead and many injured while trying to hoist the National Tricolour on this land. Thousands were put behind bars to suffer horrible conditions. Amongst them was the respected social and political personality, Pt. Prem Nath Dogra.

Above all, in this movement, the most towering Opposition leader in Parliament, Dr. Syama Prasad Mookerjee was arrested for entering our state without a permit, which was equivalent to a visa needed to visit a foreign country. After his arrest, Dr. Mookerjee was lodged in a hut which was meant for gardeners of the Nishat Bagh, on the outskirts of Srinagar.

Dr. Mookerjee died on the black night of June 22nd-23rd in 1953 under circumstances that are even today shrouded in mystery. No enquiry was held despite a strong demand from different quarters, including his aged mother Yog Maya and then Bengal Chief Minister B.C. Roy.

All this happened several decades ago, which makes it quite challenging to retrieve authentic and consolidated information. It was really important to go back to those times and do a thorough research and meet people who had contributed and played a crucial role. Unfortunately, some of them have left us and some others could not be of much help due to lack of authentic data.

As Pandit Prem Nath Dogra was the driving force, it was considered essential to take a look into his life to learn about his great contribution. During this research, it was an honour to meet Mulkh Raj Pargal, who was 92-years old and also a member of Pt. Prem Nath Dogra Memorial Trust, but unfortunately, he couldn't contribute much as he left us soon thereafter.

I am indeed thankful for this opportunity to connect with our history because of which I had the privilege of meeting Gopal Sachar, a veteran journalist, who was closely associated with Panditji and the Praja Parishad/Bharatiya Jana Sangh for about 22 years (1950-1972). Upon narrating the purpose of my visit,

Gopal Sachar readily agreed to extend a helping hand in the best possible way.

He handed over a 60 year-old file of the weekly *Jai Swadesh*, which was an official organ of the Praja Parishad, saying, "This was the property of Praja Parishad and now the BJP should take care of it." This document of *Jai Swadesh* proved to be of great help in approaching the families of Praja Parishad leaders and activists at far-off places. In addition to some papers and documents, he also provided several photographs that included some rare ones pertaining to the life and activities of Panditji and others.

I also came across a personal diary maintained by the prominent Praja Parishad activist, the late Sanji Ram, when he was behind bars, which revealed the horrible conditions and cruelties that were inflicted on the patriotic activists.

Several years ago, the late Sanji Ram published this diary in the form of a booklet, titled *Vish Dhara-370*.

It was heartwarming to have our national president, Amit Shah inaugurate our library during his visit to Jammu on 30th April, 2017. This library has been named after the great social and patriotic leader, Nanaji Deshmukh.

This inauguration proved to be a big impetus in our efforts to collect more and more information to help weave together this book on the history of the Praja Parishad.

Experience

In the efforts to collect data, pictures and facts on the important functionaries of Praja Parishad and Bharatiya Jana Sangh, there were some great experiences I would like to share.

- Some people connected with the leaders and activists were quite cooperative in providing photographs and information they had about the role of their elders.
- A few people promised to support this drive about the big role of their elders but despite persistent efforts, refused to come forward. Efforts are still on to obtain the recorded information which they can provide.

- Interestingly, some people offered to record the statements of their elders who had contributed in some way, but efforts are still on to obtain authentication in such cases.

However, some material has been provided by Rajan Verma, son of the then General Secretary of Praja Parishad, Durga Dass Verma. Also, a few photographs were provided by the then Jammu city president, Amarnath Gupta. Prof. Vidhya Bhushan provided some files of records.

It was a great learning experience for me while this was happening at long last. The last six months have brought me closer to our history and it is my belief that the readers would be able to learn how the country and the society was served by the great Dogra, Pt. Prem Nath.

A big thanks to all the senior party members and others who extended their helping hand in collecting and compiling this book related to the historic movement, especially the forgotten activists who were the real soldiers of the Praja Parishad/Bharatiya Jana Sangh. Efforts would continue to be made to remember those who contributed their mite in every possible way.

(Prof. Kul Bhushan Mohtra)
In-charge: Nanaji Deshmukh Library
and Documentation Department
Bharatiya Janata Party (J&K)

Foreword

Our national movement compelled the British to leave India in 1947. The British Union Jack was rolled up and the Indian Tricolour started flying high in the skies of the ancient Indian nation that 'we, the people of India, that is Bharat' choose to shape as a democratic republic. Although the transition was not so smooth, the erstwhile princely state of Jammu & Kashmir ruled by Maharaja Hari Singh became an integral part of India.

The Maharaja, being the only legal and constitutional authority to decide on the fate of his state, signed the Instrument of Accession (IOA). The Instrument of Accession he signed was in no manner different from the documents signed by other states for the purpose of becoming a part of India.

But this plain factual and legal position has been widely misinterpreted, misquoted and deliberately misrepresented both inside Jammu & Kashmir as well as in the rest of the country. The separatists and anti-India elements spearheaded a campaign to this effect, but those who became legal and constitutional successors of the British Crown and the nationalist Maharaja were not far behind in harming the country's national interests. All this is a part of history.

The chronology of events that preceded and followed the accession of Jammu & Kashmir into India might appear to be a little complicated in the first instance but there is ample and unchallengeable clarity regarding the state's constitutional and legal status. The moment the IOA signed by Maharaja Hari Singh was duly accepted by the then Governor General of India, entire Jammu & Kashmir which was under the rule of the Maharaja, on 15th August, 1947 became an inseparable part of India. And this is what 'we, the people of India' and even our Parliament has repeatedly asserted unambiguously amid a discourse that always sought to trivialise and falsify this truth.

Amid the intellectual and physical violence that nationalist forces continue to face in parts of Jammu & Kashmir, attempts for a necessary course correction in the discourse on Jammu & Kashmir is gaining momentum. Several books, documentaries and documents depicting the Indian view and authentic position on various questions often asked about the state have been published in the past few years.

The volume of the book is intended to supplement this ongoing work of course correction. As the volume focuses on documenting the Praja Parishad movement and the legendary role played by late Pt. Prem Nath Dogra on this front, these become much more relevant. The way the Praja Parishad stood up against the evil designs of the then leadership of the state of Jammu & Kashmir, should have been properly elucidated during the yesteryears, but which was not done comprehensively despite the several attempts in the past.

I am sure that the present project will fill the gaps and strengthen the body of knowledge already generated on this aspect of the recent history of Jammu & Kashmir. Let us take it as a tribute to all the martyrs of the state, right from those who died fighting on the frontiers in 1947-48, through luminaries like the late Dr. Syama Prasad Mookerjee and up to the brave personnel of our security forces who have laid down their lives to ensure that the Tricolour that replaced Union Jack in 1947 continues to flutter fearlessly in the state.

The hard work put in by the author accompanied by the entire team that made production of this volume possible is appreciable. Let our desire and efforts for a genuine course correction in Jammu & Kashmir become stronger with every passing day. Production of this book is neither a beginning nor an end of our quest for knowing more about the state. The *manthan* must go on.

(Ram Lal)
National General Secretary (Organisation)

Message

It is heartening to note that a book about the great struggle of Praja Parishad/Bharatiya Jana Sangh for demolishing the barriers between Jammu & Kashmir and the rest of India has been put on record.

It is indeed a maiden effort by Kul Bhushan Mohtra after a lapse of 65 years of the movement. He undertook the Herculean task of contacting various personalities and organisations for collecting, collating and sifting material and photographs of various events about the life of the great leader, Pt. Prem Nath Dogra, who is the torchbearer for the coming generations. With this, a long outstanding work has seen the light of the day for which Kul Bhushan Mohtra deserves appreciation.

Pt. Prem Nath Dogra was a selfless and nationalist leader with unflinching loyalty towards the society and the country. This historical document about the Praja Parishad movement and the life of a great son of the soil will go a long way in guiding and inspiring Indians in general and that of Duggardesh in particular.

Warm regards and best wishes for such future endeavours.

(Brig. (Retd.) Suchet Singh)
Prant Sangchalak & Chairman,
Pt. Prem Nath Dogra Trust

Message

I extend my heartiest congratulations to Kul Bhushan Mohtra, in-charge Nanaji Deshmukh Library and Documents Department, Jammu & Kashmir Bharatiya Janata Party for preparing a valuable publication titled *Praja Parishad: A Saga of Sacrifices* which throws light on the happenings that followed after the accession of J&K state with India. This book highlights the patriotism and sacrifices made by the workers/activists of Praja Parishad/Bharatiya Jana Sangh. The publication gives a detailed account of the Praja Parishad movement for removing the barriers against the integration of the state with the rest of the country. I hope this document will provide an opportunity to the BJP Karyakarta, and the common man to visualise the real picture of the events of that period and be inspired to render service for the greater cause of the motherland.

जय हिंद! जय भारत!
वंदे मातरम्!

(रविंद्र रैना)
प्रदेश अध्यक्ष,
भाजपा, जम्मू-कश्मीर

Message

It is a matter of great pleasure that Nanaji Deshmukh Library and Documents, established in the head office of Jammu & Kashmir Bharatiya Janata Party has published *Praja Parishad: A Saga of Sacrifices* containing the historical events that took place after the accession of J&K state within the Indian Union, the struggle launched by the Dogras in 1953 for complete integration of Jammu & Kashmir with India and opposing separatist tendencies that had emerged due to the incorporation of Article 370 in the Indian Constitution. The publication narrates the sequence of events of the Praja Parishad's struggle, the sacrifices made by the people under the leadership of Pt. Prem Nath Dogra and photographs of those who participated in the historical crusade.

K.B. Mohtra has put in a lot of effort to collect the material and photographs by approaching the resource persons individually and by going through the available published or unpublished material.

(Ashok Kaul)
BJP State General Secretary (Org.)

Observations

It is no easy task to dig up the past; it becomes more cumbersome when the events have taken place decades back and that too linked with a huge movement about which there is little on record in a consolidated form. More so, when its adversaries have written much to paint the struggle as black and dark by employing official resources.

It is good that Kul Bhushan has taken up the task in a challenging manner and laboured hard to knit the pieces together to weave a book, though much remains to be dug out yet.

From a journalistic point of view, the book is worth going through as certain issues linked with the world body, the U.N. General Assembly, and with small and remote places like Padli and Pargwal, find mention in it.

It is also notable that the role of all powerful politicians to dub Praja Parishad/Bharatiya Jana Sangh activist, Ram Lal alias 'Jalla Phenianwala', are touched upon in the book.

Thus, the last place and the last person have also been taken into account. For me as a person, this book is significant as I have seen, rather experienced, much about the movement.

(Gopal Sachar)
Journalist

KNOW

Our Jammu Kashmir

Region	Sq. Kms.*
1. Kashmir Valley (with India)	15,948
2. Jammu Region (with India)	26,293
3. Ladakh Region (with India)	59,146
4. Present Jammu and Kashmir State (with India)	**1,01,387**
5. Illegal occupation by Pakistan (Mirpur-Muzaffarabad 13,297 km. and Gilgit-Baltistan 64,817 km)	78,114
6. Ceded to China by Pakistan	5,180
7. Illegal occupation by China	37,555
8. Total Area Occupied by Pakistan and China	**1,20,849**
9. Total Area covered by Instrument of Accession	**2,22,236**

Jammu

2nd Largest Part Of The State

Area - Apx. 26000 Sq. Km.

No. Of Assembly Seats: 37

No. Of Lok Sabha Seats: 2

Kashmir

The Smallest Part Of The State

Area - Apx. 16000 Seats: 46

No. Of Lok Sabha Seats: 3

Ladakh

The Largest Part Of The State

Area = Apx. 59000 Sq. Km.

No. Of Assembly Seats: 4

No. Of Lok Sabha Seats: 1

POJK

AREA - 78114 SQ. KM.

COJK

AREA - 37555 SQ. KM.

Vacant Seat Of Jammu Kashmir Occupied By Pakistan = 24

Parliament Resolution on Jammu and Kashmir

(a) The State of Jammu & Kashmir has been, is and shall be an integral part of India and any attempts to separate it from the rest of the country will be resisted by all necessary means;

(b) India has the will and capacity to firmly counter all designs against its unity, sovereignty and territorial integrity;

and demands that -

(c) Pakistan must vacate the areas of the Indian State of Jammu and Kashmir, which they have occupied through aggression; and

resolves that -

(d) all attempts to interfere in the internal affairs of India will be met resolutely."

The Resolution was unanimously adopted. Mr. Speaker: The Resolution is unanimously passed on February 22, 1994

Reference: http://www.kashmir-information.com/LegalDocs/ParliamentRes.html

Contents

Emergence of the Praja Parishad

BIRTH OF PRAJA PARISHAD

Prior to the accession of Jammu & Kashmir state in 1947 with the Indian Union, there was no major political party in Jammu, unlike that in the Valley of Kashmir.

There were outfits like Naw Jawan Sabha, Muslim Conference, Hindu Sabha, Dogra Sadar Sabha and some others but their activities were confined to certain sections of communities. There were also some caste-based *sabhas* of different *biradari* (communities); however, the Rashtriya Swayamsevek Sangh (RSS) had developed a strong unit.

On the contrary, in Jammu & Kashmir, the Muslim Conference had built a strong movement against Maharaja Hari Singh since 1931. A major faction of it, led by Sheikh Mohammad Abdullah, in 1938 divided the Muslim Conference and renamed his outfit as National Conference to gain the support of Jawaharlal Nehru and some others of the Congress against the Maharaja of the state. The National Conference could not gain a mass base in Jammu because of its outlook and anti-Dogra slogans symbolising the Maharaja's Dogra antecedents when it was a dynastic rule.

After the painful communal division of India under the designs of the imperialists, when the theocratic State of Pakistan was created, its leadership not only staked claim on J&K because of it being Muslim majority but also launched a massive invasion with tribals supported by Pakistani Army, which was at that time being controlled and commanded by British commanders.

The Maharaja of the state, Hari Singh, using his legal authority signed the Instrument of Accession with Indian Union on 26th October, 1947 and thus opted for secular India, braving all pulls and pressures rather than yielding to theocratic Pakistan.

Under compelling circumstances, the Maharaja handed over the reins of power to the political friend of Nehru in Jammu & Kashmir, Sheikh Mohammad Abdullah, who pledged his loyalty to the Maharaja even when the National Conference party had little base in Jammu and other regions of the state. Many time-servers and opportunists thronged to the National Conference to show their loyalties to the new ruler and indulged in several acts of sycophancy and even that of different kinds of degradation.

These people began chanting the slogan, viz. : *'Aek rehnuma, Sheikh Mohammad Abdullah, aek tanzeem National Conference, aek jhanda, halwala.'*

Thus, an intriguing situation was created. Sensing these trends of alone 'one', the visionary Pt. Prem Nath Dogra and his colleagues felt that in a democracy, such a form could prove despotic, particularly in a state like J&K.

Pt. Prem Nath Dogra with Sham Lal Sharma, Bhagwat Saroop, Durga Dass Verma and other activists

Pt. Prem Nath Dogra and his admirers, after due deliberations for three days, decided to float a new party under the name of Praja Parishad. A young team of its activists was announced with Hari Wazir as its first president, Hans Raj Pangotra, general secretary and other office-bearers of this new party also included Sham Lal Sharma, Durga Dass Verma, Rajinder Singh, Sahdev Singh, Om Parkash Sangra, Roop Lal Rohmetra, Jagdish Raj Sahni, Mulkh Raj Arora, Hans Raj Ramnagar, Makhan Lal Aima, Jagdish Raj Khader Bhandar, Ishwar Dutt Shastri Magloor, Natha Singh, Dewarka Nath and others. Along with Panditji, Bhagwat Swaroop was named as the *margdarshak*.

RSS ROLE IN J&K

Prior to the birth of the Praja Parishad, the Rashtriya Swayamsevak Sangh had established its well-knit units (*Shakhas*) in most parts of the state, especially in the region of Jammu.

In late thirties (1939), while preparing to play its important role in the freedom struggle against the British rulers in accession of J&K, the RSS had become a hub of patriotic activities.

Madhav Ṛao Muley was the Prant Pracharak, who deputed some dedicated activists to establish RSS *Shakhas* in the state.

The first to come was Prof. Balraj Madhok in the late thirties. But as he got the job of a professor in a Srinagar college, Jagdish Abrol of Sialkot, Kedar Nath Sahni and some other Pracharaks put in their efforts to establish the RSS *Shakhas* at various places. The first one was established at Dewan Mandir in Jammu city.

Many local youth came forward to spread mostly the games. These youth included Shyam Lal Sharma, Durga Dass Verma, Dr. Om Parkash Mengi and some others.

Jagdish Abrol established his first *karyalaya* at Ved Mandir in a room. Though large numbers of youth joined the RSS network, it was generally known as a body of children and teenagers.

In the early forties, Madhav Rao Muley and some senior RSS men approached Pt. Prem Nath Dogra to lead the RSS in the state as Sanghchalak to which he agreed and a big function was held in Jammu. Some eminent RSS functionaries too joined this *samaroh*.

With this taking over by Panditji as Sanghchalak, the body attained significant respectability and fillip to its working.

ORGANISATIONAL STRUCTURE OF PRAJA PARISHAD

DIVIDED OPINION

When, in 1947, it was decided to float a political body, some senior activists were of the opinion that the new party should be named as Jammu Praja Parishad and its manifesto be titled *Naya Jammu*. This would be an answer to the Kashmir National Conference and that too to the 'Naya Kashmir'. But some others were of the view that the party should not look as confined to just one region alone and also should not sound reactionary.

Because of differences over the name, some top leaders of the RSS then advised that the new party should be named as All Jammu & Kashmir Praja Parishad because the legal authority, the Maharaja, had signed the Instrument of Accession for his entire state; and more so, it should not subscribe to the philosophy of any communal decision as Pakistan had come to be a theocratic State. Hence, the new party was named as the All Jammu & Kashmir Praja Parishad with the Tricolour as its flag and with the following objectives:

Pt. Dogra at a meeting

OBJECTIVES OF THE PARTY

The main objectives of the party were "to achieve full integration of Jammu & Kashmir state with the rest of India like other acceding states and to safeguard the legitimate democratic rights of the people of Jammu from the anti-Dogra government of Sheikh Mohammad Abdullah."

The Praja Parishad held that Jammu & Kashmir was an inseparable and indivisible part of India and based on Indian culture, the party would establish a political, social and economic order in which there would be no discrimination on account of caste, colour and faith. All the citizens would be provided equal opportunities for progress.

CONSTITUTION OF THE PRAJA PARISHAD

Any resident of Jammu & Kashmir of 18 years of age and above and who endorsed the aims and objectives of the party could become its member. He would continue to be its member as long as he regularly paid its annual membership fee that was four *annas* till he resigned, or removed from the membership, or secured the membership of any other political party.

Primary Samiti (Committee)

The first structure of the party organisation was the primary committee. Wherever there were 25 or more members of the party, a primary committee was to be constituted. The primary committee consisted of a president, a secretary and a treasurer. All the three were to be elected by the members.

Mandal Committee

The next higher organisational structure was the Mandal Samiti. For each 16 group of primary committees, there would be a Mandal Committee. All the members of primary committee were to elect the president of the Mandal Committee while he himself would constitute his executive committee consisting of a secretary, a treasurer and six members.

The Mandal Committee under its jurisdiction would be responsible for the execution of policies and programmes of the party.

Tehsil *Committee*

The next higher structure was to be the *tehsil* committee. All the members of the executive of the Mandal Committee in a *tehsil* would jointly constitute a *tehsil* committee. They would elect a president, at least two vice-presidents, a treasurer and nine members of the executive of *tehsil samiti*. They, with the consent of president of *tehsil* committee, would also elect two representatives for General Council as well as organisational secretary. The organisational secretary in cooperation with the secretary of *tehsil* committee would be responsible for the functioning as well as popularising the ideology of the party in that *tehsil*.

General Council

The constitution of the General Council was as under:

(a) The presidents, the secretaries and organisational secretaries of all the *tehsil samitis* as well as the elected representatives from each party constituency.

(b) The presidents, secretaries and organisational secretaries of all the district *samitis*.

(c) Those institutions which combined with the Praja Parishad and whose five members would be elected by the president on the order of those institutions.

(d) It would be the right of the president of Jammu & Kashmir Praja Parishad to nominate five members of the Praja Parishad.

Each member of the General Council would have to pay 5 rupees annually. It would be the main committee to run the policies and functions of Praja Parishad. During its tenure, it would have the right to solve all the problems that would come its way. It would be allowed to issue orders to other committees from time to time. The session of the General Council was to be held once a year.

Central Samiti

At the apex of the party hierarchy was to be a Central Samiti comprising 21 members, including the president. These members would be nominated by president from the members of the General Council. The president of the Central Samiti would also nominate two vice presidents, one secretary and one treasurer. The Central Committee would be responsible to the General Council for its actions, orders regarding the questions which were not defined in the party constitution. It worked to fulfil the aims of the Praja Parishad.

Pt. Prem Nath Dogra with executive members of Praja Parishad at his residence Kachi Chawni in Jammu

PRESIDENT OF THE PARTY

In the higher structure of the organisation of the party was to be a president. The president would have the highest authority. The general secretary of the party would invite nominations for the candidate desirous of contesting for the presidentship from the *tehsil* and District Working Committees of the party. The nominations were to be submitted within a fixed time. After receiving the nominations, if any candidate desired to withdraw, he could do so. On the fixed date, the general secretary would announce the names of the persons who would finally remain in the fray. He then would issue ballot papers to each member of the General Council to vote in favour of the nominated candidate he liked. After receiving the ballots papers duly filled, the general secretary would open them in the presence of all members of general body at an appointed date. The candidate with majority votes would be declared as president of the party.

PARTY FINANCE

The finances of the party included the money collected in the form of membership fee of four *annas* as well as five rupees collected from each member of the General Council. As the amount was insufficient to meet the day-to-day expenses of the party, donations from different individuals were also accepted. In order to finance the different movements launched by the party from time to time, the party got tickets printed worth Rs. 1, Rs. 5, Rs. 10, Rs. 20, Rs. 50 and Rs. 100 with the photograph of its president Pt. Prem Nath Dogra and these were then sold amongst the people. There were rumours that the then Maharaja of Kashmir also contributed to the party funds. The press tried to confirm this fact from the top party leaders still alive; however, most of these leaders denied the same.

This very much irked the Sheikh as he was already intolerant towards his adversaries. Several important activists of RSS and other small organisations were expelled from the state. These included Prof. Balraj Madhok, Jagdish Abrol, Kedar Nath Sahni, Kavi Raj, Vishnu Gupta and others.

Pt. Prem Nath Dogra and some of his colleagues were arrested and detained. He was shifted to Srinagar in the intense cold conditions in the month of February 1949. He was put under detention by slapping Section 3 of the RPC, which was notoriously known as *'Daffa Tun'*, which meant putting anyone in lockup without any trial.

He was dubbed as anti-Muslim in 1947, but ironically in 1932, Pt. Dogra was prematurely retired from service on the charge of being mild towards Muslim Conference agitators in his capacity as *Wazir Wazarat* (DC) at Muzaffarabad district of the state. The arrest and detention of Panditji by the Abdullah government resulted in strong resentment, as this government was indulging in many other acts of omission and commission.

In May 1949, the Praja Parishad launched a *satyagraha* movement to seek the release of Pt. Prem Nath Dogra. In order to crush this movement, the Sheikh-led dispensation resorted to committing all kinds of atrocities. This caused anger against the National Conference and its fellow supporters within and outside the state.

After intervention of certain national leaders from Delhi, Pt. Dogra was released from Srinagar Jail on 8 October, 1949, but these eight months in jail had severe repercussions on his health.

Pt. Prem Nath Dogra released from Srinagar Jail in 1949

In this movement, several *satyagrahis* were tortured to the extent that they were incapacitated; even to the extent of losing their ability to hear besides suffering other ill effects throughout their lives. They also included one Dina Nath of Jammu and Chuni Lal Pandoh of Reasi.

However, this prodded the Praja Parishad to play a more active role when the Abdullah government took some unhealthy decisions under communal and parochial considerations.

Th. Sehdev Singh with other activists

After his release from jail, the Praja Parishad declared Pt. Prem Nath Dogra as its president, Durga Dass Verma its general secretary, Dhanvantar Singh, Zaildar Ranjit Singh Nagri Parol, Luder Manni Sangra Koota, Sham Lal Sharma vice-presidents, secretary (Org.), Bhagwat Swaroop and Gopal Dass Sachar, in-charge of publicity matters, Makhan Lal Aima, *parbhari* (outside the state), Ram Nath Balgotra, in-charge, Kathua district, Radha Krishan Sharma (Udhampur district) and Roop Lal Rhometra (Doda district). The members of the Working Committees were announced as Chatru Ram Dogra, Shiv Ram Gupta, Sant Ram Baru, Gian Chand Mirpuri, Jagat Ram Aryan, Luder Mani Sangra, Zaildar Ranjeet Raghunath Singh Samyal and Jagdish Khader Bhandari.

The following were announced as organising secretaries:

Natha Singh (Ramban), Shiv Kumar Sharma (Kishtwar), Baldev Raj (Bhaderwah), Mulkh Raj Arora (Udhampur), Rishi Kumar Koushal (Reasi), Hans Raj Gupta (Ramnagar), Rajinder Singh and Shadi Lal Sharma (Jammu), Som Nath Dogra (Akhnoor),

Thakur Seh Dev Singh (Nowshera), Jagdish Chander Shastri (Rajouri), Narsingh Dass Sharma (Samba), Dawarka Nath (Basholi), Ishwar Dass Shastri (Hiranagar), Swaran Dev Singh (Billawar), Jagdish Singh (Kathua), Ved Parkash and Yash Bhasin (R.S. Pura).

Pt. Prem Nath Dogra released from Srinagar Jail in 1949

After his release from detention of eight long months in Srinagar Jail, Pt. Prem Nath Dogra lost no time and took stock of the fast changing developments within the state as also at the national and international levels vis-à-vis Kashmir after due consultations with the local activists and leaders with a patriotic outlook at the national level. It was decided to build a strong network of the Praja Parishad up to the village level.

The dedicated workers did a yeoman's job in establishing party units at various levels. After accomplishing the task of organising the Praja Parishad units at various levels, there was unanimous opinion that Panditji should himself head the party.

A state-level convention was convened on 10th November, 1951. In his first presidential address, Pt. Dogra gave a detailed account of the happenings and dangers looming ahead.

This maiden address at the convention was made in Jammu on 10th November, 1951.

In his 40-minute speech, Panditji pointed out to the delegates,

"This session of the representatives of the people is being held at a crucial juncture when Pakistan is out to grab the entire state of J&K with the strength and support of the Anglo-American bloc on the one hand and on the other, the Sheikh-led National Conference government is playing a dubious role. Apparently the division of the state is being opposed but little is being done to get liberated the enemy-held areas, though lakhs of people of these places have been forced to become refugees. Moreover, it is being designed to have a constitution which would be on the lines of the party bible of 'Naya Kashmir' in accordance with their slogan of Quit Kashmir."

Referring to the grave situation created by the massive enemy invasion of the state, Panditji, in his address, paid rich tributes to martyr Brigadier Rajinder Singh, the Chief of Staff of the state units and recalled how, with just about a company of the state army, he checked the advances of thousands of invaders for three days to enter the Valley of Kashmir and fought with the enemy till the last bullet and last drop of his blood, as per orders of the Maharaja. This instigated Maharaja Hari Singh to sign the Instrument of Accession with the Indian Union on 26th October, 1947 and the next day, on 27 October, the Indian troops landed at Srinagar to push back the invaders.

Pt. Dogra, in his address, also mentioned the valour shown by Lt. Col. Hira Nand Dubey, Maj. Angrez Singh, Lt. Amlok Singh, Captain Sardar Ganga Singh and others on various fronts in fighting the enemy, despite treachery by some armymen under communal influence.

In this address, the plight of the migrants from enemy-held areas was also listed.

Detailing the highly sad situation created by the internal and external elements, Panditji reminded the delegates and also the common people that all of them owed a special responsibility to save this state for India as this huge state of J&K was built by their ancestors through their blood, flesh and bones.

Pt. Prem Nath Dogra at Praja Parishad convention in 1951

He opposed the controversial moves and slogans to distance the state from the rest of India and working towards having a separate constitution. In the situation, Panditji observed, "There seems a dire need for a struggle in which we all should work for a great cause."

Panditji concluded his speech with a warning: *"Na samblo gae to mit jao gae, ae zanat nishan walo, tumari dastan tak bhi na hogi dastano mae."*

The Praja Parishad had to struggle hard to frustrate the separatist designs of Sheikh Abdullah and his companions in the Congress, Left parties and others.

Under communal considerations, the creation of district Doda and many other wrongs led to resentment against the Abdullah regime, which inadvertently contributed to the popularity and rise of the Praja Parishad. The Parishad, as one of the most important national parties in Jammu & Kashmir state, opposed the setting up of a separate Constituent Assembly for the state. It favoured the application of the Indian Constitution in Jammu & Kashmir. But due to the peculiar conditions in the state, the Praja Parishad in a special session of the party's Working Committee held on 8th May, 1951, decided to contest the elections.

All ill-conceived moves of the Sheikh administration, coupled with large-scale rejections of nomination papers filed by Praja Parishad candidates for the Constituent Assembly, compelled the party to boycott the elections. And thus the stage was set for a long-drawn struggle.

(Ref: From the documents file of the Nanaji Deshmukh Library, BJP headquarters, Jammu.)

□

Praja Parishad Stand Explained

BOYCOTT OF ASSEMBLY ELECTIONS

'Memorandum about Praja Parishad Stand (Resolution passed by All J&K Praja Parishad Working Committee on 8th October, 1951).'

Pt. Dogra submitted a memorandum to the President of India and also held a press conference at Delhi on 6th October, 1951. The resolution passed by All J&K Praja Parishad Working Committee on 8th October, 1951 is as under:

"Keeping in view the past short history of a few months of Kashmir government's partial and unjust activities in connection with the forthcoming elections to the Jammu & Kashmir Constituent Assembly and keeping in view the misrepresentation they seem to have made to the Hon'ble Pandit Jawaharlal Nehru, Prime Minister of India, with the result that he has gone out of his way in condemning the perfectly legitimate activities of the Praja Parishad in his recent speeches and statements, thereby interfering in the freedom of local elections, which he should not have been advised to do, the Working Committee deems it essential to reconsider at this juncture its line of action. The return of our president from Delhi has also made it necessary for the Working Committee to decide finally this matter. It is therefore, resolved:

1. That the statement issued by our president Pt. Prem Nath Dogra wherein it has been stated in unambiguous terms that the Parishad stands for the complete and unconditional accession of J&K state to Indian Constitution in its entirety is fully supported and endorsed by the PP as being a true reflection of the mind of Jammu's people;

2. That all assurances and guarantees of free and fair elections given by the Jammu & Kashmir government have proved to be false and in spite of the Government of India and government of Jammu & Kashmir having been fully informed of all the partisan and injustices from time to time in the shape of protests, demonstrations, notices and resolutions, no effective steps to consider the grievances or to readdress them have been taken and even our resolution of 21st September, 1951 giving the Jammu & Kashmir government ample chance for consideration has been ignored. Consequently, the circumstances created by the Jammu & Kashmir government have compelled us to decide it finally not to contest the Constituent Assembly elections under protest so long as the grievances mentioned in the statement issued by our president at Delhi are not addressed.
3. That Parishad would continue to mobilise the public opinion for the state's complete accession to India and the adoption of the Indian Constitution like other states of the Union and would do all that is needed to propagate its programme."

—Sd. Durga Dass Verma
General Secretary
All Jammu & Kashmir Praja Parishad
Jammu

IRREGULARTIES IN JAMMU ELECTIONS

The following statement was issued to the press by Pt. Prem Nath Dogra, president of the All J&K Praja Parishad, at a press conference held in New Delhi on Saturday, 6th October, 1951: "You must have read a lot about the election to the Constituent Assembly of the Jammu & Kashmir state, but I felt that you have been given only one side of the picture. So I would like to give you some facts about these elections and to leave it to you to judge for yourself in regard to the real situation in Jammu.

"THE PRAJA PARISHAD

The Praja Parishad is the strongest political party of the people of Jammu for the past so many years, just as the National Conference has been of the people of Kashmir, but ever since the present administration has been set up in the state, there has been a regular campaign of vilification and harassment of the people of Jammu. It was against this maltreatment that the Jammu & Kashmir Praja Parishad had to launch a *satyagraha* movement two years back, which was withdrawn on the definite assurance that there would be no discrimination in treatment between the people of the two provinces of J&K by the administration.

"The Praja Parishad is not a communal organisation in any sense of the term, which fact becomes clear from the fact that it has on its membership rolls hundreds of Muslims. Some of them have been addressing public meetings from the Praja Parishad platform, but the government has adopted the tactics of dubbing these Muslim members of the Praja Parishad as Pakistanis. One of them was given a beating by the local officials, while another has been externed from the state and is presently staying in other parts of our country.

Panditji with senior leaders of Praja Parishad

"Ever since the Partition of India, the Praja Parishad has unequivocally stood for unconditional accession of the J&K state to the Indian Union, while the National Conference has even till today not agreed to complete merger of the state to the Indian Union and wants only defence, external affairs and communications to be controlled by the Central Government of India. Even in the present elections, the Praja Parishad demands the application of the entire Indian Constitution to the state of Jammu & Kashmir, like all the other Part 'B' and Part 'C' states that have acceded to the Indian Union while the National Conference wants a separate constitution for the Jammu & Kashmir state for reasons best known to itself.

Praja Parishad Versus National Conference

"From the above, it is clear that there are fundamental and basic differences between the National Conference and the Praja Parishad over the question of the state's accession to the Indian Union. While the Praja Parishad stands for unconditional accession to India, the National Conference has reservations in this regard and the conflicting statements and actions of the National Conference leaders during the last four years create grave suspicious in the minds of the people of the state. The present elections to the Constituent Assembly of the Jammu & Kashmir state are also being fought on this very issue, and that is the reason why the National Conference has been making attempts to prevent the Praja Parishad from entering the Constituent Assembly.

"With this end in view, the government, which is another name for the National Conference, is adopting all means, fair and foul, to prevent the real representatives of the people from entering the Constituent Assembly. It was as a result of this policy that no Opposition candidates dared file their nominations and those who did dare file their nominations were compelled to withdraw under pressure.

Pt. Prem Nath Dogra, Bachan Singh Panchi with other activists

"In the Jammu province, this intimidation on the part of the National Conference-cum-government could not succeed, as the Praja Parishad is the strongest political organisation of this province for many years even when the National Conference had not even existed. Its activities having been confined ever since 1932 when it was born, just as the Kashmir Muslim Conference in the Kashmir Valley alone was the political party there. Therefire, attempts are being made according to a well-laid plan to prevent the Praja Parishad from having any effective voice in the Constituent Assembly.

TACTICS ADOPTED

"The first thing the National Conference government did was to decide not to hold elections in the provinces of Kashmir and Jammu simultaneously. Everyone was surprised to find that while the nominations were being filled in the Kashmir Valley, even the final lists for voters had not been made public for the Jammu province. It was only after the 'unopposed elections' of the National Conference candidates had been announced in Kashmir that the dates for nominations in Jammu province were announced, with the deliberate intention of influencing the elections in Jammu.

Pt. Prem Nath Dogra addresses a meeting of party delegates at Jammu

"IRREGULAR DELIMITATION

Another tactic adopted against the Praja Parishad was that the Parishad was given no representation on the Delimitation Committee, although at first the Praja Parishad was assured that its representatives would be associated with the committee. But later this was not done, with the result that the delimitation of the constituencies in the Jammu province was carried out in such an arbitrary way that all the strongholds of leading members of the Praja Parishad were broken up into fragments.

A public gathering before launching satyagraha *movement in 1952*

The constituencies as fixed by the Delimitation Committee are totally against to the principles of contiguity and compactness of the areas as the basis of delimitation, as laid down in the terms of reference for the Delimitation Committee, with a view to benefit the party in power.

"The following specific instances will be sufficient to prove the above contention of the Praja Parishad:

1. While fixing the constituencies for the city of Jammu, Jammu *patwar*, which is contiguous with Jammu city, was split up and a major portion of it was tacked on to the Kahna Chak constituency in Jammu *tehsil*, while the remainder was attached to the southern constituency of Jammu city, to which also was added the Bahu *patwar* on the other side of River Tawi. A protest was held and a resolution was adopted and sent to the government on 8th September, 1951, but with no result.
2. Sari *patwar*, across River Bhini, which is a natural part of the Basholi constituency, was cut off from this constituency and was attached to the Billawar constituency, because this *patwar* was taken to be in favour of the National Conference candidate standing from the Billawar constituency. This division is quite unnatural and deliberately partial.

"NO GENERAL SEATS IN THREE CONSTITUENCIES

The third method adopted against the Praja Parishad was that the areas where the Parishad was the strongest have been debarred from sending any candidates other than members of the Scheduled Castes, although the population of Scheduled Caste members there was comparatively very small. In India, Scheduled Castes and Tribes have been given seats in addition to general seats, but not at the cost of the general electorates, except in those areas where the entire population consists of such castes and tribes. But in Jammu, the Delimitation Committee has set apart three constituencies of Reasi, Kahna Chak and Bishnah for the Harijans only. If instead of these constituencies being reserved, three seats had been set apart for these Harijans in addition to general seats, there would have been no injustice to the general electorate, which has thus been debarred from being represented in the Constituent Assembly, although it forms a majority of the population in all these areas.

"The most glaring instance of the unfair delimitation of the constituencies was the one in regard to Kishtwar, which has the largest population of Harijans, as no representation has been given to Harijans there. The reason is simple. The Harijan candidate of the Praja Parishad in this area, Jagat Ram Arya, was sure to get elected by an overwhelming majority. He was a member of the Praja Sabha or the Legislative Assembly of the state last time. The government first tried to win him over to the side of the National Conference. Upon his refusal, he was arrested and sent to jail. He was however, ordered to be released by the High Court as a result of a *habeas corpus* application. The government then prevented his entry into his home district, Kishtwar, by interning him in Srinagar. When there were protests against this all around, the Delimitation Committee debarred Kishtwar from returning a Harijan candidate, thus making it impossible for the Praja Parishad candidate Jagat Ram Arya to get elected to the Constituent Assembly.

"The Praja Parishad protested against these injustices but to no effect.

"OUT OF THE WAY POLLING STATIONS

"The fourth handicap placed in the way of the Praja Parishad coming out successful was to fix the polling stations at out-of-the-way places, where the National Conference government resources alone could carry the voters, and not in central places.

"41 OUT OF 65 NOMINATIONS REJECTED

"The fifth and the most atrocious attempt that was made against the Praja Parishad was that no less than 41 out of the 65 nominations filled by the Praja Parishad for 27 of the 30 seats from the Jammu province were rejected on the most flimsy grounds, while not a single nomination paper of any National Conference candidate was rejected, although the Praja Parishad filed very serious objections against a number of them.

"As the Praja Parishad had expected trouble in connection with the nominations, it had taken the precaution of filing the nominations of more than one candidate from 24 constituencies; and in some places, the number of Praja Parishad nominees was even three or four. But, determined as the returning officers were not to let the Praja Parishad contest these seats, all the two or three or four nominations of the Parishad candidates were rejected on one ground or the other. The details of the rejection of these nomination papers would therefore prove very interesting and deserve to be mentioned in some detail.

1. In the Billawar constituency, four nominations were filed for Dhyan Singh, Tara Chand, Thakur Das and Ram Chand. All the four nominations papers were rejected on the ground that the proposers and seconders of these candidates were not able to produce State Subject Certificates, though no such condition is necessary according to the election rules.

   As against this, the nomination paper of the National Conference candidate named Ram Chandra Khajuria was accepted, although his proposer and seconder too could not produce any State Subject Certificate. In addition, his name was entered in the official electoral roll as Amar Chand and not as Ram Chandra.
2. For the Hiranagar constituency, the Praja Parishad filed four nomination papers for Baldev Singh, Rudramani, Ram Dutt and Jawala Prakash. The nomination papers of the first three choices were rejected on the basis of the State Subject Certificate and that of the last-named candidate alone was accepted as the returning officer said that he personally knew the proposer and seconder.
3. For the Basholi constituency, the Praja Parishad filed three nomination papers in the name of Tara Chand, Jagdish Sharma and Ram Chand. The nominations of the first two were rejected on the same ground of the State Subject Certificate but the nomination of Ram Chand was rejected on the plea that he was a government servant,

although he had brought with him his resignation letter duly accepted by his officer. The resignation was not considered 'sufficient'.

As against this, the nomination paper of the National Conference candidate Mahant Ram was accepted as valid, although he had not attached with his nomination the form of declaration specifying his election agent, the filling of which was compulsory for all candidates.

4. For the Kathua constituency, the Praja Parishad had set up no less than five candidates, named Chagar Singh, Surendra Nath, Prithvi Singh, Ranjit Singh and Vidya Parkash. The nominations of the first two were rejected on the same plea of State Subject Certificate. The nominations of Prithvi Singh and Ranjit Singh were rejected on the ground that they had been arrested in connection with a political movement in Jammu; the nomination of the fifth candidate alone was accepted, as no fault could be found with his nomination paper.

   As against this, the nomination paper of the National Conference candidate, Major Piar Singh was held valid, although he had not attached the necessary declaration as required by the rules.

5. For the Ramnagar constituency, three nomination papers were filed by the Parishad for Hansraj, Amrit Sagar and Shiva Charan.

"The nomination paper of Hansraj was rejected on the plea that he was not sure of his serial number on the official electoral roll. According to the original electoral roll, his number appeared to be 490, but in the revised list it was given as 491. As a precaution, he filed two separate nominations papers, one giving the number as 490 and the other, 491, but both were rejected on the ground that the candidate was not sure of his serial number.

"The nomination paper of Amrit Sagar was rejected on the plea that he was not able to produce a certified copy of his entry in the electoral roll, although he carried an official copy of the roll which contained his name.

"The nomination paper of Shiv Charan was rejected on the plea that he was not able to produce a certified copy of his entry in the electoral roll given as Lala Shiv Charan, while the nomination paper merely stated Shiv Charan, even though his father's name and all other particulars tallied fully.

"As against this, the nomination paper of the National Conference candidate Lala Hem Raj was held as valid, although his name was entered as Lala Hum Raj.

"In addition, the nomination papers of Raghunath Singh and Dhanvantar Singh from the Samba constituency, of Shiv Lal from RS Pura and Shyam Lal from Akhnoor and others were rejected on the basis of clerical mistakes or minor printing errors. The nomination paper of Dharampal, a Praja Parishad candidate, was first accepted for the R.S. Pura constituency, but he was later beaten and made to withdraw it.

"Favour towards the National Conference Candidates:

Compared to these impediments put in the way of the Praja Parishad, the National Conference candidates were favoured as is illustrated by the following:

1. The name of Shrimati Ram Dei, who had been set up by the National Conference for the Jammu city southern constituency, appeared in the electoral rolls as Mrs. Brigadier Rajendra Singh and not as Ram Dei. Yet her nomination paper was accepted.
2. The name of the National Conference candidate from Samba–Sagara Singh as well as that of his seconder–did not tally with the entries in the electoral roll. Even then his nomination paper was held valid.
3. The father's name of Chella Singh, the National Conference candidate from the Chhamb constituency, according to the State Subject Certificate was Barita, but in the electoral roll it was entered as Brita Singh. In addition, he was a Jat in the State Subject Certificate, but was entered as a Sikh in the electoral roll. Still, his nomination was held valid.

"Although the election rules laid down that the objections regarding all nominations papers should be decided on one and the same day, in the Kathua constituency, they were held over for the second day on the plea that both the presiding officers had fallen ill simultaneously, with a view to help the National Conference.

"The above instances are only illustrative and not exhaustive. How far the elections in Jammu can be and free fair can easily be gauged from these.

"Official Interference

In addition to this, the entire administrative machinery of the National Conference government has been geared to carry out propaganda of the most malicious type against the Praja Parishad, under the direct supervision of the Deputy Prime Minister of the state, who had been touring the Jammu province and intimidating the people against supporting the Parishad.

Pt. Prem Nath Dogra, Rishi Kumar Koushal in a meeting with activists

"The Deputy Commissioner of Kathua, accompanied by the minister Girdhari Lal Dogra, has been touring and addressing public meetings in favour of the National Conference candidates. He has cancelled the firearm licences of many people in the border areas who did not support the National

Conference candidates, but issued gave fresh licences to those who opposed the Praja Parishad.

"In the same way, the *tehsildar*, and the *naib tehsildar* of Ramnagar worked in favour of the National Conference as against the Praja Parishad.

"The above points are some of the handicaps which have made it impossible for the Praja Parishad to get a fair deal in the elections.

"I went to meet the Minister of States, N. Gopalswami Ayyangar, to point out to him all these irregularities in the hope that he would be able to secure a fair deal for the Praja Parishad in Jammu, but I regret to find that beyond some vague assurances, he has not been able to assure me that the Praja Parishad could expect justice and fairplay in these elections.

"If the Government of India and the state government want the formation of a truly representative Constituent Assembly for the Jammu & Kashmir state, the least they must do is:

1. To hold an independent, judicial inquiry into the rejection of the nomination papers of the Praja Parishad candidates, thereby enabling the party to contest in all the 27 constituencies from where it had originally put up its candidates.
2. To appoint some Supreme Court judge to conduct the elections in Jammu, to assure perfect impartiality.
3. To prevent government servants from working for candidates of any party in the state.

"I am really sorry that I have to give publicity to all these facts, but things have now gone so far that we cannot help it. We have tried our utmost to settle matters locally, but the leaders of the National Conference and the state government have refused to listen to the most genuine grievances of the people of Jammu in connection with these forthcoming elections.

"DECISION IN JAMMU

The Praja Parishad is now faced with the problem of deciding whether to contest the elections under these circumstances or to withdraw from the elections, exposing their mockery in their entirety. This matter will be decided by the Praja Parishad in Jammu on my return there, when a meeting of the Working Committee will be held to consider the entire situation.

— (Sd) Prem Nath Dogra
6th October, 1951

(Ref: From the historical documents of Praja Parishad available at Nanaji Deshmukh Library, Jammu.)

□

Background

History

HARI SINGH AND PRAJA PARISHAD

The Maharaja of J&K had opted for a secular India instead of theocratic Pakistan. He braved all the pulls and pressures. The Maharaja used his legal authority in signing the same Instrument of Accession, which was signed by more than 550 Rajas and Nawabs of the princely states.

And thus, legally and constitutionally, this state too came to be an integral part of the Indian Union this would not have been feasible but for legal authority of Maharaja Hari Singh.

Sheikh Abdullah did not reconcile towards the Maharaja although the Sheikh had pledged his loyalty to seek his release and become the emerging administrator in 1947 and Prime Minister of the state in 1948.

After assuming power, the Sheikh influenced his friend, the all-powerful Prime Minister of India, Jawaharlal Nehru to send Maharaja Hari Singh into exile at Bombay.

Led by Pt. Prem Nath Dogra, the Praja Parishad opposed the measure arguing that this would be a folly and would encourage communally infested separatist elements in Kashmir. The PP pleaded for similar treatment to Maharaja Hari Singh as accorded to the other princes and nawabs.

But the National Conference and Congress as also their cronies accused the PP and Pt. Dogra of being agents of dynastic rule, i.e. *rajvadashahi*. This was done to mislead the public opinion as to the PP's stand.

Respectful to the Maharaja

Pt. Prem Nath was quite respectful to the Maharaja despite being prematurely retired from his government. He was critical of the appeasement policies of Prime Minister Jawaharlal Nehru towards the Sheikh and attempts to humiliate Maharaja Hari Singh, treating him as his opponent.

Pt. Dogra in a procession

Panditji felt that Jawaharlal Nehru had not done justice to the king who had opted for India with a national outlook, braving all the pressures to merge Pakistan, which the Maharaja also felt was created under a design.

Maharaja Hari Singh minced no words in voicing his feelings that many problems in Kashmir were the creation of excessive pampering of the Sheikh, who was never consistent in his behaviour and approach and had been changing colours even on national issues.

Pandit Prem Nath Dogra made it a point to call on the Maharaja when he visited Mumbai in the late fifties as a leader of the Bharatiya Jana Sangh.

VINDICTIVE NEHRU

According to some historians, the genesis of the Kashmir imbroglio lies in the animosity between Sheikh Mohammad Abdullah and Maharaja Hari Singh, and political friendship of Jawaharlal Nehru with the Sheikh. This friendship had made the powerful Nehru vindictive towards Hari Singh to the extent that at the instance of his friend, Maharaja Hari Singh was forced out of his state to live and die in exile in 1962 at Mumbai, despite the J&K state legally becoming an integral part of India after his signing of Instrument of Accession with the Indian Union. Many writers have termed this act of Nehru as not only injustice, but also a blunder.

This can be gauged from an incident after the Maharaja was ousted from his state.

After the Maharaja had left his state on 23rd April, 1949, a few months later, Prime Minister Nehru visited Jammu and along with the Sheikh was taken out in a procession. At Purani Mandi near the office of Rajput Sabha, Nanak Singh Jamwal, an activist of the Sabha had put up a hoarding at the reception gate with the demand:

"Maharaja Hari Singh ko wapas lao"

At the end of the procession in the Parade Ground, on the northern side, a public meeting was held. In the course of his speech, Nehru stamped his foot repeatedly and in a raised voice said thrice:

"Maen kahata hoon Hari Singh naheen ayegaa,
naheen ayegaa, naheen ayegaa."

Pt. Nehru addresses a meeting at Jammu

These angry words made many people leave the venue of the meeting and Nehru's declaration also gave impetus to the activities of Praja Parishad as the party was already demanding a similar treatment for the state's Maharaja, like that of other rajas and nawabs of the country.

Evidently the reason for Nehru being against the Maharaja was that in 1944, the Sheikh-led NC had launched a 'Quit Kashmir' movement along the lines of the 'Quit India' movement. Generally, the slogan of National Conference was 'Dogra Kashmir *chhor do*' although the common Dogra people had nothing to do with it as Maharaja's rule was a dynastic monarchy, but the anti-Dogra slogans were generating obvious feelings against the National Conference in the land of Dogras.

In 1946, when the Sheikh was arrested and a case was lodged on him with sedition charges, Nehru, against the advice of other Congress national leaders of that time, tried to come to plead Sheikh's case in the court but the Maharaja had forbidden his entry in the state. The display of anger by Nehru was also an indication of how vindictive he was.

It is pertinent to mention here that adverse conditions were created to such an extent that in 1962, when the upright Maharaja Hari Singh breathed his last, no member of his family was on his side, except for his close aide, ADC Capt. Dewan Singh.

Article 370 as Enshrined in the Constitution

1. Notwithstanding anything in this Constitution,
   a. the provision of Article 238 shall not apply in relation to the State of Jammu & Kashmir;
   b. the power of Parliament to make laws for the said state shall be limited to:
      i. those matters in the Union List and the Concurrent List which, in consultation with the government of the state, are declared by the President to correspond to matters specified in the Instrument of Accession governing the accession of the State to the Dominion, Legislature may make laws for that state; and
      ii. such other matters in the said lists, as with the concurrence of the government of the state, the President may by order specify.

Explanation: For the purposes of this article, the government of the state means the person for the time being recognised by the President as the Maharaja of Jammu & Kashmir acting on the advice of the Council of Ministers for the time being in office under the Maharaja's proclamation dated the fifth day of March 1948;

   c. the provisions of Article 1 and of this Article shall apply in relation to that state;
   d. such of the other provisions of this Constitution shall apply in relation to that state, subject to such exceptions and modifications as the President may by order specify:

Provided that no such order which relates to the matters specified in the Instrument of Accession of the State referred to in paragraph (i) of sub clause (b) shall be issued except in consultation with the government of the state:

Provided further that no such order which relates to matters other than those referred to in the last preceding proviso shall be issued except with the concurrence of that government.

2. If the concurrence of the government of the State referred to in paragraph (ii) of sub clause (b) of clause 1 or in the second proviso to sub-clause (d) of that clause be given before the Constituent Assembly for the purpose of framing the constitution of the state is convened, it shall be placed before such Assembly for such decisions as it may take thereon.
3. Notwithstanding anything in the foregoing provisions of this Article, the President may, by public notification, declare that this Article shall cease to be operative or shall be operative only with such exceptions and modifications and from such date as he may specify:

Provided that the recommendation of the Constituent Assembly of the state referred to in clause (2) shall be necessary before the President issues such a notification.

ARTICLE 370: AN EVIL

There were several reasons for launching the big agitation of 1952-53. The Praja Parishad was opposed to the incorporation of Article 370 in the Indian Constitution granting separate status to Jammu & Kashmir state. This was taken by the Praja Parishad as discriminatory and obnoxious as it would encourage divisive and fissiparous tendencies and prove to be a psychological barrier. However, the Praja Parishad's warnings were ignored.

It is pertinent to recall that the Maharaja Hari Singh of J&K had signed the same Instrument of Accession that was signed by about 560 other princely states of India. The other states agreed to fully adopt the Indian Constitution but the Sheikh-led National Conference leaders pleaded for a separate status in Constituent Assembly because of their state having a Muslim-majority identity.

In the Constituent Assembly of India, while framing the Constitution, this state was represented by the top leaders of the National Conference, viz. Sheikh Mohammad Abdullah, Mirza Afzal Beg and Molana Mohammad Sayeed Masoodi from Kashmir and a little-known Moti Ram Biagra from Jammu. There was no representative of Ladakh.

In the draft of the Constitution, originally the name of this state was inserted simply as Kashmir, but later, on objection raised by some members from Bengal and others, the amended name was corrected as Jammu & Kashmir. Not only this, the Kashmiri language alone was included in the 8th Schedule of the Constitution. It was only in 2002 during the NDA rule led by Atal Bihari Vajpayee, that the Dogri language could find a place in the Constitution. Thus, Dogri had to wait for about 50 years to get recognition at the constitutional level as a regional language.

It is noteable to mention here that Article 370 was not included in the original draft of the Constitution prepared by the then Union Law Minister and founding father of the Constitution, Dr. B.R. Amebedkar. Ignoring the reservations made by most of the national leaders of the party not to pamper the Sheikh, Nehru entrusted the task to another minister, Gopalaswami Ayyanagar to pilot the Article 370. Several members of the Constituent Assembly, including Maulana Hasarat Mohani raised serious objections over this discriminatory step. To pacify the agitated members, they were assured that this Article would "wither away with the passage of time."

But in Jammu & Kashmir, Pt. Prem Nath Dogra was not convinced about this assertion by Nehru. He was of the strong opinion that it was easy to opt for any wrong course of action but difficult to get rid of it.

Panditji quite often had been observing:

"Lamhon ne khata ki, sadion ne saza paee."

The result has been obvious.

The events of the history indicate how visionary Pt. Dogra was. Even today, after about seven decades, this temporary provision not only existed in the statute book but too the descendants of the Sheikh and some other controversial elements are harping for undoing what had been intended in the state by constitutional provisions and restoration of what is being demanded as autonomy, and even *azadi*.

Many legal and far-sighted people opine that Article 370 has become a psychological barrier between this state and the rest of India, resulting in numerous problems, including secessionism and backwardness of J&K on many accounts.

Adoption of Flag of Jammu & Kashmir

The so-called national movement in the state had from the very beginning a distinctive growth and character. Although the Indian National Congress did support the All Jammu & Kashmir National Conference in its struggle against the autocratic rule of Maharaja, the National Conference did not merge with the Indian National Congress.

However, the National Conference adopted a red flag with a white emblem of a plough in the centre as a symbol of its political organisation in 1939. The same flag was accepted as the party flag in 'Naya Kashmir'.

□

Major Issues

VISIONARY LEADER

Pt. Prem Nath Dogra was very much alive to the happenings around, especially in J&K.

He knew how the Jamaat-e-Islami was becoming active and hundreds of *madrassas* had been opened to spread their ideology of radicalisation.

The people of Kashmir were known as peace-loving and refraining from any kind of violence. But in the to events of modern history, the seeds of radicalisation were sown by leaders of the National Conference and the Congress themselves, the fruits of which are being reaped by the enemy. The founder of Pakistan, Mohammad Ali Jinnah, was invited to Kashmir by Sheikh Mohammad Abdullah and his colleagues as far back as in early 1944; so was the Muslim Conference. Upon their invitation, Jinnah and his sister Fatima Jinnah came to Jammu on 8th May, 1944. According to an account given by Mohammad Sarver Abbasi, Vice-Chancellor of Muzaffarabad University, upon his entering the state. Jinnah was received by the National Conference leaders, Bakshi Ghulam Mohammad and others at Suchetgarh. A warm welcome was arranged for the Muslim League leader by the Muslim Conference and partly by National Conference.

In the evening, in Jammu city, the Muslim Conference arranged a big public meeting at Eidgah in the city. This was done by Choudhary Ghulam Abbas and his colleagues of the Muslim Conference.

JINNAH IN SRINAGAR

The next day, 9th May, 1944, upon the entry of Jinnah in the Valley, a big reception was accorded to him by the National Conference. A function in this regard was held at Pratap Park, Srinagar, at which the reception address in honour of Jinnah was read by Pandit Jia Lal Kilam.

Kilam cleverly inserted at the end of his speech that "such receptions are held in honour of great men whosoever visits Kashmir."

These words irked Jinnah and in his speech, while expressing his gratitude for according this royal reception, he too cleverly remarked that he was of the belief that this reception was not for his person but for the Muslim League which he headed.

Jinnah stayed in Srinagar for over two months and enjoyed reception parties and *ziafatien* (feasts), etc. He listened to the views of both the National Conference leaders as also of their adversaries led by Mirwaiz of Kashmir, Yusuf Shah, and head of the Muslim Conference. On his return, after over two months' stay in the Valley, he travelled via the Uri-Muzaffarabad Road and at a function at Murree, Jinnah announced his unequivocal support to the Muslim Conference of Mirwaiz.

This statement of Jinnah, Sheikh Abdullah was annoyed to the extent that he pledged, "I will never accept the two-nation theory of Jinnah till the last drop of my blood."

This statement of the Sheikh came as be a boon for Jawaharlal Nehru and thus both of them came to become close friends. This made the Sheikh become the Prime Minister of J&K and all-powerful Sheikh ultimately became a problem on many accounts.

The happenings of 1952-53 agitation by the Praja Parishad jolted the Sheikh, who otherwise had unbridled authority. The powerful Sheikh Abdullah came in contact with certain foreign diplomats, who injected in him the virus of an independent Kashmir, and the was also enshrined in the National Conference manifesto, the *'Naya Kashmir'*.

With this dream in his mind, Sheikh Abdullah began to get jittery because of the Praja Parishad agitation for putting J&K at par with other parts of the country. He started showing signs of his inner worry. Not only this, he had also begun to disrespect senior leaders in New Delhi, like Maulana Abdul Kalam Azad and others.

Sensing serious developments in the days to come, the Sheikh's own colleagues on 9th August, 1953, deposed and jailed him. His deputy, Bakshi Ghulam Mohammad now became the Prime Minister of the state. And thus, a new era began for the state and also for the Praja Parishad.

The agitated Sheikh's supporters floated a new outfit under the title of Plebiscite Front, which gave new impetus to sowing seeds of separatism.

For many reasons, Jawaharlal Nehru did not wish to keep his friend in jail any more; hence, a big change was effected in the Kashmir policy in the early sixties. Under a plan, Prime Minister Bakshi Ghulam Mohammad was removed from power. After some important happenings, a senior National Conference leader, G.M. Sadiq was installed as Prime Minister of the state on 29th February, 1964. The Sheikh and his colleagues were released on 8th April, 1964. The court cases against the Sheikh were withdrawn and it was decided to fight the Sheikh 'politically'.

In the 1967 Assembly elections, the Sheikh-led Kashmir Plebiscite Front gave a call for boycott of Congressmen with the slogan of *'Tark-e-Mawalat'* (social boycott) by terming them as 'insects of the dirty lane'. Such moves by the Sheikh caused an embarrassing situation for the Congressmen in the Valley of Kashmir.

To contain the influence of Sheikh Abdullah, the ruling Congress activists, who were the old adversaries of the Sheikh including the scions of Mirwaiz Yusuf Shah and others (even some who had earlier left for Pakistan-occupied Kashmir), were persuaded to return. Mohammad Umar Farooq, who was installed as the Mirwaiz of Kashmir, formed the Awami Action Committee with a secessionist stance and slogans.

The then Pradesh Congress chief, Syed Mir Qasim and some other senior Congressman enjoying feast with Mirwaiz of Kashmir and head of Awami Action Committee, Maulana Mohammad Farooq after Sheikh Abdullah had termed them as 'insects of dirty lane'. What politics! Adversary becomes friend to meet the challenge of another one

As part of their plan to counter the Sheikh, an official body but with secret functioning was created. It was known as FSO (Field Survey Organisation). It was headed by some experts in political matters. Because of such moves the Jamaat-e-Islami also emerged on the Kashmir scene. Several *maktabs* and *madrassas* were opened in the Valley. Some other such extremist outfits too mysteriously came up.

A senior journalist wrote an article with some details on how the tentacles of the Jamaat-e-Islami were being spread to radicalise Kashmir.

The visionary Pt. Prem Nath Dogra was alarmed to read this write-up. He straight went to the Chief Minister G.M. Sadiq and asked what was happening.

(Up to 1965, the nomenclature of the state executive was as Prime Minister. It was changed on 30th March, 1965 to that of Chief Minister.)

Sadiq asked Pandit Dogra to see Syed Mir Qasim, who was then Revenue Minister and also the state president of the Congress. When Pt. Dogra asked Syed Qasim that what was happening, the latter's reply was, "Do you know the meaning of *Tark-e-Mawalat?*"

After all, we too have to live in Kashmir. You know that iron cuts iron (*lohe ko loha katata hai aur zehar ko zehar*)."

Pt. Dogra understood the feelings of the Congress leader but felt that what was being done was not good for the future.

CONGRESS REACTION TO ADVICE

Interestingly, after cautioning by Pt. Dogra against sowing the seeds of radicalism in Kashmir, the ruling Congress leaders substantially enhanced the funding of FSO and extended its area of operation towards Jammu for weakening the Jana Sangh. Some of its activists went astray.

It is noteable here that for first time in the 1972 Assembly elections, the Jamaat-e-Islami won five seats in Valley and became the major Opposition group in the House and the Bharatiya Jana Sangh was relegated to second position with just three members.

Ali Shah Geelani, leader of the separatist Hurriyat Conference at that time, became the deputy leader of the Jamaat-e-Islami group, with Saif-ud-din Qari as the leader.

In 1975, in the wake of Indira-Sheikh accord, Sheikh Mohammad Abdullah took over the reigns of power and his first move was to disband the FSO. (But one report said the Qasim-led Congress government itself in the last Cabinet meeting had decided to disband the controversial FSO before handing over power to Sheikh Abdullah in the last week of February 1975.) And in the 1977 Assembly elections, the Jamaat-e-Islami could muster just one seat.

After the death of Sheikh Abdullah in 1982, the radical outfits combined to form the Muslim United Front (MUF). In the 1987 Assembly elections, the performance of the MUF improved, but it created problems, alleging that some of its wining candidates were declared defeated. They also included Mohammad Yusuf Shah, a young man of Amira Kadal. The same Shah is now the chief commander of Jehad Council operating from Pakistan/PoK.

The wrongs of the National Conference and that of the Congress done in the wake of the Rajiv-Farooq accord in 1986-87, led to great resentment in Kashmir. Pakistan, taking advantage of the anger, exploited the youth and provoked them to take up guns and thus armed terrorism broke out in Kashmir.

No doubt, Pakistan is behind the menace of cross-border terror but the love-hate relationship of the Congress and National Conference is no less responsible for the sad situation in this state, more so, in the troubled Kashmir Valley, for sowing the seeds of radicalism.

In this regard it is also notable that the leaders of these pseudo-secular parties did not learn any lesson from the happenings of the past. In 1983, the then BJP president, Atal Bihari Vajpayee had termed the relationship of Congress with that of the National Conference as those of jilted lovers who create problems.

JAGMOHAN'S BOLD STEPS

After the alarming situation developed in 1990, the then J&K Governor Jagmohan, took some bold steps for correcting the wrongs of the past. These also included the winding up of about 200 *madrassas* and other such educational centres. These were brought under the control of the State Education Department and their teachers and other staff were adjusted after due screening. With the result, in 1996, the number of such *madrassas* and religious centres dropped to a big zero and in 2008, it was 34. But about a decade back, in 2008-2009, the Centre provided a special grant of some crores for 'imparting quality education' in *madrassas* and *maktabs* with the result that a large number of *madrassas* and other such bodies for religious education began to sprout, not only in the Valley, but also in many sensitive areas of Jammu. The number of such religious institutions has gone up to over a thousand, both registered and unregistered. In this regard, an amazing account is also apparent from the answer of a Q.D. in the Assembly.

Regarding: Educational Institutions
Unstarred A.Q. No. 126: Prof. Chaman Lal Gupta:
Will the government state?

<table>
<tr><th></th><th>Questions</th><th></th><th>Reply</th></tr>
<tr><td>a.</td><td>Year-wise the amount received under Central schemes for providing quality education in educational institutions for minorities and the assistance provided to each such body along with the number of students and teachers therefore;</td><td>a.</td><td>The details are at Annexure 'A'.
24th February, 2014</td></tr>
<tr><td>b.</td><td>Separately, the number of local/non-local teachers in these institutions giving the name and residential particulars of non-local teachers;</td><td>b.</td><td>The details of local and non-local teachers in madrassas are detailed below and list of non-local teachers is detailed at annexure 'B':
<table>
<tr><th>S No.</th><th>Divison</th><th>Local Trs.</th><th>Non Local Trs.</th><th>Total</th></tr>
<tr><td>1</td><td>Jammu</td><td>337</td><td>17</td><td>354</td></tr>
<tr><td>2</td><td>Kashmir</td><td>521</td><td>Nil</td><td>521</td></tr>
</table></td></tr>
<tr><td>c.</td><td>The number of registered and unregistered madrassas and other such institutions as in 1996, 2002, 2008 and as on date; and</td><td>c.</td><td>The details of registered and un-registered madrassas is detailed below:
<table>
<tr><th></th><th>1996</th><th>2002</th><th>2008</th><th>Present</th></tr>
<tr><td>Registered</td><td>Nil</td><td>23</td><td>23</td><td>298</td></tr>
<tr><td>Unregistered</td><td>Nil</td><td>9</td><td>11</td><td>165</td></tr>
</table></td></tr>
<tr><td>d.</td><td>Whether this assistance is provided to all schools for minorities, including those run by Sikhs; if not, the reasons therefore?</td><td>d.</td><td>No sir. The assistance is provided to madrassas under Centrally-sponsored 'Scheme to Provide Quality Education in Madrassas' (SPQEM) which seeks to bring about qualitative improvement in madrassas to enable Muslim children attain standards of the national education system in formal education subjects.</td></tr>
</table>

It is worth taking note of the moves for more and more radicalising of Kashmir (J&K). The activities by terrorists have been targeting the state educational system. During the nineties alone, terrorists had set ablaze as many as 800 government and private buildings and other structures. These included nearly 600 schools and other educational buildings. The purpose was obviously to keep the younger generation away from educational bodies.

To what extent educational institutions had been the target of anti-national elements is evident from the fact that during 2016, large-scale violence was seen in south Kashmir where about 40 buildings were set on fire. Of these, as many as 34 were schools.

More significant was that during those days of serious violence and strikes, the *madrassas* and other such bodies hummed with unusual activity. Many of them linked with such institutions were found indulging in stone-pelting and other such unlawful acts.

How much this number has gone up is anybody's guess. Many have come up in most sensitive border areas. At least four *madrassas* have been opened for Rohingya immigrants in Jammu alone.

In this connection, a passage from the book, *My Frozen Turbulence in Kashmir,* authored by former Governor Jagmohan, also makes noteable reading.

BANNING OF SUBVERSIVE ORGANISATIONS

"With the interrogation of the persons arrested, the ruthless manner of operations by the subversive organisations became still clearer. To undermine their operational effectiveness, I decided to declare unlawful some of the more dangerous organisations.

Governor Jagmohan in Kashmir

"On 16th April, 1990, I issued orders under the State Criminal Law Amendment Act, declaring eight organisations unlawful. These were: Jamaat-e-Islami, J&K Hizbul Mujahideen, J&K Liberation Front, Students' Liberation Front, Mahaz-e-Azadi Islami Students League, People's League and Islamic Jamiat-e-Talaba.

"I made it clear to the public that the organisations in question had been banned because of their secessionist and terrorist activities, for which ample proof existed. These organisations, I further pointed out, were building up a general atmosphere of subversion and terrorism and were sowing the seeds of the disintegration of India.

"One immediate and significant result of the orders was that the offices and bank accounts of Jamaát-e-Islami were sealed and their cadres scattered. Publicity material could not also be easily produced and distributed. The Friday gathering could not also be addressed from the mosques by the Jamaát-e-Islami's leaders who either fled or were arrested."

"One of the root causes of the current turmoil in Kashmir was the role played by Jamaát-e-Islami and its auxiliary agencies, like Falah-i-Aam. As brought out in the earlier chapters, these bodies had been laying the seed-bed of fundamentalism and fanaticism through the numerous schools and *mudrassas* run by them. Narrow ideas were planted in the impressionable minds of children. The present crop of fundamentalism in Kashmir which has weakened the indigenous Kashmir's Islam is largely a result of unchecked activities conducted through schools and *madrassas* run by the Jamaát-e-Islami and Falah-i-Aam Trust. While discussing the Kashmir issue in the Pakistan Press and Parliament, the chief of Pakistani Jamaát-e-Islami said that Kashmiris had woken up and understood the true meaning of Islam and resorted to *jihad* against India.

"I, therefore, decided to immediately plug the foundation-head of subversion and fanaticism in Kashmir. I also banned the Falah-i-Aam Trust and declared its activities unlawful. The closure of 157 schools run by the Trust was the obvious consequence of this decision. For 15,000 students of these 157 schools, arrangements were simultaneously made for admission to the government-run educational institutions where normal education was imparted."

A difficult task was smoothly and speedily performed where by virtue of judicial orders passed by the high-powered tribunal headed by Justice G.D. Sharma, eight militant organisations banned by Governor Jagmohan in the year 1990 were confirmed under vide SRO 146, dated 16 April, 1990. The Jamaát-e-Islami of J&K was declared as an unlawful association. vide SRO 147, dated 16th April, 1990; the Islamic Students League was declared as unlawful association vide SRO 148, dated 16th April, 1990; the Islamic Jamiat-e-Talaba was declared as unlawful association vide SRO 149, dated 16th April, 1990; the Mahaz-e-Azadi was declared as unlawful association vide SRO 150, dated 16th April, 1990; the People's League was declared as unlawful association vide SRO 151, dated 16th April, 1990; the Jammu & Kashmir Liberation Front was declared as unlawful association.

Justice G.D. Sharma

(Ref: Jagmohan (1991), My Frozen Turbulence in Kashmir, *Allied Publishers, New Delhi.)*

GENERAL VIEW

It is beyond any doubt that the roots of problems in Kashmir are not only local ones; they lie outside the borders. But an outsider alone cannot cause much harm. What has been happening in Kashmir is a mixed picture.

In this regard, the question is that when the *madrassas* and other such bodies were disbanded on specific grounds, what was the need to provide grants, and that too by the Centre? More so in the name of minorities, although in this state the operators of *madrassas* and other such outfits do not come from minorities of the state.

In J&K, Hindus, Sikhs, Buddhists and Christians are the real minorities; no such assistance has ever been provided to them.

In view of all this, there are many who feel that if the advice of visionary Pt. Prem Nath Dogra had been taken, the many complex problems would not have cropped up.

The patriotic moves of the Praja Parishad/Bharatiya Jana Sangh in this regard were very clear.

CEASEFIRE

Nehru and Sheikh counselling

Pt. Dogra was opposed to a ceasefire in 1948, especially when the Pakistani invaders were on the run and the Indian forces were marching rapidly in liberating the enemy-held areas of the state.

He was of the view that holding of state territory by Pakistan would become a bone of contention between the two neighbours. Moreover, Pakistan had no legal authority; her position was nothing other that of an invader.

But Prime Minister Nehru was guided by other considerations. He was obtaining more guidance from Sheikh Abdullah than anybody else on Kashmir. But the Sheikh was not interested in those areas as he had little following outside the Kashmir Valley. And thus, the people of the enemy-held areas were left at the mercy of mauraders. It is noteable that in Pak-held areas, there was a population of about 35 per cent Hindu, Sikhs and other miniorties before the invasion, but now, not a single person from these communities is left there. All of them have been eliminated or forcibly converted to Islam.

A Sikh boy who could not migrate was converted by the jihadis *to Islam*

Among two brothers, one was converted to Islam in PoK, as he could not migrate to this side.

The signs of the painful communal division of India still remind us of how a terrible situation was created. The armed tribesmen launched a massive attack to grab the state of for annexing to the theocratic State of Pakistan.

The invaders supported by Pakistan Army, entered this state in the third week of October, 1947. Poonch and Muzaffarabad areas were their first target. In the Plandri and Rawala Kot areas of Poonch, a large number of invaders indulged in loot and plunder.

Thus, Sardar Chatterpal Singh was separated from his wife and three male children, namely Paramjit Singh: 9 years and 6 months, Bhagat Singh: 5 years and Rajinder Singh: 3 years under hapless circumstances before reaching the migrant's camp in Jammu. After finding no clue of the where abouts of the members of his family, Chatterpal entered into a second marriage. But he and others continued with their efforts to find the fate of the family members left in Pak-held areas. Ultimately information came that the wife had died and his three children, like others, had been converted to Islam by the *jihadis*.

Not only this, many Muslims had been forced to leave and they left for the Gulf countries as also the UK. In their place, Pakistanis and other outsiders were settled. The entire demographic character some regions had been changed.

After the ceasefire, the UN Assembly, with some preconditions to be the filled by Pakistan on 5th February, 1949, adopted a resolution for holding a plebiscite to decide the future of the state although India, including Sheikh Abdullah made it clear that "not the accession but the Pak aggression is the issue", in accordance with the provision that the Maharaja was entitled to opt for India or Pakistan.

Indian forces had landed in the state only after the Maharaja had completed the formalities of signing the Instrument of Accession.

Pt. Prem Nath Dogra was not only against the ceasefire but also did not favour knocking at the doors of UNO as he rightly feared that the Kashmir issue would become a pawn of international politics as nations were divided between power blocs.

UN RESOLUTION FOR PLEBISCITE

On 5th February, 1949 the UN adopted a resolution for plebiscite with the pre-conditions that Pakistan would vacate the occupied areas and conditions would be created for the conduct of the plebiscite. But instead of withdrawing its troops from occupied areas, Pakistan first resorted to cleansing of the minorities and also the liberal Muslims from the so-called Azad Kashmir. In their place, outsiders like Punjabis and even Afghans, were settled there.

Amazingly, even after totally changing the demographic character and fiddling with the geographical position by illegally gifting away large areas of this state to China, Pakistan and its cronies in Kashmir, the Kashmiri Muslims, rant for plebiscite to decide the future of J&K by referring to UN resolution of 5th Feburary, 1949 and ignoring the fact that this resolution was strictly on the pre-condition that Pakistan would withdraw its forces and create a situation for ascertaining the views of the people of the state.

Far from doing so, the invaders are still occupying large areas of J&K, including the most strategic areas of Gilgit and Baltistan.

In Pak-occupied Jammu & Kashmir before 1947, about 35 per cent population comprised of Hindus, Sikhs and other minorities. But over the years, now not a single member of these communities can be found there. Many were massacred during the painful days of 1947-48 while others were forced to become migrants.

Not only this, instead of vacating its troops in accordance with the requirements of the UN resolution, Pakistan has raised several cantonments of permanent nature and also established training centres for not only its army; several places are being used for training and lodging of terrorists. Some of the top terrorist commanders too live in the illegally-occupied Kashmir.

MIRPUR DEVASTATION

Prior to the Pakistani invasion of the state in 1947, Mirpur was the second biggest city of the Jammu region. It was a flourishing trade centre. It was known for having men of high calibre, like Lala Ayodha Nath, elected members of the Maharaja's Praja Sabha, Chaudhary Ram Lal Sadavarti, Chaudhary Gian Chand, the editor of the *Sadaquat* weekly, Raja Mohammad Akbar, editor and philosopher, Judge Harbans Lal, Mahasa Roop Chand, Jagdish Chander Gupta and many others from different spheres of life. The relations between various communities were cordial as the name of this city, named after two saints, Mir and Puri, suggests.

During the painful days of 1947, the religious zealots made several attempts to grab the city, but their attacks were repulsed by the army supported by the nationalists. But on the fateful night of 24-25 November, the invaders supported by Pakistani troops succeeded in capturing the historic city because of the withdrawal of the state army under mysterious circumstances.

The highly communalised invaders resorted to barbaric acts of massacre of thousands of innocent women, children, the aged and others who could not move out.

In this regard, horrible eyewitness accounts of the bloodbath have been given by C.P. Gupta in his write-up in the *Daily Excelsior*, dated 5th March, 2017.

What a terrible and heart-rending scene it was! The author witnessed it at the age of 16, when Pakistan with its fully armed battalions, like hungry wolves, pounced upon the innocent and unarmed population of Mirpur city, now in PoK, when out of the total population of 25,000 men, women and children of tender age, more than 18,000 people were brutally killed in three days of carnage on 25, 26th and 27th November, 1947. The only 'crime' of the people of Mirpur was that they had unitedly vowed to protect Mirpur, their land of birth, from the Pakistani raiders even at the cost of their own lives.

Trouble began when on 26th October, 1947, Maharaja Hari Singh, the then ruler of Jammu & Kashmir state, signed the Instrument of Accession after which Jammu & Kashmir became an integral part of India. This could not be digested by the Pakistani regime. It planned a nefarious design in connivance with the Pathans. This led to a secret agreement between Pakistan and the Pathan mercenaries, according to which, if Mirpur city was forcibly occupied, the captured women would be taken by the Pathans and the immovable land of Mirpur and movable property, viz. gold, cash etc., would be the share of Pakistani regime. This was named as 'Zan and Zar' agreement. Before carrying out the armed attack, the Pakistani regime, in the first week of November 1947, managed to a secret manner, to send a bag of pamphlets written in Urdu, in the city of Mirpur, in which it was written that the Pakistan government would assign a special status to Mirpur in Pakistan if the citizens of Mirpur amicably surrendered themselves and allowed the Pakistani army to occupy the territory of Mirpur without any hindrance. The literate and the elderly persons of the city met in the evening and decided outright to reject the proposal of the Pakistani regime and the refusal was conveyed through the shower of bullets from each defence picket of the city. This invited a brutal attack on Mirpur from the enemy.

The small and ill-equipped state police force stationed at that time at Mirpur was fully assisted by the young civilian population of the city. On the midnight of 24th November, 1947, under a thick cover of artillery shelling and bursting of grenades which are normally used during an openly declared war, the Pakistani army launched a major attack on the southern side of the city, which was spiritedly resisted by the depleting garrison force for six hours. Although the pickets put up a tough resistance, the enemy came in, wave after wave, and after six hours of ceaseless fighting, the defence line of the city was overrun by several Pathans. Alarmed at the most critical situation, the Flying Death Squads of the city engaged themselves ferociously in hand-to-hand combat with the infiltrators and killed all the raiding Pathans at the cost of the lives of many young men of the Mirpur community. Though the people of Mirpur displayed tremendous grit and tenacity, the end seemed gloomy and dreadful because that operation depleted the city's stock of ammunition to nearly zero. Further, due to the irony of fate, the old model wireless set installed in the police camp at Mirpur suddenly developed some technical snag and went out of order, leading to disruption in the radio link with the state police headquarters at Jammu and the Government of India. Despite the war-like situation created by Pakistan, the Government of India, due to political rivalry between the then Prime Minister of India and the Maharaja of Jammu & Kashmir state, did not send the army although at that moment, the Indian Army was stationed at Jhanghar, which is at a distance of only 20 miles from Mirpur.

In that critical situation, the state administration headed by Wazir Wazarat of Mirpur decided to clandestinely retreat to Jammu, leaving behind the hapless civilian population of the city to face the wrath of the marauders. It was the moral duty of the state administration to ask the citizens of Mirpur to vacate the city and march towards Jammu under their protection but far from doing their duty, the Wazir Wazarat and his police officers galloped away on their horses and left the city in the wee hours of 25th November, leaving behind their own wounded soldiers who were crying in pain because of their wounds in the Police Line Hospital. This cowardly departure of the state administration from Mirpur city sent a triumphant signal to the enemy. At that moment, the entire population of the city of Mirpur felt themselves as hanging between the jaws of the enemy, which was very eager to devour the flesh and even the bones of the people of Mirpur for refusing to give shelter to the Pakistani invaders.

Immediately after the departure of the state administration from the city, a fully-armed battalion of the Pakistan army assisted by Pathan raiders entered the city from all sides at the stroke of 8.30 a.m. and raising terrible sounds of their war instruments, pushed the local population into one corner of the city. The terrified men, women and children in utter chaos and confusion in the midst of heavy firing from all sides and in the choking atmosphere due to smoke billowing out of the burning houses of the city, scattered and went forth in caravans in different directions, without knowing where they were going. They were intercepted by the enemy at various places who like hungry wolves unleashed terror and brutal savagery which rendered the whole area an open graveyard of dead bodies. Many seriously wounded, uncared for persons were battling for life in the whirlpool of their own blood. By sunset, the entire area from Mirpur city to the foothill was fully covered with dead bodies and critically injured persons. Ultimately, in the gathering darkness, Nature had to forcibly convey a signal that the graveyard was full and no further entry of any dead body was possible. That brought a temporary halt to the day's carnage.

This was not the end of the misery of the people of Mirpur. At night fall on the same day, an ill-fated group of about 2,000 captured persons was brought to a place known as Kas Guma, a colony of retired Muslim soldiers. The enemy encircled the captives and asked them to surrender all the cash and jewellery which they had with them. Thereafter, the males were asked to remove their clothes and lie down in a row. They were tortured brutally and killed in batches, throughout the night. The women and girls were taken to unknown places by the Pathans as per their 'Zan and Zar' agreement with the Pakistani regime. Next day, the enemy drove another group of about 2,000 persons and brought them to a village known as Thathal. They also met the same brutal treatment as at Kas Guma during the day. Finally there was a massacre at Ali Beg where, about 5,000 captives were huddled up in an old deserted, unhygienic and ruined *gurudwara* building. In the beginning about 50 to 100 young men were daily taken on pick-and-choose basis to be killed in the open fields. Besides, on an average basis, about 15 to 20 aged captives died every day due to the severe cold weather, starvation, illness and mental shock.

On 1st December, a young Muslim attorney named Mohammad Ibrahim, being very soft in tongue and well known to many Hindu officers of Mirpur, visited the Ali Beg prison and showed his lip sympathy to the intelligentsia who were brought there as captives. He also shed crocodile tears on their pitiable condition and assured them that he would do his best to talk with the concerned authorities of the Government of Pakistan to get them employed in factories on a daily wage basis till they were at Ali Beg camp as captives. He distributed Muslim caps and mufflers to some of them as a token of friendship, but these gestures were in fact subtle signals and indications to the Pakistani soldiers to massacre these persons first. The next morning, the enemy soldiers drove a group of educated people out of the prison on the pretext that they would be taken back in the evening with their earnings after utilising their services in factories during the day. Those wearing caps and mufflers unknowingly occupied the front line to get priority in getting jobs at factories but they never came back as they all were slaughtered on the bank of the Jhelum canal.

In mid-January 1948, a team of ICRC (International Committee of Red Cross) arrived and took charge of the camp, supplying the much-needed food and medicines to the captives. On March 18th, they managed to get the captives released in exchange of the same number of Muslims who were in India and willing to go to Pakistan. The freed captives, at that time were not more than about 1,600 as the rest had either been killed, dead or kidnapped. The liberated persons were mostly aged and unable to even walk. They reached Amritsar where they were given a tearful and touching reception by their relatives and the general public.

In the memory of Mirpur martyrs of 1947, a Shaheedi Smarak was constructed by the government of Jammu & Kashmir at a conspicuous place in front of the main entry gate of the Government Medical College at Mahespura Chowk, Bakshi Nagar, Jammu. The Jammu Development Authority dedicated the said Smarak to the Mirpur community and which was unveiled by Sushma Choudhary, I.A.S. and the then Financial Commissioner on 25th November, 1998. The said Smarak is also the starting point of 'Mirpur Road' which was named so, on the same day, viz. 25th November, 1998 to pay tributes to the martyrs of Mirpur, under the patronage of late Harsajan Singh, who at that time was the Chairman of the Legislative Council of Jammu & Kashmir state.

On 25th November every year, thousands of Mirpuris residing in Jammu city and its peripheral colonies, march in *prabhat pheris* coming from different sectors of Jammu city and all assemble at the said Mirpur Shaheedi Smarak to pay heartfelt tributes to the martyrs of Mirpur who sacrificed their lives for the sake of their motherland, as a result of which the Jammu & Kashmir state remained an integral part of India.

(Ref: Original documents/records available in the Nanaji Deshmukh Library, Jammu.)

□

The Praja Parishad's Struggle against Separatist and Communal Politics

The Praja Parishad movement played a key role in opposing the separatist and communal tendencies of Sheikh Abdullah and Nehru's endorsement, even tacit encouragement, in the years following Jammu & Kashmir's accession to India. It campaigned vigorously for the state's complete and total integration with the rest of the Indian Union in the face of stiff resistance from Sheikh Abdullah and his henchmen. Numerous workers and leaders of Parishad suffered at the hands of the Sheikh's administration and many of them laid down their lives to uphold the unity of the country.

For a better appreciation of the Parishad's role in the state's politics and its impact on New Delhi's otherwise myopic policies on Jammu & Kashmir, it is important to take a brief look at the period immediately after Maharaja Hari Singh signed the Instrument of Accession. Sheikh Abdullah, who had found an ally in Jawaharlal Nehru, was becoming increasingly audacious by the day. Not content with Nehru's hands-off policy on Jammu & Kashmir, which forced Sardar Patel (much against his wishes) to play a non-participatory role as far as this state was concerned, Sheikh Abdullah began to dream of an independent state of which he would be the sole arbiter.

Sheikh Abdullah embarked on this mission in April 1949 through an interview to Michael Davidson of *The Observer*, in which he spoke on the impropriety of the Maharaja's accession, declared that he wanted to live in peace with both India and Pakistan and promoted the concept of an independent Kashmir which would be underwritten not only by India and Pakistan, but also the UK, the USA and the UN.

A furious Sardar Patel made his disapproval known in no uncertain terms. Nehru, ever willing to indulge Sheikh Abdullah, was forced to take note of the serious implications of the statement. What transpired between the two is not known, but Sheikh Abdullah finally disowned the statement on 18th May, 1949 and ruled out independence as an option. This was obviously a tactical retreat, because he began talking of secession soon after returning from a trip abroad, in late 1949.

All this apart, even before Maharaja Hari Singh had signed the Instrument of Accession which paved the way for Sheikh Abdullah's rise to political power, the National Conference had made clear its anti-Hindu, more specifically anti-Dogra bias, especially towards the residents of Jammu. Abdullah's concerns were limited to the Muslims of the Valley while his contempt was reserved for the Hindus.

Pt. Dogra at the satyagraha

The simmering resentment against Sheikh Abdullah's advocacy of self-determination, his pronounced communal bias, the 'Quit Kashmir' movement of 1946 and finally Pakistan's move to smash and grab Kashmir led to the birth of the Praja Parishad in November 1947. The Parishad's first president, Hari Wazir joined the army as a commissioned officer of the Indian Army and died in Kashmir. Pt. Prem Nath Dogra took charge of the organisation soon after and the Parishad emerged as the only representative party of Jammu dedicated to "achieve full integration of Jammu & Kashmir state with India like other acceding states and safeguard the legitimate democratic rights of the people of Jammu from the communist-dominated communal government of Sheikh Abdullah."

ACCESSION AND AFTER

Immediately after he signed the Instrument of Accession, Maharaja Hari Singh, on the advice of Government of India, set up an emergency administration headed by Sheikh Abdullah. This was replaced by an interim government, constituted by proclamation of the Maharaja in March 1948, and also headed by Sheikh Abdullah. The unique feature of the interim government was that it ruled by decree and reduced the Maharaja to nothing more than a rubber stamp and in a short time, adopted policies which were clearly aimed at Islamisation of the state polity and its isolation from the mainstream of India's democratic political culture.

The United Nation's intervention in the dispute with Pakistan, invoked by Nehru's misplaced trust in Lord Mountbatten and against the advice of Sardar Patel and other colleagues, and the subsequent Security Council Resolution envisaging a plebiscite under international supervision, almost challenged the state's accession to India. The National Conference lost no time in taking advantage of the Kashmir dispute between India and Pakistan to provide a mechanism to ensure protection for the Muslim majority of the state from being dominated by the Hindu majority of India.

The National Conference adopted four main strategies to achieve this goal:

a. It tried to interpret Article 370 as the exclusion of J&K from the Indian Constitution by forcing a separate constitutional relationship with the Union of India through this Article.
b. The Conference leaders abandoned their commitment to secularism and instead shifted their emphasis on consolidating the Muslim identity of the state; in a sense,

it was going back to the days of Sheikh Abdullah's identity as the leader of the Muslim Conference.

c. It insisted on the right of the Constituent Assembly of J&K which was instituted in 1951, to determine the future disposition of the state with regard to accession and also began discussing independence as the third option along with the other options of acceding to India or Pakistan. It began to work surreptitiously to consolidate Muslim opinion in the state against India and to prepare the ground for the secession of Jammu & Kashmir.

SHEIKH'S ANTECEDENTS IGNORED

Contrary to popular belief foisted upon the people by the Congress and the National Conference, not to mention other political parties, Sheikh Abdullah had cherished the dream of an independent Kashmir from the very early stages of his political career, which began as a rabble-rouser. He saw himself essentially as the leader of Kashmiri Muslims and promoted this view that he founded the Muslim Conference in 1932. He changed the nomenclature of his organisation to National Conference in 1938, not because he wanted to abandon his original stand, but because it suited his design and strategy.

Along with exploiting the religious appeal of his movement, he also exploited 'Kashmiriyat' to the hilt and launched an agitation after agitating against the Maharaja's regime and thus built up an essentially anti-Dogra Muslim movement in the Valley. Sheikh Abdullah's political game suited British strategic interests in the region and it is not entirely coincidental that the British should have made no effort to hide their sympathies for him and his agitation.

The 'Quit Kashmir' movement which Sheikh Abdullah launched in 1946 should not be seen as an 'uprising against a despotic ruler'; it had a specific political connotation that is not in consonance with the popular perception. The agitation was aimed against the Hindu ruler of the state as he was painted as an alien and aimed at establishing an independent Kashmir.

Nehru legitimised this separatist streak of Sheikh Abdullah of excluding J&K from the purview of the States Ministry and handing it over to Ayyangar under his direct supervision—a decision whose implications are too obvious to be stated.

FALLOUT OF NEHRU'S FLAWED POLICY

Having armed himself with unbridled power, Sheikh Abdullah began to ride roughshod, doing all he could to implement his political designs with the help of his friend Nehru in Delhi. He was extremely ruthless in suppressing the dissent raised by the Praja Parishad, using all the might of the official machinery to let loose a reign of terror. Nehru was fully aware of what was happening in J&K, but he chose to support Sheikh Abdullah's policies rather than chastise him. So much so, he blamed the Parishad for provoking his friend and, when cornered on the floor of Parliament, would not hesitate to throw a tantrum and thus escape criticism.

The following is a chronological history of events culminating in the martyrdom of the then Bharatiya Jana Sangh president, Dr. Syama Prasad Mookerjee on 23rd June, 1953 while being held a prisoner by Sheikh Abdullah.

Early in 1949, the Praja Parishad was targeted by Sheikh Abdullah's regime for persecution, leading to clashes. Pt. Prem Nath Dogra, who had by then emerged as a popular leader with a large following in the Jammu region, was arrested. By the summer of that year, the Sheikh's prisons had as many as 294 Parishad workers rotting behind bars without trial. This action of his distressed many Indian leaders,

Lathi charge on Praja Parishad activists

including senior parliamentarians, though Nehru cheered from the sidelines. Some members of the Constituent Assembly intervened on their own and succeeded in bringing about a temporary truce. The arrested Parishad workers and leaders were released. A defiant Sheikh Abdullah, to cock a snook at the non-Muslim residents of Jammu & Kashmir, began making public statements to belittle Maharaja Hari Singh and the monarchy, hoisted the National Conference flag at official functions and atop public buildings, and adopted resolutions espousing autonomy and started advocating independence.

15th January, 1952: Sheikh Abdullah came to Jammu where he spoke at an official function at Gandhi Memorial College. By then he had institutionalised the practice of hoisting the National Conference flag. The flag was hoisted and the students were asked to salute the flag. When they objected, the students were penalised.

To oppose this move, the students decided to go on a hunger strike to force the government to revoke its inhuman and undemocratic order. Those brave men who went on hunger strike for 38 days in 1952, for the diginity and honour of the national flag the tricolour were Vishva Pal, Tilkraj Sharma, Capt. Ram Saroop, Ved Chauhan, Om Parkash Gupta, Hari Saran Sharma, Dwarika Nath Gupta, Hardev Sharma, Ram Saroop Gupta, Ghian Chand Sanothra, Kewal Krishan Sharma, Ram Mohan Katyal, Ved Mitter Gandothra, Hansraj Sharma, Kuldeep Raj Verma, Ram Nath Sharma, Inderjeet and Prof. Chaman Lal Gupta, etc.

Activists gathering from all nooks and corners at Jammu for a public meeting

8th February, 1952: A huge procession was taken out in Jammu by the residents to express solidarity with the students. The people spontaneously participated in the protest, sending shock waves among Sheikh Abdullah's administration which retaliated in the only manner it knew. The army was called in and a 72-hour curfew imposed. The official action showed that it had Delhi's, that is, Nehru's sanction. The students were released but Praja Parishad leaders, including Pt. Dogra, were arrested. With the protest showing no signs of dying, Nehru rushed his confidant, Gopalaswami Ayyangar, in April 1952, to broker peace. The Parishad leaders were released, but Sheikh Abdullah was incensed: he felt Nehru had let him down and retaliated by taking decisions that further distanced J&K from the rest of the country.

Crowd showing their strength

Pt. Dogra's Views on the Students' Agitation

An open enquiry into the present incidents and its background will enable the true facts of the situation to come to light and will be helpful in removing much of the misunderstanding about the Parishad, which had been caused by its systemic misrepresentation for quite some time past. The Praja Parishad therefore, hopes that the people of India, including that of Jammu & Kashmir state will appreciate the Parishad's demand for an independent commission to enquire into the Jammu incident.

Praja Parishad circles are shocked to read the government Press note, dated 8-2-52, in the last para of which the government has charged that the demonstrations by the students of the colleges and schools, both boys and girls, and inspired by the Praja Parishad organisation, which openly wants to subvert authority and bring into existence chaotic conditions in the state.

This is a mere travesty of facts and is intended to bring into disrepute the only opposition party in the state The true facts are that the Parishad has all along extended fullest cooperation to the government and has never done anything subversive to the authority. The Praja Parishad is out and out for bringing about harmonious and peaceful conditions in the state and welding together all dissident elements. Its pro-India stand is the only cause of the cold war that is being waged against it by the party in power. In spite of so many provocative speeches and statements issued by the government, the Parishad has never deviated from its peaceful path.

I want to make it known to the public and government that my organisation has no hand in the students' movement and has kept aloof all the time. The Parishad with all the emphasis at its command demands that an independent commission be appointed to enquire into the false and unfounded accusations levelled against It. To prove the bonafides of the government against the people of Jammu, the recent utterances of the Hon'ble Deputy Prime Minister before the respectable citizens of Jammu on 7th February, 1952 should serve as a pointer. Therein he openly threatened the people of Jammu that he would destroy the country lock, stock and barrel and make it over to Pakistan.

Dated Jammu the
8th February, 1952

—(Sd.) Prem Nath Dogra
President
All Jammu & Kashmir Praja Parishad

Resolution Passed by Working Committee of Praja Parishad, on 25th February, 1952 at Pathankot

The Jammu & Kashmir Praja Parishad, during the past four years of its existence as the only party in Opposition in the state, has successfully worked for creating political awakening in the people, particularly those living in Jammu province and who are comparatively backward because no political party had worked among them before the Praja Parishad. It stands for a progressive economic programme, abroad and non-sectarian social path for J&K and close integration of the whole of the state with India, like all other acceding states. It wants full application of the Constitution of India to the state and is opposed to the semi-independent state for which the party in power has been working.

The patriotic and pro-India stand of the Parishad has made it suspect in the eyes of the party in power. It has been trying to suppress the Praja Parishad in different ways. The leaders of the Parishad were arrested and detained without trial early in 1949 and were not released when the Praja Parishad launched a mass *satyagraha* movement. The Praja Parishad was forced to boycott the elections to the Constituent Assembly because of the rejection of 44 nomination papers filed by Praja Parishad nominees on most flimsy grounds. To keep the voice of Praja Parishad out of the Indian Parliament, the J&K state plans to nominate the state representatives to the Indian Parliament instead of holding elections for the purpose. The Praja Parishad has been corresponding with the Government of India on the question of election of state representatives to the Parliament. It was as it should be educating the public opinion in the state as well in favour of election of the state representatives for the Parliament instead of nominating. All this was being done by the Parishad in the most peaceful and constitutional manner.

The Praja Parishad had nothing to do whatsoever with the present happenings in Jammu, which began on the 15th January when students of the local government college protested against the hoisting of the party flag of the National Conference along with the national tricolour. Its leaders and workers scrupulously kept themselves aloof. As citizens, some of the leaders of the Praja Parishad, did lend their helping hand to the authorities to end the students' agitation They even succeeded in evolving an agreed compromise formula, which was approved by the Deputy Commissioner of Jammu and other authorities on the 6th February, but Bakshi Ghulam Mohammad, the Deputy Prime Minister who returned to Jammu the same day, torpedoed the efforts of the citizens and rejected the compromise formula evolved by them. That created consternation among the students and relatives of the hunger-striking students and resulted in the demonstration of 8th February, which was crudely handled by the authorities.

The way the Jammu & Kashmir government has exploited the situation to suppress Praja Parishad is no secret now. It let loose a reign of terror on the people of Jammu. Scores of men and women workers and sympathisers of Praja Parishad, including our president Pt. Prem Nath Dogra have been arrested and detained without trial, or warrants of arrests. Externment orders have been issued against hundreds of others. All this, the Praja Parishad is convinced, has been done with a set plan to crush the Parishad. The ban imposed on the *Milap* and *Pratap* Urdu dailies of Delhi, most widely circulated in the state, and which voiced the feelings of the people of Jammu is an additional proof of it.

The Praja Parishad Working Committee strongly condemns these most undemocratic and fascist methods of the Kashmir government. It challenges the government to place any evidence it has against the Parishad before any court of law. It demands of the government to institute an independent enquiry committee to look into the happenings of Jammu, release Praja Parishad leaders, cancel warrants against others and remove the ban on the entry of *Milap* and *Pratap* in the state.

The committee also prays to the Government of India to take a realistic view of the situation in Jammu. The Parishad is a friend of India, a better friend, we claim, than the National Conference. It espouses the cause which is dear to every Indian today. The government must protect and respect the legitimate rights and aspirations of the people of Jammu and not ride roughshod over them to please the party in power. The committee further takes the opportunity to thank the public and press of India who have sympathised with the just and patriotic cause of the Parishad and hopes that the Indian public will continue to extend its helping hand to the Parishad in the achievement of its patriotic objective of making Jammu & Kashmir state one with India, exactly like the other acceding states.

Tribune dated 11th February, 1952: Need for Enquiry

A 72-hour curfew was imposed in Jammu following the unruly demonstration by what has been described as a violent crowd of 2,000 demonstrators, who tried to force their way into the Secretariat. It was staged on Friday on a small scale inside the local college as a protest against the imposition of fine on two students and which is reported to have culminated in a procession towards the Secretariat in defiance of the District Magistrate's order banning meetings and processions. On the way, so the report says, the demonstrators among whom were also women, attacked police officers and men on duty, and on reaching the Secretariat, they indulged in open lawlessness. The police made two *lathi*-charges and fired two rounds to disperse the mob and bring the situation under control. Bakshi Ghulam Mohammad, Deputy Premier of Jammu & Kashmir has stated that it was an organised attempt on the part of Praja Parishad to subvert authority and create confusion in the state. The government, according to him, is holding enquiries into Friday's incidents and will make the findings public at the proper time. The press communiqué issued by the State Information Bureau and the statement of the Jammu District Magistrate show that the trouble was brewing ever since January 15th, when 10 to 15 students in the Government College in Jammu demonstrated against the National Conference flag alongside the Indian Union flag. Some of the student demonstrators were punished with fines. The District Magistrate alleges that a large crowd of students mobbed the cinema halls in an attempt to force admission at concession rates and that, as a consequence, he had to impose a ban on meetings and processions. If all the acts committed by the government are correct, the Praja Parishad stands condemned. No government will and can spare an organisation which resorts to or instigates violence to attain its objectives. A spokesman of Praja Parishad, the leaders of which are now under arrest, has, however, denied that the Praja Parishad had anything to do with the demonstrations. The allegation that the Parishad had organised demonstrations is a travesty of facts and intended to bring into disrepute the only Opposition in the state. Mere assertion on one side and denials on the other do not lead to any positive conclusion, especially when the question of law and order is concerned. In these circumstances, the only way to reach the truth is to hold an independent, impartial and sifting enquiry into the whole affair. According to Bakshi Ghulam Mohammad, the Jammu & Kashmir government was in possession of the pre-arranged plans of certain political parties in the state to subvert authority and bring about a state of confusion. That is all the more reason why an enquiry should be ordered. Once such an enquiry establishes the fact that the Praja Parishad had deliberately incited the forces of lawlessness and that it wanted to subvert authority by resorting to violence, it will be discredited for all times to come and will lose whatever support it has.

National Herald dated 12th February, 1952

The Parishad has denied having had anything to do with the demonstration and demanded an impartial enquiry into the false and unfounded allegations levelled against it. Subject to the demands of security, a thorough enquiry is called for and that there was a prearranged plan to create confusion in the state and if the statement of the Principal of the Government Gandhi Memorial College about Parishad workers having taken active interest in the students' agitation is based on fact, the government will be strengthening its own position by ordering such an enquiry.

Hindustan Standard dated 10th February, 1952

If the Parishad has been at the back of the deplorable happenings in Jammu city, with intent to subvert authority and create chaos in the state, it deserves the strongest condemnation. In the interest of security of Kashmir, in which the whole of India is vitally concerned, the serious charge made against the Parishad should be fully investigated and, if it be found true, suitable action should be taken. The question of proof however, remains. We hope the government of Jammu & Kashmir as well as that of India will publish the evidence in possession to establish the charge as true. That publicity will itself be corrective. Things hatched and nursed in the darkness of secrecy usually fade with the sunlight of publicity, and the earlier it is done, the better.

Searchlight, Patna dated 13th February, 1952

The disturbances in Jammu city on Friday last which necessitated a *lathi* charge by the police and calling in of 72-hour curfew was unfortunate. According to a press note issued by the government of Jammu & Kashmir, the demonstrations were organised by the Praja Parishad, but a leader of the latter organisation has categorically denied the charge. Whosoever inspired and organised the violent demonstration did the state no good. One wonders if communists had no hand in misleading the students. An enquiry into the incident should unravel the mystery.

Amrit Bazar Patrika, 13th February, 1952

The disturbances, according to the press note recently issued by the Kashmir government, were organised and inspired by the Praja Parishad, which wants to subvert authority and bring into existence chaotic conditions in the state. Several leaders of the Praja Parishad including its president, have since been arrested and Bakshi Ghulam Mohammad, Deputy Premier of Kashmir has expressed his firm determination to maintain law and order in the state. But why do the Praja Parishad and its political association create such conditions in the state? What are their grievances? What are their political aims and plans? If they have been indulging in subversive activities to gain their political ends, precautionary measures have been taken by the government of Jammu & Kashmir to keep them in check till future. No light has been thrown on these matters till now, either by the authorities of the Kashmir government or by any spokesman of the Parishad. It is therefore, only logical to expect that an adequate explanation will soon be forthcoming from the state government.

Shibban Lal Saxena's speech in Parliament on 3rd March, 1952

It has been tried to be made out that it was a movement without support. But, the admission that a thousand Hindu women took part in the protest procession in which thousands of other people also took part and the fact that the Indian military had to be called in to control the situation, shows that the movement had large public appeal behind it. There is therefore, a clear case for a public inquiry to discover the truth. I hope Sheikh Abdullah will appoint a committee which will inspire confidence and will see that such things do not happen again. I had hoped that he would set standards which other people would follow. I am disappointed. If such things had happened in other Indian provinces, the whole country would be shaken. I expect that in Jammu, he will try to deal with the situation with tact and intelligence and see that the present tangle is soon resolved.

Statement in Parliament by H.V. Kamath on Jammu Affair during the general debate on Budget for 1952-53 on 3rd March, 1952

My hon'ble friend Prof. Shibban Lal Saxena has referred to Jammu & Kashmir and I would not repeat the points that he has made out. But I would certainly say that I hope that our troops and army in Jammu & Kashmir will not in any way lend themselves to be used or exploited for the suppression or for dealing with the internal disturbances in Jammu & Kashmir. And I would like to say, before I close, that it is rather a paradox that the Praja Parishad of Kashmir, which stands for complete integration of Kashmir with India and even the abolition or deletion of Article 370 from the Constitution, should be looked down upon as a hostile body.

10th April, 1952: In a no-holds barred speech at Ranbirsingh Pura, Sheikh Abdullah mocked the Union and expressed misgivings about the utility of Jammu & Kashmir's continued association with India, accusing 'powerful sections' of trying to establish a 'Hindu raj'. The speech was clearly aimed at rousing communal passions among his constituents, both in the Valley and in Jammu. Derisively characterising the demand for the full applicability of the Indian Constitution to J&K as 'unrealistic, childish and bordering on lunacy,' he thundered: "Many Kashmiris are apprehensive as to what will happen to them and their position if, for instance, something happens to Pandit Nehru." The cat was out of the bag: Sheikh Abdullah's politics had been dependent on Nehru's support.

Statement issued by Pt. Prem Nath Dogra on 12th April, 1952 after his release from jail

The Jammu College boys' hunger strike has come and gone, but the trail it has left behind has been rather acrimonious. The government issued a press communique on 8th February last, justifying the extraordinary measures to suppress the students' agitation wherein the Praja Parishad was implicated and accused of 'subverting authority'—a not uncommon shibboleth copied from the British masters in India and 'inspiring the student to violence',–an unwarranted and unsubstantiated charge. I at once contradicted the government's allegations and demanded an open, impartial and independent commission of enquiry to punish the guilty, but instead, I was arrested with my colleagues that very night under the dark cover of 79 hours' curfew clamped on the city. After two full months of detention in the icy cold cells of Srinagar Jail, I have now been released, but I still find that not all my arrested comrades have been set at liberty.

The present arrests have, however, confirmed the impression that the government claiming to be the representative of democracy arrests people, detains them in jails for indefinite periods without trial and resorts to undesirable restrictions on the liberty of the people. This is no democracy. Everyone in the state, holding a political opinion different from that of the party in power but in no way anti-national, is unsafe in the present regime—a state of affairs which does not add to the fair name of the government.

My arrest was made at a time when I was in correspondence with the President of the Indian Union in the matter of choosing members for the Indian Parliament from the state of Jammu & Kashmir by election, like other Part 'B' states of Hyderabad, Mysore, etc., and not by nomination as has now been done. Persons of unrepresentative character have been elected in defiance of the people's genuine demand. The general feeling among the public has been that these unjustified arrests were simply resorted to gag the popular voice and suppress opposition constitutionally started by the Praja Parishad. It is no tall talk that the Praja Parishad stands for unequivocal and complete accession to India with full application of the Indian Constitution and the jurisdiction of the Supreme Court of India to the state. Everyone in the state has been simply disappointed and shocked at the speeches of Sheikh Abdullah and his Revenue Minister Mr. Beg declaring that the state is independent in all respects and that the Constituent Assembly and their party are sovereign for all purposes, even to the extent of making the state a 'republic within a republic'. The position taken by these two leaders of the National Conference is not only unpatriotic but a challenge to the very Government of India of uncertainty from economic starvation on the other hand and to the Union of India to which we claim from the rooftops to have acceded. It bespeaks ingratitude which no citizen of Kashmir would endorse. I and my party want to reiterate in clear terms that our state has acceded to India for all matters and if any attempt is made to restrict or limit the full accession by continuing the unwanted Article 370 in the Indian Constitution, we shall not hesitate to offer any sacrifice to resist it.

In the interest of India and the state, I would respectfully urge the President of the Indian Union:

1. To appoint an independent commission to enquire into the recent college boys' hunger strike and the government's charge of the Praja Parishad's hand therein, as also the unwarranted and vindictive measures taken by the government.

2. To have the unwanted Article 370 deleted from the Constitution of India so as to extend the full benefits of the said Constitution to the people of the state of Jammu & Kashmir together with the jurisdiction of the Supreme Court.
3. To cancel the nomination of 10 members from the state to the Indian Parliament and order their election, like in other Part 'B' states.
4. To undo the disintegration of the Jammu province into the unwanted administrative units of Doda and Poonch, Rajauri, to restrain the government from the intended move of breaking Ladakh province.
5. To issue a directive to the government of the state that all talks of a 'republic within a republic' is unconstitutional and that no member of government party or an individual should indulge in such irresponsible declarations, which are calculated to strengthen the enemy's hands when the fate of the state is hanging in balance.
6. To order appropriate measures being taken by the Government of India to grant an equal status to the people of the state with the people of India and remove unwanted and restricted barriers or customs.

In the end, I want to thank my countrymen who, despite grave and extreme provocation, have given proof of their tolerance and patience by silently bearing the vagaries of the government in power. I assure them that the Praja Parishad will not rest content until it attains the cherished goal for which it considers no cost too high and no sacrifice too great and expects every true citizen of the state to offer and lend it his or her support—unstinted and sincere.

Before closing, I would like to sound a note of friendly warning to the government that it should behave as true servants of the people and not get puffed up with power to suppress people's legitimate aspirations by resorting to tactics once employed by the foreign government in India.

12th April, 1952 — Prem Nath Dogra
Jammu — President

15th April, 1952: Faced with a barrage of criticism, Nehru was forced to mildly deplore the 'tone' of Sheikh Abdullah's speech, but ever willing to bail his friend out of a sticky situation of his own making, he blamed the Praja Parishad! Emboldened by Nehru's action, Sheikh Abdullah proceeded with setting up the apparatus of his despotic rule.

10th June, 1952: Sheikh Abdullah, without consulting New Delhi and as a Chairman of the Basic Principles' Committee of the J&K Constituent Assembly, presented an interim report recommending the abolition of monarchy and election of a head of state to be called 'Sadar-e-Riyasat'. Two days later, the recommendation was unanimously accepted and the Drafting Committee was asked to submit a proposal within a month. Days before taking this decision, the Constituent Assembly had unilaterally adopted a new state flag, replacing the old standard.

19th June, 1952: Alarmed by these decisions which were fast alienating the state from India and leading to the creation of Sheikh Abdullah's fiefdom, the Praja Parishad presented the President with a memorandum, demanding the application of the Indian Constitution to J&K, jurisdiction of the Supreme Court, extension of Fundamental Rights to the people of the state and the right to fly the national tricolour.

26th June, 1952: A huge demonstration was organised by the Praja Parishad outside Parliament to press its demands. Inside the House, Nehru was pilloried by members for his myopic policies and favouring Sheikh Abdullah. N.C. Chaterjee ridiculed the idea of a 'republic within a republic' while Dr. Mookerjee categorically asserted that notwithstanding Nehru's claims to the contrary, Sheikh Abdullah was neither impartial nor secular. A cornered Nehru found the going tough but, as usual, sought to lay the blame elsewhere. He blamed the Maharaja and the UN for the trouble in J&K and insisted that the state's accession was complete "although it is limited to three subjects."

Demonstrators sitting in front of Parliament in New Delhi

Once again, Nehru had left an escape clause for his friend who, all this while, was busy scheming on how to assert his independence: First, he tried to convince Nehru into allowing him to raise his own militia which would be armed by India but report to him. Then he refused to hand over communication to the Centre and later he began using his trade agent in Delhi and Bombay as 'diplomatic missions'. Even as the Praja Parishad was trying to prevent Sheikh Abdullah from fulfilling his dreams, Nehru was striking a deal which would have far-reaching consequences and for which the nation continues to pay a heavy price.

12th July, 1952: A delegation of National Conference leaders, headed by the Revenue Minister Mirza Afzal Beg, was invited to Delhi by Nehru for talks which lasted till July 20th. From July 16th to 23rd, in-camera discussions were held between Nehru and Sheikh Abdullah where a concrete shape was given to the latter's plans of creating a 'republic within a republic'. The plan, known as the Delhi Agreement of 1952, was disclosed by Nehru in Parliament where he gave a short summary on July 24th. Full details were provided by Sheikh Abdullah to the J&K Constituent Assembly on August 11th. The highlights of this deal were:

a. Residuary powers would be vested in the state government.
b. Kashmiris would get Indian citizenship but Indians living in other states would not be entitled to citizenship

rights in J&K. The State Legislature was empowered to regulate rights and privileges of permanent residence as the "Government of India appreciated the need for such a safeguard."

c. While Sheikh Abdullah was not particularly bothered about the fundamental rights of citizens, he secured the legislature's discretion on the extent of their applicability.
d. There would be limited jurisdiction of the Supreme Court. As for civil and criminal matters, its jurisdiction was left open to further discussion.
e. Sheikh Abdullah secured the right to fly the state flag along the national tricolour.
f. The Head of State would be recommended by the legislature and recognised by the President.
g. Sheikh Abdullah refused financial integration and this was granted.
h. Article 352 would have limited applicability. Emergency could be declared in J&K on grounds of internal disturbances only with the concurrence and approval of the state government.

A triumphant Sheikh Abdullah flaunted the deal as a slap in the face of the Praja Parishad and the non-Muslim residents of the state. He began demolishing whatever remained of the system that was not to his liking.

11th August, 1952: Sheikh Abdullah warned: "I would like to make it clear that any suggestions of altering arbitrarily this basis of our relationship with India would not only constitute a breach of the spirit and letter of the constitution, but might have serious consequences..."

21th August, 1952: The Jammu & Kashmir Constituent Assembly adopted a resolution abolishing monarchy and accepting the concept of an elected Head of State. On November 12th, a Constitutional Amendment was incorporated, substituting 'Sadar-e-Riyasat' for ruler.

By now, the Praja Parishad workers were seething with anger.

They decided to battle it out with Sheikh Abdullah's National Conference.

24th November, 1952: A public reception in honour of Yuvraj Karan Singh was boycotted by the people of Jammu. Festoons were pulled down, arches destroyed and all signs of official celebration removed.

26th November, 1952: Pt. Dogra was arrested with 14 other leaders, triggering the movement against *'Ek desh me do pradhan, do nishan, do vidhan.'* The Praja Parishad supplemented its demand with evidence of Sheikh Abdullah's communal politics as borne out by his policies of breaking up Hindu majority districts for electoral purposes, making Urdu a compulsory subject, filling up of important posts with Muslims, sacrificing the economic interests of the non-Muslims and rigging elections to deny Hindus a legitimate voice.

Panditji garlanded by the people of Jammu

By the closing days of the year, the agitation was no longer limited to Jammu. In state after state, the Bharatiya Jana Sangh, under the leadership of Dr. Mookerjee, rallied people to the cause of protecting J&K from the evil designs of the Sheikh Abdullah-Nehru duo. The support was spontaneous and overwhelming.

HISTORICAL *SATYAGRAHA*

In Jammu, the Praja Parishad with Pt. Dogra at its helm, launched a historic *satyagraha* for full and final accession of the state to India, abrogation of Article 370, application of the Indian Constitution to the state and the abolition

Satyagraha *activists*

of customs duty and the permit system. Pt. Dogra and Shyam Lal Sharma offered the first *satyagraha* along with 200 volunteers. This unleashed a powerful movement all over Jammu region and whose ringing slogan was, *'Ek desh mein do nishan, do vidhan, do pradhan nahin chalengey, nahin chalengey.'* More than 10,000 volunteers offered peaceful *satyagraha,* but instead of listening to their demand, Nehru turned a blind eye to the repression that was unleashed by Sheikh Abdullah against the Parishad.

□

Section-50

During the National Conference rule, especially in the late fifties, the imposition of Section 50 (later on changed to Section 144) of the CrPC was a regular feature in Jammu city and many other places. No meeting or rally could be held without the prior permission from the Wazir Wazarat (DC) despite the freedom of speech and expression being the major part of the NC bible, viz. the 'Naya Kashmir'.

During the *satyagraha* movement, it was difficult to have even a small procession at the time of courting arrests, but for the purpose of defying Section 50, some novel methods were evolved. One of these was the use of cinema gatherings. To this end, some youths had become experts.

Adv. Onkar Seth

Adv. Vikram Mengi

Adv. Vijay Bharti

Advocates Onkar Seth, Vikram Mengi, Vijay Bharti and Durgadass driver and other teenagers were taken as experts in arranging gatherings for *satyagrahis.*

Sometimes, even marriage parties or other such fake functions were arranged by these youths for courting arrest by the *satyagrahis* and making the task of the police difficult.

Narsingh Dass Sharma, Murari Lal, Sat Grover
(disguised as bridegroom satyagrahi *Ram Nath Minhas)*

(Ref: Original Documents of Praja Parishad available at Nanaji Deshmukh Library, Jammu.)

SHEIKH ABDULLAH'S ATROCITIES

The intensity of the Praja Parishad's movement had a deep and stirring impact on every family in the region. People joined the agitation spontaneously. Sheikh Abdullah, taken aback by the agitation, responded by resorting to ruthless suppression of dissent. Sixteen people were shot dead by his police while hoisting the national tricolour on government buildings. Hundreds of people were injured and thousands put behind bars. Bullets, *lathis* and a systematic campaign of looting, harassing and raping of woman by National Conference workers was the order of the day. Individuals were humiliated by both officials and party workers in myriad ways. All this failed to dampen the spirit of the nationalists. *Satyagrahis* carrying the tricolour and a copy of the Indian Constitution in their hands and a photograph of Dr. Rajendra Prasad (then President) around their neck continued to court arrest.

Mela Ram was the first victim of police firing at Chhamb.

This was followed by the martyrdom of Krishan Lal Bali, Baba Ramji Dass and Beli Ram at Sunderbani. Behari Lal and Bhikam Singh were shot dead at Hiranagar. Their bodies were not handed over to their relatives; instead they were burned after being doused with kerosene. Nanak Chand, Basant Ram, Baldev Singh, Sain Singh, Waryam Singh and Trilok Singh were shot dead at Jaurian. Devi Saran, Shivaji and Bhagwan Dass succumbed to bullet injuries at Ramban in Doda district. But all was not lost and the voice of protest raised by the Praja Parishad against the despotism of Sheikh Abdullah and his separatist policies were not ignored by nationalists in Delhi, represented by the other parties too. Dr. Syama Prasad Mookerjee lent his immediate support to the Praja Parishad's struggle and the Jana Sangh took up the issue at the national level, launching one of the most emotive nationalist campaigns in post-Independent India.

□

Incidents during the Movement

Incidents at the Time of the Movement

The Praja Parishad *satyagraha* spread to the farthest villages and assumed the form of a mass movement. It is being carried on peacefully and non-violently in spite of the gravest provocations from the side of the government. Not a single incident of burning any government building has taken place so far, in spite of the fact that most of the leaders of the movement have been arrested and put in jail. But the repression on the side of the government to suppress this legitimate and peaceful movement has crossed all limits. It has let loose the brute force of the police and militia on the people of Jammu who are being subjected to most inhuman treatment inside and outside the jails.

The following report gives a greater idea of the repression now going on in Jammu:

Protest demonstration

About two thousand people have offered *satyagraha* so far, but about 1,200 of them have been sent behind bars. The treatment meted out to the rest of the *satyagrahis* has been that they were kept in the police lock-up for the whole day and then loaded on trucks and lorries during the night to be left off at distant and desolate places after giving them a thorough beating. Some of them were thrown into the Ranbir Canal as a result of which, four persons caught pneumonia and one of whom, belonging to Jammu *tehsil*, has since died.

In the severe cold of December, when the temperature in Kashmir falls below the freezing point, a batch of about 100 prominent persons amongst those arrested was transferred to Srinagar Jail from Jammu Central Jail. They could not bear the severe cold of Kashmir to which they were not accustomed and hence have been undergoing terrible suffering since then.

Women at the satyagraha

A few days later, another batch of prisoners was loaded for Srinagar via Banihal Cart Road. Upon refusal of permission to cross the pass by the military authorities as it had become snow-bound, the prisoners were kept at Banihal at the foot of Pir Panjal although no sub-jails exists there. In the benumbing cold and heavy rains, the *satyagrahis* were not allowed to ease themselves for 48 hours or move out to attend to the call of nature. During the first 10 days they were given very meagre food eight times only, instead of 20. To protest against this inhuman treatment, the prisoners had to go on a hunger strike. Seventy-four of them were kept in a sericulture insect-breeding house. As a result, a number of them fell ill, of whom the condition of Masat Ram and Charan Dass became critical.

Some of the *satyagrahis* were subjected to barbarous torture in the Police Lines of Jammu after their arrest. The examples of this sort of torture can be cited in the case of Bhagwat Swaroop, B.A. Thakur, Nanak Singh, secretary of the Rajput Sabha, Shiv Ram, a prominent worker of the Harijan Mandal and Vishwapal. They were not only given shoe-beating but even the hair of the private parts of their body was pulled out. Rishen Dass from Rinshal (R.S. Pura *tehsil*) was so mercilessly beaten in the local *thana* that he fell unconscious several times. In a number of cases, the *satyagrahis* were forcibly pulled out from the procession, caned in the open and dragged by their legs to the police stations.

Fire has been opened on peaceful processions 11 times and *lathi*-charge has been made at 31 places, resulting in the death of a number of persons, out of whom the remains of 19 persons have been traced so far. The chronological report of these *lathi*-charges and killings is given below:

Satyagrahis *protesting*

On 26th November, immediately after the arrest of Pt. Prem Nath Dogra, police *lathi*-charged the people who had assembled to listen to Pt. Dogra, so severely and indiscriminately that an Inspector of the Indian Intelligence Bureau was also severely injured.

Protest demonstration at Udhampur, 1952-1953

The *lathi*-charge at Udhampur on 29th November resulted in severe injury to a number of women. The severest *lathi*-charge was made at Bhaderwah on 17th January on a peaceful procession led by Chaudhary Khushi Mohammad, the *tehsil* president. He and scores of others were severely injured. The *satyagrahis* were stripped naked and humiliated in many ways. At Jaurian, a severe *lathi*-charge was made on a peaceful procession on 28th January as a result of which, one woman died.

Firings: The first shot was fired by the police on a Parishad procession at Samba on 27th November, but it did not result in any fatal casualty.

The first to die of police bullets was Mela Ram at Chhamb on 15th December. The government at first denied any casualty but when his body was brought to Jammu, the government had to admit the fact.

On 29th December, three persons were shot dead when the police opened fire on a peaceful procession at Sunderbani, a village about 25 miles from Jammu. Their dead bodies were burnt at dead of the night and their remains too were not given to their next of kin. Here too, the government first denied any casualty but admitted the fact after three days when the names and the addresses of the dead became known to the people.

Women's gathering for the Jammu cause

On 11th January, the worst firing took place at Hiranagar, a *tehsil* about 40 miles from Jammu on the Pathankot-Jammu Road in the presence of two ministers of the state government. The number of dead as a result of this firing has not yet been ascertained. The dead bodies of two of them, Bihari Lal and Bhikam Singh, were found half burnt in a *nullah* near the Indian border, the next morning. But according to the report of the fact finding mission sent by the People's Party, 13 people are still missing and 20 were injured as a result of this firing, which appeared to be more in the nature of display of might, rather than to deal with any particular situation, real or imagined, according to the report.

The last firing took place at Jaurian village, about 30 miles to the west of Jammu on 30th January. A procession of 3,000 villagers from the surrounding villages was first tear-gassed and then fired upon while it was carrying the dead body of the woman, who had succumbed to the injuries received as a result of the police *lathi*-charge on the previous day, to the cremation ground. According to the authorities, five people were killed and one was injured. But according to the report of Sardar Bachan Singh Panchi, who was deputed by the State Akali Dal to visit the place to ascertain the true facts, a much larger number of persons were missing. The names and addresses of nine of them have so far been traced. The number of injured according to this report runs over into 200, 20 of whom were seen by him in one village alone. Not a single dead body was restored to the guardians of the deceased.

Crimes Perpetrated on Women: The worst part of this campaign of repression is the cruelties and crimes perpetrated against women who have sympathy for the movement.

A women's procession in Jammu on 11th December was repeatedly tear-gassed and *lathi*-charged as a result of which many women, including small girls, received severe injuries. One girl remained unconscious for a full 12 hours; another was refused admittance in the hospital because of her precarious condition. Two female *satyagrahis*, who were leading the procession, also became unconscious and were taken to jail in a bad condition.

Women's procession at Jammu

On 6th January, the police arrested four women *satyagrahis* who were leading a procession in Jammu city. They were kept in the police lock-up for the whole day. At 11 o'clock in the night, they were taken out of the lock-up and thrown out on the roads.

On 17th January, three girl students of Mahila College were abused, manhandled and assaulted by an inspector of police while they were dragged by their hair.

On 26th January, 10 women *satyagrahis* who were picketing at the bus stand, were manhandled by the police. A police officer abused them in the most filthy language. Their leader, Kumari Sharda, was arrested. As a result of the ill-treatment in jail, she fell ill. After seven days, when it was found that her condition had become precarious, she was thrown out of the jail in an unconscious condition.

On 27th January, the police raided the house of a *nambardar* in the village Rothua at 2:00 a.m. in the night. He was not at home. They asked about him from the two young women who were present at the time. On their being unable to tell the police the whereabouts of the *nambardar,* they were stripped of their clothes, criminally assaulted and then carried to jail. They were maltreated in the jail as well.

SEARCH AND LOOT

On 3rd February, the police raided the village of Gho Manhasen in Jammu *tehsil*. It forcibly entered the house of Thakur Rachpal Singh who was in jail and looted 12 *tolas* of gold and 500 rupees from his safe.

His wife was maltreated and the maid servant in the house was stripped naked and criminally assaulted by the police.

Ten women of Udhampur had to go on a hunger strike as a protest against the ill-treatment of the *satyagrahis*, particularly women, inside and outside the jails.

Women's procession at Udhampur

The worst feature of these crimes against women was that the police were sent after giving spirituous drinks to them, so that they might handle the *satyagrahis* in a cruel and insensitive manner so as to strike terror amongst the people.

Since the beginning of non-cooperation and civil disobedience, the second phase of the *satyagraha*, the Kashmir militia and police have let loose a reign of terror in the countryside.

The Jammu, Akhnoor and Reasi *tehsils* were first chosen for this campaign of terror. The residents were totally thrown at the mercy of police and militia who were raiding the villages in batches to terrorise the people. A few glaring cases are given below:

In the village of Gho Manhasen, Santoo Mahajan was threatened in his own house and three pairs of earrings along with 200 rupees were looted.

In Kunkerian, a search of many houses was carried out and the household belongings of Mewa Singh, who was later arrested, were thrown out.

The severe beating of Kartar Singh of Gho Manhasen resulted in the fracture of his knees and a severe wound in the interior of his mouth. Sansar Singh Chib and Santoo were severely injured.

On 8th February, the house of Pt. Abhey Ram in the village Gajansoo was searched and his whole family was thrown out.

On this very day, at 4:00 p.m., in the village Saharan, the houses of Messrs Baldev Singh and Fakir Chand Mahajan were raided. After search, six Harijans were beaten. The same day at 5 p.m. in village Karlop, the houses of Messrs Ram and Nand Lal were raided and keys were forcibly snatched from the womenfolk by threatening them. At 7:00 p.m. in village Plora Harmukandpura, the house of Ram Chand was searched and about two *tolas* of gold along with 13 rupees in cash were taken away. Here, two persons were injured as a result of the police beatings. On 7th February, the house of Chhaju Ram in Garota was searched and the inmates immorally harassed. Becoming disappointed at not having found anything in the house of Pt. Sita Ram of village Seri Pandilan, his family members were abused and terrorised. A neighbour was arrested and then let off.

In this cruel hunt for Praja Parishad workers and terrorising of people, the police party reached Palwal and searched Ram Chand's house. Having found nothing there, it made its way to Kot. Here the houses of Munshi Lal Chaman Dass and Pt. Dheroo Ram were ransacked, but nothing was found. This irritated the unscrupulous police officers, who lost all their mental balance and arrested a minor aged 10 along with a postmaster. Both of them were released in Domana the following day, after being inflicted with severe beatings.

On 9th Feburary, in village Paryal, the house of Budhi Singh was damaged. His son Keor Singh and sister were beaten in his presence. When he raised a hue and cry, he too was beaten. Since then, he has been lying in bed. The house was thoroughly searched and Rs. 800 in cash was taken away. Keor Singh was also arrested. Vakil Singh's house was raided and all the sweets and other items which he had collected for the marriage of his daughter were confiscated. Rs. 300 in cash also was taken away. After raiding the house of Indir Singh and confiscating some of his belongings, the 'victorious party' returned.

In village Laddora, the house of Dewan Chand was raided and his brother was beaten. A local Harijan, who stood nearby, was ordered to give him a further shoe-beating. Upon his hesitation to comply with such an order, he too was beaten. On their return journey, the police party took away one tin of kerosene oil and a truck full of fuel.

On 11th February, the police again raided the villages of Gho Manhasen and Rathoa. The son of Kaka Ram was severely beaten and his house searched but the police could not recover Ram Piari. At Rathua, the keys were obtained from a 10-year old daughter of Ch. Ram La Tempo and again his house was searched. Bajura Yogi of Rathoa was severely beaten. The police declared that anybody found giving water to his bullocks would be severely punished. The police ordered for kerosene oil so that his house could be set on fire.

On 13th February, at 10 in the morning, the house of Shatrugun of village Marh was raided. A chair and ornaments of the women first were confiscated. The moustaches of Ghaju Ram Harijan were cut off along with a part of the hair on his head. Durga Dass Harijan was beaten and arrested but upon a bribe of Rs. 40/- was released. During the day, while perpetrating these criminal atrocities, the houses of all of the four villagers were raided. At nightfall, when the police began to return, the villagers heaved a sigh of relief.

On 14th February, the police marched towards Grohta through Agaur. Reaching there, the house of Kaviraj Chhaju Ram was attacked but it proved fruitless and the police had to return empty-handed.

Being irritated at the applications made in the court by the inhabitants of Sangrampur against the inhuman treatment meted out to them, on March 22nd, the police again besieged the whole village. The helpless and innocent people, both young and aged, men and women, fled from the village, being terror-stricken, but many of them, including Dhani, a *mahajan*, relived the scene of the Pakistani invasion. Dhani, a Harijan, was beaten while running. Shib Ram Lengah, Chhatro Dass and Ram Dass were severely manhandled. Blood gushed out from the head of Chhatro Dass. At Domana, a village about 8 miles from Jammu on the bank of a canal, a sweetmeat shop was plundered of all its sweetmeats, which was the only source of family income.

A many as 28 persons, arrested in a procession at Billawar, were cruelly beaten at midnight. In this extremely cold part of Jammu, they were provided with no bedding and were forced to spend full three days without water and food. Some of the *satyagrahis,* having been beaten at the pitiless hands of the police and militia, suffered from swellings.

In village Billawar of Basholi *tehsil,* a military man who had been beaten, succumbed to his injuries on 19th March, 1953.

Some villagers, on their way to shop in the nearby village and another group of villagers going for worship in a temple in the adjoining village, were cruelly beaten.

In Ramkot area, the Kashmir militia and police in hundreds entered the villages, beat the menfolk and terrorised and manhandled the women and looted their property. The people of the area consequently left their homes and have taken recourse to living in jungles to avoid police atrocities.

A maid-cook of Rachpal Singh of Jammu *tehsil* was stripped completely naked by the police in the course of a search of his house.

How brutally the police *lathi*-charged the people can well be imagined from the fact that the skulls of two villagers, Bhagat Singh and Teja Singh, were broken.

Two military personnel, Baikunth Singh and Pritam Singh in Akhnoor, who were on leave, were arrested by the police, while on their way to the canteen and kept under custody for a full 15 days.

Hundreds of militiamen and policemen, with the help of the Muslims of the area, raided and looted the village Kawana of *tehsil* Nowshera.

About 100 Kashmiri militiamen raided the village of Koat Mehra the near Pakistan border and *tehsil* Akhnoor and looted property worth Rs. 4,000 after having severely beaten the residents of the village.

□

Bullets for Hoisting Tricolour

What kind of conditions were created in J&K by the Nehru-backed Sheikh government can be judged from the fact that as many as 16 youths were shot dead at different places for hoisting the national tricolour as the Sheikh regime, discarding the Maharaja's flag, had adopted the National Conference party flag with some minor changes in the state flag. The Praja Parishad was opposed to this approach.

The first incident of such firing took place at Chhamb on 14th December, 1952. In this firing a young man, Mela Ram was shot dead. His body was brought to Jammu for cremation, resulting in high tension and anti-government demonstrations.

The second where such firing and other brutalities took place was at Hiranagar, a *tehsil* headquarters in Kathua district. In this police action of 11th January, 1953, two youths were shot dead. The killed youths were Behari Lal of village Chhan Morian and the other was Bhikam Singh of Hiranagar Garh Mundian. One of them was married only some months earlier before this painful happening. Several others were injured and included Gian Chand Sangra, whose eyesight was badly affected.

The bodies of the martyrs were taken by police and these half-burnt bodies from isolated places were picked up by Diwarka Nath, an activist of Praja Parishad and taken to Delhi.

In this regard, an account has been given in the booklet written by Sanji Ram Gupta. Titled *Vishdhara 370*, it carries many details about certain horrible acts to suppress the Praja Parishad movement.

JOURIAN EPISODE

The most cruel acts were committed on 30th January, 1953, at Jourian, a small town about 55 kms from Jammu in the then border area of Akhnoor *tehsil*.

The police, backed by the state miltia, let loose tear-gas and then firing on a gathering which was organised for hoisting the Indian tricolour.

In the firing, six persons were killed on the spot and several others were injured. One of the injured expired later on.

To spread terror in the area, several village houses were damaged and people beaten even in the adjoining areas.

Firing at Sunderbani

In police firing at Sunderbani, three persons who dared to hoist the tricolour on government buildings were shot dead. The last and fifth such incident took place at Ramban on March 1953. In this firing, three men were killed.

Significantly, most of the martyred youths were in their twenties. Thus, the *Tiranga* found some place in this part of the country.

Samadhi *at Jourian Mela Ram Chamb, Nanak Chand Jourian, Basant Ram Math, Baldev Singh Rathi Danda, Sain Singh, Waryam Singh Bhopur, Trilok Singh Pragwal on 14th December, 1952 and 30th January, 1953*

Samadhi *at Sunderbani*
29th December, 1952, Krishan Lal, Baba Ramji Dass, Beli Ram

Samadhi *at Hiranagar*
11th January, 1953, Bikam Singh

Samadhi *at Hiranagar*
11th January, 1953, Bihari Lalji

Samadhi *at Ramban, 1st March, 1953, Shib Ramji Balihot Ramban, Devi Sharanji Balihot Ramban, Bhagwan Dassji Kanthi Ramban*

Dr. Mookerjee's Role and His Martyrdom

Sardar Patel, who had spent the last years of life toiling day and night to create the Union of India and coping with Nehru's quirks, died on 15th December, 1950. This left Nehru in sole command of India's destiny. More importantly, there was nobody to ask uncomfortable questions about his handling of J&K affairs. But Nehru had to reckon with Dr. Syama Prasad Mookerjee, president of the Bharatiya Jana Sangh, who took it upon himself to steer the polity on a nationalist course. By the time the new Parliament was convened, as *The Times of India* commented, 'the mantle of Sardar Patel had fallen on Dr. Syama Prasad Mookerjee,' he did not shy away from accepting the responsibility.

Responding to the President's address to the new Parliament on 21st May, 1952, Patel referred to Sheikh Abdullah's separatist politics, which had begun to shape by that time and said that India's unity and integrity were at stake. Nehru interrupted to inform Parliament, "I know more about Kashmir than Dr. Mookerjee." Undaunted, Dr. Mookerjee pressed with his point: "I would like to know, are Kashmiris Indian first and Kashmiris next or they are Kashmiris first and Indian next, or they are Kashmiris first, second and third and not Indian at all. That is a very important point we have to settle."

Dr. Mookerjee had hit the nail on the head. He had succinctly presented the problem and sought a clear answer. Nehru, of course, responded by signing a deal with Sheikh Abdullah in June-July that year, virtually legitimising the separatist and communal policies of the National Conference and formalising J&K's 'special status'. The deal came as a body blow against the non-Muslims of the state as they had launched an agitation against Sheikh Abdullah under the leadership of the Praja Parishad. The import of the deal was lost on the Congress and other Opposition parties, but Dr. Mookerjee, who had by then been in touch with the Praja Parishad and briefed by Pt. Prem Nath Dogra, saw through the game.

The following are the important milestones then onwards in the Jana Sangh's campaign to save J&K from separatist and secessionist designs: a campaign initiated by Dr. Mookerjee and kept alive by the BJP.

Dr. Syama Prasad Mookerjee with Pt. Dogra at Jammu & Ch. Ram Narayan (MP) on 10th August, 1952

14th June, 1952: Dr. Mookerjee gets a resolution passed by the Working Committee of the Bharatiya Jana Sangh, emphasising that "Jammu & Kashmir is an integral part of India and declaring that the decisions of the state's Constituent Assembly concerning an elected president and a separate flag coupled with the recommendations of its Basic Principles Committee that Jammu & Kashmir will be an autonomous republic are in clear violation of India's sovereignty and the spirit of India's Constitution. The committee takes a serious view of this development and wants to remind the people and the Government of India that the Cabinet Mission scheme of 1945

Dr. Syama Prasad with Sheikh Abdullah and Bakshi Ghulam Mohammad in Srinagar on 10th May, 1952

envisaging a weak Centre with only three subjects was opposed by the Congress and a large section of Indian opinion as being inimical to India's unity and interests. The fissiparous tendencies of the Muslim League, however, succeeded in dividing India and leading to disastrous consequences. To allow the J&K state to proceed along the same path now looks like permitting history to repeat itself. It might mean a fresh call to disruptive elements in India to break its unity and integrity, which has been achieved at such tremendous cost." The resolution also called upon the people to observe 29th June, 1952 as Kashmir Day in support of the Bharatiya Jana Sangh's stand.

26th June, 1952: Dr. Mookerjee speaks in the Lok Sabha on the question of J&K having a separate flag, an elected Head of State and Article 370 on the basis of which Sheikh Abdullah wanted a separate constitution for the state. "You cannot have divided loyalty. Sheikh Abdullah has said, 'We will treat both flags equally.' You cannot do it. It is not a question of fifty-fifty. It is not a question of parity; it is a question of using one flag for the whole of India, that includes Kashmir. There is no question of having a separate republic of Kashmir having a separate flag." He referred to the incongruity of Article 370 and provided details on the suppression of civil rights, elimination of Hindi, division of Jammu along communal lines, expropriation of *dharamarth* property and funds, communalism in services and discrimination against Jammu and the 'iron curtain' which Sheikh Abdullah had drawn around the state. "If you just want to play with the wind and say we are helpless and let Sheikh Abdullah do what he likes, then Kashmir will be lost. I say this with great deliberation that Kashmir will be lost."

24th July, 1952: Nehru unveils in Parliament the deal he has struck with Sheikh Abdullah, which marked a victory for the latter's politics.

7th August, 1952: Dr. Mookerjee attacks the agreement in the Lok Sabha and warns Nehru, "What you are going to do may lead to the Balkanisation of India, may lead to the strengthening of the hands of those who do not believe that India is a nation but a combination of separate nationalities." He went on to ask the Prime Minister, "Was Sheikh Abdullah not a party to the Constitution of India? Did he not accept this constitution in relation to the rest of India, including 497 states? Is it not good enough for him in Kashmir?" Nehru vaguely referred to the 'special status' of the state, condemned the Praja Parishad and blamed everybody except the real culprits.

9-10th August, 1952: The Praja Parishad organises a convention in Jammu to explain to the people the disastrous consequences of the 'Delhi Agreement'. Pt. Dogra invites Dr. Mookerjee to attend. On his way to Jammu, Dr. Mookerjee responds to surging crowds at every railway station with the slogan, *"Hum vidhan lengey ya balidan dengey."* Upon reaching Jammu, he was invited by Sheikh Abdullah for talks.

10th August, 1952: Dr. Mookerjee has a six-hour meeting with Sheikh Abdullah and which is also attended by his deputy, Bakshi Ghulam Mohammad. Sheikh Abdullah tells Dr. Mookerjee that his actions are dictated by political compulsions and the need to keep fundamentalist Muslims in check. At one point, he raises his voice. Dr. Mookerjee responds by telling Sheikh Abdullah that his policies and speeches make him look and sound like Jinnah.

Pt. Prem Nathji Dogra with Dr. Syama Prasad Mookerjee at Jammu, August, 1952

11th August, 1952: Dr. Mookerjee tells Pt. Dogra and other Parishad leaders not to precipitate action and instead educate and inform the people about the dangerous policies of Sheikh Abdullah. He assures full support to the Praja Parishad if Sheikh Abdullah persists with his policies. Clearly, he wanted to prevent turmoil in the state. On his return, he has a lengthy talk with Nehru and asks him to give a hearing to Pt. Dogra, and listen to the grievances of the non-Muslims of J&K. Nehru contemptuously rejects the suggestion. In Srinagar, Sheikh Abdullah moves swiftly to put his plans into action.

8th November, 1952: Pandit Dogra meets Dr. Mookerjee at Jalandhar where the latter had gone for the Punjab Provincial Jana Sangh Conference and briefs him about the fast deteriorating situation in the state. Dr. Mookerjee asks Pt. Dogra to take all issues into consideration before launching an agitation and assures him of full support of the Jana Sangh to mobilise public opinion in favour of the Praja Parishad.

17th November, 1952: Sheikh Abdullah plans to hoist the new 'state flag', a minor modification of the National Conference flag, on the state's Secretariat. Praja Parishad responds by saying that only the tricolour shall fly in Jammu. Sheikh Abdullah, taken aback, postpones the hoisting and seeks Nehru's help. Nehru responds by rushing armed police to his friend's rescue. With the help of these forces, Sheikh Abdullah cracks down on the Praja Parishad.

26th November, 1952: Pt. Dogra and Shyam Lal Sharma, organising secretary of the Praja Parishad, are arrested from the main square of Jammu city for hoisting the national tricolour. The arrests and subsequent atrocities on Parishad workers and all nationalist people of Jammu marked the beginning of the historic *satyagraha* against *'Ek desh mein do nishan, ek desh mein do vidhan, ek desh mein do pradhan, nahin chalenge, nahin chalenge.'*

14th December, 1952: Jana Sangh observes J&K Day to express solidarity with the Praja Parishad agitation. There is tremendous and emotive response to the call all over the country; in the last week of December the first plenary session of the Bharatiya Jana Sangh is held in Kanpur after Dr. Mookerjee's re-election as party president. In his address to the session, Dr. Mookerjee says, "Even at this late stage, I would appeal to Mr. Nehru and Sheikh Abdullah to cry a halt and not to stand on false prestige. They must open negotiations with the Parishad leaders and arrive at a settlement which will be fair and just to all. Meanwhile, our active sympathies must be extended to all those in Jammu for facing bravely the wrath of the authorities and silently suffering for a noble cause." Exuberant members demanded that the BJS serve an ultimatum to Nehru's government to act or face the party's wrath. Dr. Mookerjee suggests trying to bring about a peaceful settlement. A resolution is adopted, authorising Dr. Mookerjee to write to Nehru and Sheikh Abdullah and explore the possibility of a solution.

9th January, 1953: Dr. Mookerjee writes to Nehru: "...I know that you do not see eye to eye with many of us on this issue. Yet I am writing to you in the hope that you will keep an open mind and

The nine great sons of Bharat Mata given to Dr. Syama Prasad Mookerjee by RSS during the formation of the Bharatiya Jana Sangh in 1951.
From left to right: (1) J.P. Mathur (2) Nanaji Deshmukh (3) Jagannathrao Joshi (4) Balraj Madhok (5) Deendayal Upadhyaya (6) Atal Bihari Vajpayee (7) Kedarnath Sahani (8) Yagnadutt Sharma (9) Sundar Singh Bhandari

try to appreciate the viewpoint of those who may differ from you on this matter. It is vitally important that the circumstances that have led to the present movement should be impartially reviewed and effort made to arrive at a speedy and peaceful settlement which will be fair and just to all concerned...Repeated efforts were made by the Praja Parishad leaders and others to have an amicable settlement by constitutional means. Representations were sent to Dr. Rajendra Prasad, to yourself, to the Minister of States and to Sheikh Abdullah...Apparently the authorities concerned paid no heed to such manifestations of public opinion and even treated them with contempt. On the other hand, some of the matters regarding which acute controversy had been raised were proceeded with by the authorities themselves with undue haste, thus precipitating a crisis...It is high time that both you and Sheikh Abdullah should realise that this movement will not be suppressed by force or repression... The problem of J&K should not be treated as a party issue. It is a national problem and every effort should be made to present a united front...The state of J&K is a part of the Indian Union and as such, it is perfectly open to the rest of the people to interest themselves in the affairs of the state... The people of Jammu are not prepared to sever their connection with India under any circumstances, plebiscite or no plebiscite. The greater the delay in having this moot question decided once for all the greater will be complications and possibilities of unrest...Once it is settled that a final decision has been taken on the question of accession, two matters will have to be taken up. One relates to recovery of one-third territory of J&K which is now in occupation of Pakistan. How are we going to get this back? You have always evaded this question. The time has come when we should know what exactly you propose to do about this matter. It will be a sort of national disgrace and humiliation if we fail to regain this lost portion of territory. The other question relates to the extent of accession of J&K state with India. If the people of Jammu demand that the accession should be on the same lines as in the cases of other states, they don't say anything that is arbitrary or extraordinary.

"This is their natural wish and they are guided by patriotic and national motives...A copy of this letter is sent to Sheikh Abdullah with a note: 'The issue at stake affects not only your state but the whole of India and I hope you will move before the situation further deteriorates.' "

10th January, 1953: Nehru replies to Dr. Mookerjee, "...I am quite prepared and I am sure that Sheikh Abdullah is prepared to consider any grievances of the Jammu people and try to rectify them where this is possible. But the demands of the Praja Parishad are basic constitutional issues which cannot be given effect to for obvious reasons. They are trying to decide a very difficult and complicated constitutional question by methods of war. It does not require much thought that this method cannot yield those results, whatever the merits may be..." Soon after this, Nehru and Sheikh Abdullah launched a vituperative campaign against the Praja Parishad and the Bharatiya Jana Sangh.

3rd February, 1953: Dr. Mookerjee writes to Nehru, "I have no desire to carry on a protracted correspondence with you in this matter. But the issues involved are so serious that I am taking the liberty of writing to you again. One common feature of the speeches has been abundance of abuses and vituperation which you have poured forth on those who differ from you. You have all sorts of base motives and have even dubbed us as betrayers of the country's interests. I have no desire to emulate you in this respect. I have read your speeches and those of Sheikh Abdullah with considerable care, but unfortunately they evade the real issues..."

He then made the following points:

1. The Parishad has considerable popular backing. As one who knows the mass mind, you will realise that no popular movement can be crushed by force.
2. The first question raised is when and how will the accession of J&K state to India be finally settled? My own suggestion has been that the Legislative Assembly of J&K, which has been elected on adult franchise, may accept a resolution accepting final accession and the matter may be considered as irrevocably decided so far as India is concerned. Please be specific on this issue and let us know that if this suggestion is not acceptable, what your alternative proposal for finalising the accession is.
3. We do not want partition of the state, but you seem to forget that J&K has already been partitioned by Pakistan and the real question is whether you and Sheikh Abdullah

propose to acquiesce in this partition. You have always evaded this question. Please do not sidetrack the issue and let the public of India know when, if at all, we are going to get back this part of our cherished territory.

4. The third point relates to the subjects in relation to which accession will take place. The Praja Parishad wants, and we wholeheartedly agree, that the entire state of J&K should be governed in accordance with the same constitution that applies to the rest of India. Is there anything communal or reactionary or anti-national about it? It is amazing how the move of separatism pursued by Sheikh Abdullah and his colleagues is being applauded by you as national and patriotic; and the genuine desire on the part of the Praja Parishad to secure the fundamental unity and integrity of India and to be governed as common Indian citizens is being dubbed as treacherous conduct. Your letter and your speeches give no satisfactory answer to those basic points raised by the Praja Parishad.
5. There are many grievances of the people of Jammu regarding internal administration. Delay in dealing with them is intensifying the agitation.
6. It is undoubtedly true that we should do nothing which may weaken India's position or strengthen the hand of our enemy. This aspect you must bear in mind as Prime Minister of India."

He sends a copy of this letter to Sheikh Abdullah, adding a note, "It is a tragic you completely misunderstand those who are differing from you and are proceeding in a manner which may be disastrous to India, including the state of J&K. I still hope you will be able to rise equal to the occasion and find a way for peaceful settlement."

5th February, 1953: Sheikh Abdullah replies to Dr. Mookerjee's letter from Jammu Tawi, enclosing pamphlets issued by his government to justify its policies. He emphasises on J&K 'special status' apropos Article 370.

5th February, 1953: Nehru replies to Dr. Mookerjee's letter: "According to my thinking, the agitation of the Praja Parishad is not only communal but is supported by communal and narrow-minded elements in India. Believing this as I do, the only course that I can follow is to resist this utterly misconceived agitation. That is our government's opinion and they propose to adhere to it and pursue this policy. If needed, the agitation continues, it will be for us to consider what other further steps government can take in the matter." Nehru followed this up by ordering the preventive arrest of Bharatiya Jana Sangh leaders on the eve of the party's meeting in Delhi.

8th February, 1953: Dr. Mookerjee writes to Nehru, "Apparently you are not in mood even to understand the views of those who differ from you. I, and many others, honestly feel that the demand on the part of a section of our countrymen living in the state of J&K to see that their state is finally integrated with India and is governed according to the Constitution of free India is not an unpatriotic or disintegrating or communal move. Let me assure you, we are ready to face your wrath and fury. You will forgive me if I fail to appreciate your repeated reference to possible international support and sympathy. On the other hand, your policy in this behalf has added to complications both at home and abroad. Statesmanship requires that you should instead of being haunted by false internationalism, firmly create conditions for national solidarity."

10th February, 1953: Nehru replies to Dr. Mookerjee, "I have no doubt that you wish well for India, but the fact remains that our conceptions of what is well for India appear to differ. Because of this, our past lives have moved largely in different spheres. I would suggest that you exercise your influence to put an end to this agitation in Jammu."

12th February, 1953: Dr. Mookerjee writes to Nehru, "...The only way this can done is to make the sponsors of this movement appreciate that you and Sheikh Abdullah are prepared to discuss all matters with them with an open mind and arrive at decisions which would meet their legitimate demands. The points for consideration are as follows:

1. Finality of accession to India through a resolution to be adopted by the Constituent Assembly of the state.
2. Adoption by the state of the provisions of Indian Constitution regarding such matters as Fundamental Rights, citizenship, financial integration, abolition of customs duty, Supreme Court, emergency powers of the President and conduct of elections. These are to be implemented within a stated time.
3. In respect of the rest of the Indian Constitution, Sheikh Abdullah should indicate what deviations, if any, he desires to be made. These are to be considered on their merits.
4. Jammu & Kashmir, as finally agreed, will be a part of the Indian Constitution.
5. Provincial autonomy to Jammu and Ladakh without changes of boundary.
6. Acceptance of the supremacy of Indian flag.
7. Policy regarding liberation and occupation of the Pakistan-held territory.
8. A Commission of Enquiry with a majority of judges from outside the state to go into all grievances, including the Dharmartha Trust, excesses committed by the police and compensation to the families of sufferers, especially who have been shot dead.
9. Restoration of pensions, properties, etc., to people against whom confiscation order might have been passed."

12th February, 1953: Nehru sends his reply, arguing that the only solution lay in autonomy for J&K, "I am sure that the right course is for this agitation to be withdrawn."

12th February, 1953: Dr. Mookerjee writes to Nehru, who had pleaded helplessness because of 'ongoing talks in Geneva', "...What you and Sheikh Abdullah have to decide first is whether you are willing to talk with the Praja Parishad leaders. I would implore you to do so..."

13th February, 1953: Dr. Mookerjee realises the futility of correspondence with Nehru and writes to Sheikh Abdullah: "It is not safe to base one's present attitude towards grave political issues solely on past relationship with one's opponent. You yourself started as a leader of a communal party and yet it would be highly improper to judge your present aims by making elaborate research into your past history, starting from Aligarh. You are now developing a three-nation theory, the third being the Kashmir nation. These are dangerous symptoms and are not good for your state or for the whole of India. I would beg you not to stand on false prestige but to agree to discuss all disputes with the leaders of the Praja Parishad even at this last stage."

15th February, 1953: Nehru, briefed by Sheikh Abdullah, replies to Dr. Mookerjee, "...subject to our holding fast to the principles which have guided us, and the policies which we have pursued, the government will gladly do, all in its power, to bring about normalcy and peaceful cooperation in the J&K state. But this agitation was not of our seeking and the first step should be to withdraw the agitation completely..."

17th February, 1953: Dr. Mookerjee writes to Nehru yet again, "...After considering the matter fully and also your determination that the movement must be withdrawn completely as a first step, may I suggest the following procedure for your consideration:

1. The movement is withdrawn.
2. Order for release of prisoners is given and there will be no victimisation.
3. You and Sheikh Abdullah call a conference, say, after a fortnight, where all political and constitutional matter are discussed with an open mind.
4. Both parties reiterate that the unity of the state of J&K will be maintained and that the principle of autonomy will apply to the province of Jammu as a whole and of course, also to Ladakh and Kashmiri Valley.
5. The new constitution to come into force as soon as possible and elections to take place within, say, six months.
6. The question of flag is to be clarified and the Indian flag

should be in use every day just as is done in all other parts of India.

7. Implementation of the July agreement will be made at the next session of J&K Constituent Assembly after the issues left vague have been properly clarified. In respect of Fundamental Rights, citizenship, Supreme Court, President's powers, financial integration and conduct of elections, provisions of the Indian Constitution will apply. Exception however, may be made with regard to conditions for acquisition of land...
8. The terms of reference of the Commission of Enquiry will be widened and all grievances will be examined by it.
9. The commission now includes four persons. Chief Justice, Accountant General and Chief Conservator of Forests and the Revenue Commissioner. The last three gentlemen are administrative officers under J&K government and they can hardly inspire confidence. The Commission should be reconstituted with two judges from India and Chief Justice of J&K so that its impartiality and representative character may not be questioned.
10. Regarding finality of accession and other political matters, the conference will consider these points from every aspect and agreement ought to be reached which will be to the best interests of India including J&K."

NEHRU DID NOT BOTHER TO REPLY HIS LETTER

18th February, 1953: Sheikh Abdullah writes to Dr. Mookerjee, "I will frankly state that the present leadership of the Praja Parishad is avowedly disruptive and communal in its aim and purpose. Consequently, it will not be possible for us to have any common meeting ground with them." Dr. Mookerjee decided to make a last effort by writing to Sheikh Abdullah.

23rd February, 1953: Dr. Mookerjee writes to Sheikh Abdullah, "I have been unable to understand your refusal even to talk to the representatives of the Praja Parishad. If you...feel determined to crush a particular political party that may be opposing you and adopt force and other methods for the purpose, then you cease to be a democratic leader. You then become a fascist. But even then, your success is doubtful, for in all such cases, history has proved that the movement goes underground and ultimately the mighty dictator loses the battle of true freedom..."

5th March, 1953: BJS observes J&K Day all over the country. Once again it receives tremendous response. Earlier, the BJS-Mahasabha had captured three of the four seats to the Delhi Assembly to which by-elections had been held on the strength of its Kashmir campaign. Nehru first imposed a ban on public meetings, but gauging the public mood, lifted it just before the March 5 meeting in Delhi where it was decided that Dr. Mookerjee, N.C. Chatterjee and Nand Lal Shastri would lead a procession the next day, from the railway station, carrying the ashes of victims of Sheikh Abdullah's atrocities.

6th March, 1953: Dr. Mookerjee and his colleagues are arrested at Chandni Chowk for violating prohibitory orders, provoking widespread protests and consolidating the party's Kashmir campaign.

11th March, 1953: Dr. Mookerjee and others released after Babu Ram Narain Singh, MP, files a *habeas corpus* petition. Dr. Mookerjee tours several states and is greeted by full-throated support for the Bharatiya Jana Sangh's campaign on Kashmir. He decides to visit J&K without a permit.

8th May, 1953: Dr. Mookerjee boards the train to Jammu from Delhi. He is accompanied by Vaidya Guru Dutt, Atal Bihari Vajpayee, Tek Chand and Balraj Madhok. He issues a press statement, saying, "The *satyagraha* movement has been continuing in Jammu for nearly six months, leading to the arrest of about 2,500 persons and to the killing of more than 30 *satyagrahis* by police firing. In Delhi and Punjab, the movement has been going on for more than two months and has led to the arrest of more than 1,700 *satyagrahis*.

"A large number of *satyagrahis* are pouring into the capital of India from various parts of the country, giving the movement an all India character...In Jammu, in spite of the iron curtain, people have not succumbed to fear and are ready to face the wrath and fury of the authorities whose repressive measures continue unabated...It is strange that one cannot enter the state without a previous permit from the Government of India...entry is barred to those who think or act in terms of Indian unity and nationhood...My object of going to Jammu is solely to acquaint myself with what exactly had happened there and the present state of affairs...."

11th May, 1953: At Pathankot. Dr. Mookerjee is informed by Deputy Commissioner of Gurdaspur that the government has allowed him to proceed without permit and "though no limit has been put on the number of companions you can take with you, I will advise you to take only a few." Dr. Mookerjee reaches Madhopur check-post on the Ravi Bridge at 4 p.m. The jeep carrying him and others is stopped half-way across the bridge by Kashmir policemen and Dr. Mookerjee is handed an order of the Chief Secretary of the state dated 10th May, 1953, banning his entry into the state. When Dr. Mookerjee insisted on going to Jammu, he was given an order of arrest under the State's Public Safety Act issued by the Inspector General of J&K Police and dated 11th May, 1953, stating that Dr. Mookerjee "has acted, is acting and is about to act in a manner prejudicial to public safety and peace." Dr. Mookerjee got down from the jeep along with Vaidya Guru Dutt and Tek Chand. They were put under arrest before being taken away. Dr. Mookerjee told his companions, "Go tell our countrymen that I have entered J&K state, though as a prisoner."

12th May, 1953: Dr. Mookerjee and his two companions are imprisoned in a small cottage near Nishat Garden which is designated as a sub-jail. The sub-jail is not equipped with any facilities, not even a telephone.

13th May, 1953: N.C. Chatterjee, a leading legal illiumanry, demands an explanation from Nehru as to how Dr. Mookerjee could have been arrested after being allowed to proceed by the DC of Gurdaspur. Nehru denies that the DC met Dr. Mookerjee.

18th June, 1953: Barrister U.M. Trivedi, who had gone to Srinagar to argue his habeas corpus at Kashmir High Court to secure his release, met Dr. Mookerjee for three hours. He found him weak and cheerless. The next day, Pt. Dogra, who was taken from Jammu to Srinagar to meet him, also found Dr. Mookerjee in a poor state.

19-20th June, 1953: On the night of June 19th, Dr. Mookerjee developed pain in the chest and high fever. On June 20, Dr. Ali Mohammad diagnoses it as dry pleurisy and prescribes Streptomycin injections, despite Dr. Mookerjee informing him that he had been advised by his family physician to avoid this drug as it did not suit him. Vaidya Guru Datt was to say later that Dr. Mookerjee that day requested the Superintendent of Jail to inform his relatives about his illness. No such information was conveyed.

21st June, 1953: A sub-assistant surgeon, who was the jail doctor, pays a cursory visit. Dr. Mookerjee's chest pain becomes intense and his fever increases. He remains untreated. He is unable to talk to Pt. Dogra who had been fetched from Jammu to discuss the possibility of ending the agitation as by then, Sheikh Abdullah had begun to face dissension in his own ranks. Bakshi Ghulam Mohammad wanted a settlement with the Praja Parishad.

22nd June, 1953: Dr. Mookerjee suffers a severe heart attack at 4 a.m. His temperature plummets and he begins to perspire. The jail superintendent is requested to fetch a doctor. Dr. Ali Mohammad arrives at 7:30 a.m. and suggests Dr. Mookerjee's removal to the state nursing home. The two co-detenus want to accompany him, but are denied permission. Permission to remove Dr. Mookerjee to hospital is secured only at 11:30 a.m. and he is taken in a taxi. The hospital is at a distance of 10 miles and he is kept in a room on the first floor. Trivedi meets him at 5:30 p.m. and is confident that he will able to secure a release order the next day.

23rd June, 1953: At 3:45 a.m. Trivedi is picked up from his hotel. Vadiya Guru Datt and Tek Chand are picked up from the sub-jail. They are taken to the hospital where they are informed that Dr. Mookerjee died at 3:40 a.m. Witnesses claim later that as he lay gasping, Dr. Mookerjee was denied oxygen.

Only a judicial enquiry could decide whether he died or was murdered, which was never conducted in spite of the fact that Dr. Mookerjee, the leader of the Opposition in Parliament, died in mysterious circumstances in Srinagar Jail.

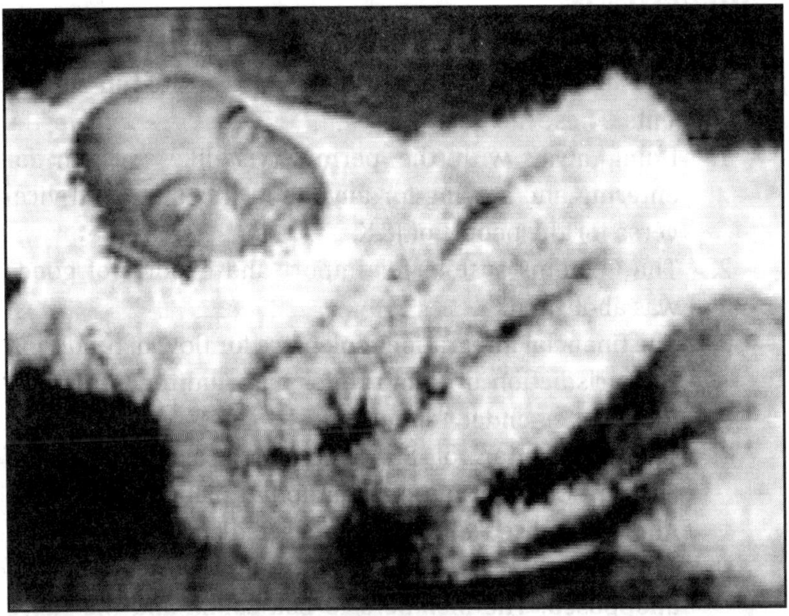

The last journey

In his death, Dr. Mookerjee secured from Nehru what had been denied to him in life. A storm of protest blew across the country and public anger kept on mounting. Nehru found himself increasingly cornered, even by his own colleagues in the government. Sheikh Abdullah, meanwhile, prepared for his final push. Finally, Nehru was left with no further defence of his friend. On 9th August, 1953, after losing the confidence of his colleagues in the Cabinet when refused further cooperation, the Sheikh was dismissed from office and jailed. Nehru had to acknowledge that Sheikh Abdullah was indulging in anti-national activities and working against the country's interests. The Praja Parishad's demands too, had to be conceded, but on this front success was partial.

The biggest success, however, was that Sheikh Abdullah could not fulfil his dream of breaking free India and Nehru was prevented from helping his friend to fulfil this dream.

ACHIEVEMENTS

The hard struggle for demolishing the barriers between Jammu & Kashmir and the rest of India has resulted in several achievements. These include:

1. Doing away with the permit (visa-like) system for entering and staying for anyone in this state and vice-versa for the people of J&K.
2. The Customs system for import and exports of goods was abolished.
3. The financial integration took place for flow of funds and the jurisdiction of Comptroller and Auditor General of India got extended to the state.
4. The jurisdiction of Supreme Court as also that of Election Commission of India found place in this state. And 'unopposed' successes to elected bodies came to an end, whereas earlier, majority seats were manipulated unopposed. The members to Lok Sabha and the Rajya Sabha were earlier nominated instead of elections.
5. The nomenclature of the Sadar-e-Riyasat to that of the Governor and that of Prime Minister to the Chief Minister were changed to become in line with other states.
6. Most of the Indian laws got extended to benefit the people of the J&K too.
7. Freedom of the press is also one of the major achievements.

(Ref: Gupta, Chaman Lal (2010), Article-370: A Thorn, *Art Printers, Jammu.)*

□

Resume of the Big *Satyagraha* Movement of 1952-53

The following is the full text of the presidential address delivered by Pt. Prem Nath Dogra in the meeting of the General Council of all Jammu & Kashmir Praja Parishad on 6th September, 1953

Brother delegates,

We are meeting after about a year of momentous events. It was on the 8th August last year that we met here in a convention to chalk out our course of action, checkmate the policies of separatism which were intended to make Jammu & Kashmir an independent state with a separate flag, separate constitution and a separate head. We pointed out the dangers of that policy and pleaded with the Government of India to put a stop to it, which, we warned them would spell disaster both for the state and the rest of India.

On the occasion, we had the privilege of having with us that noblest and bravest of the sons of Mother India and who has since made the supreme sacrifice by laying down his life for our cause which, he had the foresight to realise, was the cause of India's unity. How we wish that he had been with us today here to guide our deliberations! Our hearts are heavy with grief, but we have to go ahead to complete his mission and that alone will be our real tribute to that great martyr.

Dr. Syama Prasad Mookerjee on that occasion counselled us to have patience and promised us that he would use his good offices to make the Government of India see the dangers of their policy on Kashmir. He made heroic and persistent efforts to do so. We too made further efforts to catch the ears of powers that be in Delhi. We implored them to give us at least a hearing. But they could not rise above their prejudices and Dr. Mookerjee was ill-advised to trust them, who treat his compatriots and countrymen worse than political untouchables.

In those circumstances we were forced to take resort to the path of self-sacrifice, through peaceful non-violent *satyagraha* to awaken the conscience of the Indian people and government and also of the government of Jammu & Kashmir with a view to make them conscious of the dangers of Sheikh Abdullah's policy of unbridled separatism and to persuade them to change it in the wider interests of the people of the state and for the unity of India.

THE *SATYAGRAHA*

Our *satyagraha,* which began on the 17th November, 1952 continued without break till 7th July, 1953 when it was withdrawn. During these eight months, terrible engines of suppression were let loose against us by the government of Kashmir with the help of the Government of India.

The most virulent kind of propaganda campaign was also started against us, within and outside the state. Not merely courage, forbearance and restraint in the face of gravest provocation and above all, faith in the justice of our cause shown by the people of Jammu, proved too much for the might of both the governments. Their bullets, *lathis,* gas bombs as also their systematic campaign of looting, harassing, dishonouring women in most barbaric manner and of humiliating the people in various other ways was done to break the spirit of the people. Ultimately the oppressor has to admit his defeat. His failure to cow us down had become as potent as the vindications or the cause for which we struggled.

TRIBUTE TO MARTYRS

I take this opportunity to pay on your behalf and my behalf our humble tribute to all those martyrs and fighters known and unknown, who responded to the call of the Parishad and laid down their lives or suffered in other ways. Their sacrifices and sufferings have not gone in vain. They have put new life in our people and instilled a new confidence in them. They have ensured our existence as a free and honourable people in our own homeland as an integral part of India.

THANKS TO THE PEOPLE OF INDIA

The role played by the people of India in our struggle which in its ultimate analysis was the struggle for the unity of India has been equally glorious. Under the leadership of Dr. Syama Prasad Mookerjee, the Bharatiya Jana Sangh, the Hindu Mahasabha and the Ram Rajya Parishad extended their active support to us. They made our cause their own, shared our sufferings and grief and thereby proved that unity of India is a living faith in the hearts of the Indian people. Even those who did not actively help us had a word of sympathy for us. In fact it will not be an exaggeration to say that the Congress rulers of India stood isolated in the policy they pursued towards us. The country was with us and it made the greatest sacrifice in the death of Dr. Mookerjee for our cause.

I take this opportunity to thank my countrymen outside the state on behalf of the people of the state for their deep and continued sympathy and interest in us.

OUR STAND VINDICATED

The hollowness of the propaganda made against us by both the governments and those who take their clue from the men in power has been thoroughly exposed by now. The events have proved that we were right and that our critics were either misinformed or their judgement had been clouded by prejudices and party's spirit. Our demand for abolition of customs, protection of Supreme Court, etc., was as much for the good of the people of Kashmir as of Jammu. In fact, the people of Kashmir stood to gain much more than the people of Jammu by the economic and other reforms demanded by the Parishad. The Wazir Committee, which consisted entirely of officials and could not be suspected of partiality for the Parishad, has in its report substantially vindicated the stand of the Parishad about land reforms and other economic matters. It is a pity that this report has not been made public so far.

But the real success of our movement lies in the fact that the Government of India as also majority of the ruling group of Kashmir ultimately realised the dangers of the separatist policies of Sheikh's party in power in the state; yet, the fact remains that he has been dismissed mainly on those grounds for which he was opposed by the Parishad. But for our movement, he might have continued to deceive the people of Kashmir and of the whole country and might have succeeded in his deep-laid conspiracies with foreign powers. There cannot be a surer vindication of the stand of any movement than the one provided by the recent course of events in Kashmir for our movement.

THE CHANGE OF GOVERNMENT

But the change of the government in itself is not of much significance as far as the Parishad is concerned. Ghulam Mohammad and two of his Cabinet colleagues were members of Abdullah's government as well, and they too must share the blame for his anti-national policies. They cannot shield themselves by saying that they were not heard and that Sheikh Abdullah had became a dictator. What did the so-called representative of Jammu in the Abdullah government do when inhuman torture and repression was being perpetrated on the people of Jammu? What did they do to save the life of our great leader, Dr. Mookerjee, whose life was a national trust in their hands? One of them even tried to defend Sheikh Abdullah by issuing the statement which gave entirely wrong facts about Dr. Mookerjee's death.

NO CAUSE FOR JUBILATION

There is no question of our jubilation over the change. We had no grudge against the person of Sheikh Abdullah; we were opposed to his policies which, as is now admitted by all concerned, have proved ruinous to the state. Our attitude towards the new government will depend on the policies it pursues. If it will honestly work for the betterment of the lot of the people and for bridging the gulf that the Sheikh Abdullah government had created between the people of Jammu & Kashmir on the one side and between the state and the rest of India on the other, it will have our cooperation in the fullest measure. We did offer our cooperation to Sheikh Abdullah as well when he took over the administration of the state but he spurned it. Had he cared to listen to those who did not agree with him, the situation today might have been quite different. I hope that Bakshi Ghulam Mohammad will not follow in the footsteps of Sheikh Abdullah in this respect. No doubt he has begun very well, but so had Sheikh Abdullah. It is for him to prove by his actions that he is a different man. Let us hope that he will do so. In that case, he will find we are his best friends.

OUR COOPERATION

Our cooperation however, will be the cooperation of equals and not that of a subordinate with master. We want the people of Jammu, Kashmir and Ladakh to live and prosper as equal partners in the discharge of duties and responsibilities that have fallen on their shoulders. We want different parts of the state to remain united in the bonds of freedom and mutual trust, unmitigated by any feelings of domination by one part over the other so that the state as a whole may grow as an indivisible part of India, which is the common motherland of us all.

ACCESSION AND PLEBISCITE

As regards the fundamental question of the state's future affiliation, the Praja Parishad has made its stand clear. We consider the accession of Jammu & Kashmir state to India as final and irrevocable. There may be difference of opinions about the degree of cohesion but we do not think any loyal citizen of the state can ever question the fact of accession.

HARMFUL AND UNCALLED FOR

It is why we consider the talk of plebiscite to decide the future of the state as wholly harmful and uncalled for. Jammu & Kashmir state has since times immemorial been an integral part of India geographically, culturally as well as economically. It became legally and constitutionally a part of India when the Maharaja signed the Instrument of Accession. The common sufferings of the people of the state and the rest of the country in defence of the state against Pakistani aggressors during the last six years have cemented with blood the age-old ties binding us with the rest of India. The supreme sacrifice of the greatest son of India has further strengthened these ties. It is impossible for us today even to entertain any thought which might tend to break or weaken these ties. We are determined to remain an indivisible part of Mother India and no power on earth can deflect us from our resolve. We will resist to the last man any effort to cut ourselves from India, plebiscite or no plebiscite.

PAKISTAN HAS NO LOCUS STANDI

We cannot understand the insistence of Pakistan on plebiscite. In the first place, Pakistan has no business to interfere in the internal matters of the state and India. The offer to ascertain the will of the people was made by the Government of India to the people of the state, if so decided by them. Secondly, Pakistan cannot talk about plebiscite which is essentially a path of peace, so long as she continues to be in aggressive occupation of one-third part of the state and so long as her press and radio continue to cry for *jihad*. She must know that cries of war and plebiscite cannot work together. She must make up her mind as to what she really wants. Pakistan is mistaken if she thinks that her threats can cow down the people who have had the foretaste of what Pakistan means during the Pakistani invasion in 1947. Furthermore, to allow Pakistan to be party to any plebiscite in the state is to create religious frenzy in the state and which has become the hallmark of Pakistan today. India and the people of the state cannot allow the poison of religious fanaticism to be injected into the body politic of the state once again. We, therefore, call upon the Government of India to give any encouragement by entering into pacts about plebiscite with Pakistan. The people of the state do not want it because they are convinced that it cannot serve any useful purpose and will only disturb the peace of the state and vitiate it. The Praja Parishad cannot be party to it.

NEED OF VIGILANCE

We also want the Government of India to be more vigilant about the developments in the state. It cannot be absolved from the responsibilities for the policies of Abdullah government which had jeopardised the very existence of the state. The government must also take immediate steps to stop the machinations and intrigues of the agents of foreign countries which are very active in the Valley.

REFUGEES TO BE REHABILITATED

The condition of the refugees from the Pakistan-occupied areas of the state also demands immediate attention of the government. Many of them are still wandering in other parts of the country. They yearn to be back in the state. Those who are in the state have not yet been rehabilitated. The previous government had been very callous towards them. We expect the Bakshi government to take immediate steps to resettle them so that their misery is ended.

OUR DUTY

While it is our duty to press the government to take steps to improve the condition of the people, we ourselves cannot afford to sit idle. During the last six years of its existence, the Praja Parishad had to launch a *satyagraha* movement a number of times to make the voice of the people heard by those in authority. It has been a period of continuous struggle or preparation for struggle. Our people have suffered a lot during this period. Many of them have been utterly ruined. They deserve our attention first. We should set up a committee to enquire into cases of repression and hardships. It will have to move in the areas and collect evidences and submit its report to the Parishad. We will have to do whatever little we can to help them. I also expect the Kashmir government to take immediate steps to compensate them. That is the least it can do to expiate for its sins of omission and commission. It is also necessary to create an atmosphere of goodwill and cordiality in the state.

MEMORIAL TO DR. MOOKERJEE

It is also our duty to do something to perpetuate the memory of those who have laid down their lives for our cause. The greatest of them was Dr. Syama Prasad Mookerjee. It is our duty to set up a befitting memorial to him and other martyrs. For that purpose, we should set up a Dr. Mookerjee Memorial and Jammu Martyrs Memorial Committee to collect funds for raising the memorial. I hope the people of the state will contribute liberally towards the memorial fund.

ENQUIRY INTO DR. MOOKERJEE'S DEATH

It is a matter of deep pain that the circumstances for the death of Dr. Mookerjee still remain shrouded in mystery and grave doubts have been expressed about the events leading to it. We should reiterate our demand which is also the demand of 370 million people of India that the government should institute an impartial commission, consisting of judges of the Supreme Court, to enquire into this matter. Otherwise, those doubts will turn into confirmed belief, which would not be in the interest of the government and will also shake the foundations of democracy in the country.

COMPLETE THE ORGANISATIONAL STRUCTURE

We have also to address ourselves to the organisational work. A draft constitution is being placed before you. I hope you will pass it. It will be our duty to organise the countryside on the basis of this constitution in the shortest possible period. A time-table for this purpose will soon be announced. The Praja Parishad is an organisation of the masses and workers and it has received the fullest support of all sections of society. It is for us now to harness this universal support and give it a permanent standing by speeding up the work of our organisation in the remotest villages.

THREE-FOLD CONSTRUCTIVE PROGRAMME

At the same time we have to turn to constructive activities. So far, our attention and energies were mainly concentrated on the struggle. The struggle had its advantages. Besides creating awakening in the people, it has brought into the forefront persons who can serve as servants of the people and who have the ability and statemenship to carry their cause to success. But now that we have got some respite from the struggle, we must turn our attention to equally important work of internal reconstruction. There is a large field and scope for it. Our people are backward and neglected. They need our guidance and help. The constructive activities can take many forms. I recommended the following threefold programme for your consideration:

1. Ours is a land of villages. Villages have been the centre of social, economic as well cultural life of our people. There can be no improvement in the life of the people so long as the villages remain neglected and the trend of educated people moving out of the villages to towns and cities continues. I would like you to improve the life of villages through construction of link roads, planning and lining of villages streets, opening of schools and reading rooms and taking in your hand such other things as can be accomplished by voluntary effort of the local people. Many of the villages have some families of ex-servicemen. They can give the benefit of their experience for the improvement of village life. Efforts should also be made to start cottage industries in the villages, wherever possible.
2. Many of our people are illiterate and absolutely ignorant about ordinary rules of health. As a result, the general health of the people is declining rapidly. The Parishad

workers may take in their hands the work of educating the people particularly in respect of rules of health. Something must also be done to check the growing evil of liquor consumption.

3. Though many of the evils of casteism and barabarism have been removed and the people of Jammu have been working as one man under the leadership of the Parishad, some more effort is needed to create social cohesion in our society. We must pay particular attention to the backward sections of our society and create in them a sense of confidence and oneness with the rest of the community through our behaviour. Attention must also be paid to our Muslim brethren who must be made to feel that they are one of us. The Muslims of the state have the same blood and are inheritors of the same culture as the Hindus. It is the duty of the Parishad workers to rekindle in their hearts love for that heritage and also for the common motherland through development of social relations with them.

The speeches of our new Premier, Bakshi Ghulam Mohammad have created hopes in the minds of the people. They show an insight into the real problem of the state, but it is essential that the hopes created are speedily fulfilled. I am happy to note that he has already taken some steps in the right direction, but much however, remains to be accomplished. I trust that his enthusiasm in this respect will continue unabated till the economic rehabilitation of the people of the state is achieved.

THE GOAL YET TO BE ACHIEVED

But even more important for us is the question of fuller unity of our state with the rest of India. We have already made some progress towards the achievement of this goal, but much still remains to be done. For that, we will have to be active and vigilant. I hope that the state government has by now realised the intensity of the feelings of the people on this question and it will take speedy steps to bring about financial integration of the state with India and do such other things as are necessary to bring the state into the position in which, like other acceding states, or will be entitled to claim all those benefits which other states derive from the Centre and without which it will not be possible to develop the resources of the state; and this will not improve the economic conditions of its people.

Jai Bharat!

□

Objections to a Separate Constitution

On 1st April, 1954, Panditji submits a memorandum on the constitutional setup of J&K state to the President of India, New Delhi

His Excellency the President of Indian Union, NEW DELHI

May it please Your Excellency,

1. In connection with the constitutional proposals which have been recently made by the J&K state authorities to the Central Government, this representation is most respectfully submitted on behalf of the Praja Parishad of that state for Your Excellency's kind and sympathetic consideration.
2. There is no doubt that these proposals constitute a little advance on the existing position. And coming as they do, in the wake of the decision of J&K Constituent Assembly to confirm and finalise the accession of this state to the Indian Union, they have been welcomed not because they take us far towards our goal, but because they seem to have been conceived in a different spirit from that which animated the Abdullah government.
3. Amidst this chorus of praise, it seems almost churlish to strike jarring notes to the people whom it represents. They have consistently demanded that the Indian Constitution be made applicable to the state just as it applies to the other Part 'B' states. In the pursuit of this objective, they have undergone great sacrifices and sufferings, being convinced that without achieving it,

there can be no peaceful and honourable life for them in this state. They were led to entertain certain hopes by definite assurances, but these proposals do not come near their fulfilment. Consequently, the people affected have on the whole received them with mixed feelings, including those frustrations.

4. In certain circles, there is a tendency to dismiss the demand mentioned in the preceding paragraph as a problem for legalistic or academic discussion and to ignore its human aspects, but those who have raised it are indeed earnest about it. To them it is a matter of life and death and they are determined to persist in it, regardless of the sufferings and sacrifices which this course might entail for them.
5. It is a pity that the Central Government has never enquired from the proper quarters why this demand is being made and how far it is justified. On the contrary, they have been more responsive to the opposite demand of the National Conference leaders, which is to effect that this state should have a special privileged status, different from that of the other Part 'B' state. The wonder is that it has occurred to the otherwise wide awake Central Government that, in ultimate analysis, both these demands, so contradictory in their formulation and intent, really spring from similar apprehensions. But the fears of the Kashmiri leaders are wholly baseless, because admittedly they have received the most generous treatment from the government and the people of India during the last six years and more. On the other hand, the apprehensions of the Jammu people are fully justified by the experience they have had of 'so called popular rule' during the same period. They have been reduced to the level of political untouchables in their homeland. Their genuine voice has been effectively shut out from the Constituent Assembly. The government formed by the Conference

Party is neither responsible nor responsive to the people of Jammu. The doors of government services are closed to them and those already in service are being pushed out. The administration is corrupt and inefficient and it is difficult for the common man to obtain redressal in the ordinary course. Naturally the people of Jammu seek those organs of the Central authority that might possibly be afforded to them. But the Kashmiri leaders desire to retain the best of both worlds; they demand autonomy for themselves in relation to the Central authorities of the Indian Union and at the same time, they stick to undiluted autocracy in the shape of an unalterable fixed majority in relation to the Jammu people. In fairness, they should accord the same treatment to the latter as is demanded by them for themselves from the Indian Union. This legitimate demand of the Jammu people is sometimes ignored on the false plea that it is confined to reactionary, communalist and vested interests.

6. The problem that has arisen between Jammu & Kashmir is essentially the same problem as has emerged between the whole state and the Indian Union. And fortunately it is also the problem that the Indian Constitution was devised to solve. Its wise framers were faced with the rival claims of competing elements in the body politic and they arrived at a nice adjustment of those claims in the framework of that constitution. This nice balance and adjustment makes it eminently fitted to provide a solution of the essentially human problem that faces us in this state. This is a strong reason why a solution of this problem should be attempted by applying the Indian Constitution in its entirety to this state.
7. Viewed against the above background, the unsatisfactory character of the new proposals becomes quite apparent, in as much as they disturb the nice balance of adjustments that the Indian Constitution in its entirety was intended to be. They mutilate its organic unity without leaving

a fair working arrangement. They seem to have been cleverly devised in order to achieve the following objectives, namely:

i. To retain as much power as possible;
ii. To part with as little of it as might be inevitable;
iii. To let qualifications and exceptions swallow what is conceded;
iv. To make the powers retain the close monopoly of an unalterable fixed majority;
v. To ensure that the resulting setup shall not be altered without the consent of that majority;

Some of the expedients adopted by the framers of these proposals in order to achieve the above objectives are mentioned below, viz.:

i. Fundamental Rights have been whittled down and reduced to a mockery;
ii. The jurisdiction and powers of the Supreme Court have been curtailed to prevent effective enforcement of fundamental and other rights;
iii. Full control over the state High Court has been retained in order that the local judiciary may not become truly independent and embarrass the executive authorities;
iv. A sort of dual citizenship has been created within the Indian Union to its eternal shame and humiliation;
v. One-way traffic from Pakistan in the matter of settlement within this state has been provided for;
vi. Direct elections to the House of the People from the state have been avoided in order that the authentic voice of the people of this state may not be heard even in the Indian Parliament;
vii. The powers vested in the central organs of authority in the Indian Union in relation to the other Part 'B' states have been curtailed even in matters of common and national interests where uniformity of action is necessary;

viii. The status of the Sadar-i-Riyasat has been made inferior even to that of a Governor and his position is precarious by leaving him at the mercy of a prejudiced and an unalterable fixed majority in the local legislature;

ix. Even the Delhi pact has not been fully implemented;

x. Certain provisions of the Indian Constitution, which are applicable to this state at present are proposed to be repealed;

xi. The capacity and powers of the Indian Union to take prompt and effective action in relation to this state at times of emergency have been crippled;

xii. Provisions relating to effective and independent audit and financial control have been omitted; and

xiii. Drastic and confiscatory 'lawless' laws are proposed to be legalised.

8. There are several other objectional features of these proposals but it is unnecessary to detail them all. Some of them will, however, become apparent as the succeeding detailed scrutiny of the proposals proceeds. Enough has, however, been said to show that these proposals give no indication of its framers being grateful for the generous treatment which they have received. On the contrary, they betray great distrust of the various organs of the Indian Central authority, including the Parliament, the President and the Supreme Court.

9. Such an important matter as constitution-making should have been circulated for public opinion before being finally passed when it is an admitted fact that this Assembly is composed of one party alone. The constitution should not have been conceived and hatched in a secret manner behind closed doors, without associating any person unconnected with the government or the Assembly even in an advisory capacity at any stage of their formulation or consideration. These facts should persuade the Government of India to examine these proposals with

special care and consult the opinion of Jammu before accepting them finally.

10. Some points calling for consideration which the detailed scrutiny of these proposals has revealed, are briefly noted below:

1. Article 3 of the Indian Constitution

The new provision which it is proposed to add to this Article will in certain respects overlap the existing provision.

2. Part II of the Indian Constitution

This part is to apply to this state from 26th January, 1950, but the state acceeded to the Indian Union from 26th October, 1947. What will be the status of the people of the state between these two dates? Will they be deemed to have been aliens during this interval?

3. Article 7

It is a proposed to add a new proviso to this article. Even Sheikh Mohammad Abdullah, ex-Prime Minister of the state, knew that the policy underlying the proposed proviso might cause apprehensions in certain quarters. He tried to allay these fears in the statement which he made before the State Assembly on 11th August, 1952, in the following words:

"It has been suggested in certain quarters that this protection has been provided only for those residents of the state who are at present stranded in Pakistan. I would like to make it clear, as I have stated earlier, that this protection will operate only when the conditions are normal and such conditions naturally presume that the resettlement of the dislocated population, whether Muslims or non-Muslims, cannot be one-sided or unilateral.

"If such is still the intention, it should be clearly and expressly stated in the proviso and not left buried in vague declaration of the ex-Prime Minister. Secondly, as the new proviso will operate to confer Indian citizenship, and also because its subject matter deals with, and affects, foreign relations, the law which is to regulate this matter should be enacted by the Central and not by the state legislature. Thirdly, as the conditions are not likely to become normal in the near future, there need be no desperate hurry in adding this proviso; it can be added when the conditions become normal. Lastly, it should be kept in view that part of the Jammu & Kashmir state which is at present in the occupation of Pakistani forces and which is sometimes mis-described as the 'Azad Kashmir territory', is not identical with, and should not, therefore be confused with the territory now included in Pakistan." The framers of the proposed proviso have ignored this distinction. They probably had the former territory in view but have used the latter expression to describe it. They seem to have fallen into this error because they have copied blindly the language of the existing proviso without realising that it becomes inaccurate in the context in which they have used it. In view of these complications and also because there is no real urgency, it seems expedient to drop the idea of adding the proposed proviso to Article 7.

4. Article 19 (Fundamental Rights)

The practical effect of adding the new clause (7) to Article 19, as has been proposed, will be that for five years there will be no 'Fundamental' Rights in the state, and thus what was intended to be granted under clause (1) will have been taken away under clause (7) for that period. It is of the very essence of the 'Fundamental' Rights which are provided in the Indian Constitution, that the Legislature should not have the absolute power to impose such restrictions on their exercise as the courts consider being unreasonable. If the legislature is made the sole absolute judge of the reasonableness of any restrictions which it might deem fit to impose on their exercise, then such rights cease to be 'fundamental' and become ordinary legal rights. It would be a more honest way of dealing with this matter if the proposed clause (7) were to be ordered as follows:

"(7) For a period of five years those citizens of India who happen also to be the permanent residents of the state of Jammu & Kashmir, shall not exercise the rights conferred under clause

(1), except to the extent to which the legislature of the state may, in its absolute discretion, permit them to do so."

As the discretion is not to be 'judicial', it need not necessarily be judicious and may be capriciously exercised.

5. Article 22 (Preventive Detention)

The proposed amendment is neither necessary nor fair; if it must be made, its duration should be limited to a period not exceeding five years.

6. Article 31 (Property Rights)

Clause (3) of this article should not be omitted as has been proposed. In the first place, it provides a safeguard which certainly is not less necessary in the case of this state than it is for the rest of India. Secondly, in the matter of land reforms, it is desirable to aim at a measure of uniformity. Thirdly, it is not clear why this clause is proposed to be omitted when the provisio to clause (1) of Article 31-A is being retained, as both refer to similar matters.

7. Article 31-A (Acquisition of Estates)

The proposed definition of 'estate' is needlessly and unfairly too wide. Secondly, the definition of 'estate' given in our law relating to land tenures which is served by the existing sub-clause (a) of clause (2) of Article 31-A could have served the purpose in view. Thirdly, it is undesirable to provide a fixed definition of 'estate' in the constitution itself, because in may become necessary to vary the definition from time to time, or place to place, or in order to suit various purposes, but constitutions cannot be easily amended even when it becomes necessary to do so.

8. Article 35-A (Privileges of State 'Subjects')

This Article, if added, will create dual citizenship and retard the growth of common nationality and classless society. It will be a bar sinister on the Indian escutcheon and a disfiguring blot on the Indian Constitution. Secondly, if its addition is unavoidable in view of the present mood of the Kashmiri leaders, its duration should be limited to a period not exceeding five years. Thirdly, even in that case, sub-clause (iii) of clause (b) should be omitted, because 'settlement' is a vague term, and it is not at all clear what it is intended to include over and above, that which is already covered by sub clauses (i), (ii) and (iv). Fourthly, it should be stipulated that sub clause (iii) must not be used to impose new, or enlarge the existing, disabilities; lastly, the saving grace of Article 35-A should be limited to existing laws and should not cover laws imposing new, or enlarging the existing, disabilities.

9. Part (IV) Articles 36 to 51 (Directive Principles)

If these Articles are proposed to be omitted, it is a matter for profound regret. These have been evolved after mature thought and long experience and should guide the course of legislation and administrative action in every enlightened state. There should be no hesitation in adopting them because they are directory, and not mandatory in the sense of being justifiable.

10. Articles 54, 55 and 81 (Parliamentary Elections)

In the first place, it is unfair to deprive the people of the state of their right to choose by direct election their representatives in the House of the People. When direct elections were held for the State Assembly, electoral rolls were prepared on the basis of adult franchise. Such rolls can be prepared also for the parliamentary elections. If the population of the state can be assumed to be 44, 10,000 for the purpose of Article 55, as has been proposed, there is no reason why the same figure should not be adopted for purposes of Article 81. Secondly, it would be a misnomer to categorise the representatives of the state as 'elected' members for purpose of Article 55, as has been proposed, when at the same time it is being clearly provided under Article 81, that they shall be 'appointed' by the President. Their status will still be that of 'appointed' members even though they might have been appointed on the recommendation of the State Legislature. At present they are 'chosen by the President in consultation with the government of the state', but it is now proposed that 'they shall be appointed by the President on the recommendation of the legislature of the state.' It would be simpler to say that thereafter the representatives of this state in both the Houses of Parliament shall be elected by the elected members of the State Legislative Assembly. Thirdly, it is wrong to provide in the constitution itself that the population of the state shall be deemed to be 44,10,00. This figure is bound to vary frequently, but the constitution should not be liable to frequent changes; perhaps the best expedient would be to make a temporary provision on the lines of Article 387, until a regular Census can be held in this state.

11. Article 73 (Executive Power of the Union)

This Article is at present in force without any modification in this state by virtue of the constitution (application to Jammu & Kashmir) order, 1950. But it is now proposed to repeal certain words from the provisio to clause (1) of this article. No reason has been given for the proposed repeal and none is apparent. Considering that clause 1(a) deals with the matters with respect to which the Parliament has power to make laws, and that the whole of Article 73 deals with the extent of the executive power of the Union, it would be better either to omit this provisio altogether or to leave it unmodified. Any tampering with it might make matters worse.

12. Article 136 (Special Leave to Appeal by the Supreme Court)

Under Article 136, the Supreme Court is empowered to grant in its discretion, special leave to appeal before itself but it is proposed to omit this Article and deny this power to that court in relation to this state. This would be a very unwise and serious omission. Without this power, the extension of the jurisdiction of that court to this state will remain illusory, and the people will not have full confidence and assurance that they are getting justice and protection of their rights like other citizens of India.

13. Article 139 (Additional Powers of the Supreme Court)

This Article is applicable to this state at present but it is proposed to repeal it. Obviously, this is a retrograde step and should be avoided.

14. Articles 149 and 150 (Comptroller and Auditor General)

It is necessary to apply these Articles to this state in the interests of sound financial administration and economy, as the present state of affairs in this respect is far from satisfactory. Secondly, such application becomes almost inescapable now that the state government is going to get its share from the common pool of certain Central taxes. The taxes to be shared are raised from the people of India as a majority of them as taxpayers are entitled to the assurance and protection these Articles are intended to supply. Thirdly, the Central Government would be failing in its duty if it did not satisfy itself that the funds supplied by it to the government of this state were being utilised properly for the intended purposes. This duty the Government of India can discharge effectively only if these Articles are applied to this state.

15. Article 255

Article 255 applies to this state under the President's application order of 1950, but it is now proposed to omit it. There is no justification for such omission.

16. Article 259

Article 259 applies at present to this state, subject to the specified modifications, but it is now proposed to omit it altogether. The retention of this Article is very necessary.

17. Article 261

The whole of this Article applies at present to this state, but it is now proposed to omit the words 'made by Parliament' from clause (2) of it. This proposal seems to have been made in ignorance of the scope and purpose of clause (2). If the manner of and the condition for, proving public acts, records and judicial proceedings of the Union and of every state are to be regulated for the whole of India on a uniform basis, as they should be evidently, the only law that can do this effectively and appropriately is the law made by the Parliament. Therefore, it is clearly to apply without any modification to this state, as it does at present.

18. Article 291 (Privy Purse Sums)

This Article should be retained, subject to certain obvious modifications.

19. Part XVII (Official Language)

This part should be made applicable to the Jammu & Kashmir state for all purposes. Considering that Urdu is not the spoken language of any considerable section of the people in any part of the state, its imposition as the official or regional language of the state and as the medium of instruction in schools or in colleges, will not be fair. In any case, Hindi should have equal status with Urdu in this respect, if not throughout the state, at least in the Jammu province. The medium of instruction in the primary or basic classes should be the mother tongue, but the guardians should have the option of declaring the mother tongue of their wards. In any case, whatever is adopted as the official or regional or mother language in the state or any part of it, it should be permitted to be written both in Arabic and Hindi characters as the option of the persons concerned and its teaching should be arranged for and permitted in both characters.

20. Part XVIII (Emergency Powers)

It is proposed to omit Articles 356, 357 and 360 and to amend Article 352. Under Article 355, which was being retained, it is the duty of the Union to protect this state, not only against external aggression, but also against internal disturbances and also ensure that the government of this state is carried on in accordance with the provisions of the constitution. The President of the Union will be deprived of the power to act effectively and promptly in discharge of the duty imposed under Article 355, if Articles 356, 357 and 360 are omitted and Article 352 is amended in the manner proposed. There should be no divorce between responsibility and power. This part should apply to this state in its entirety without any modification.

21. Part XIX Article 361 (Sadar-i-Riyasat)

There should be no confusion, vagueness or conflict about the position of the Sadar-i-Riyasat, but such is likely to be the result if reference is retained to the state constitution in the new clause (5) which it is proposed to add to this Article. Keeping in view his positions and functions, he should be free from local influences and harassment. Experience of the action he had to take in the recent Emergency should suggest caution in this respect.

22. Article 362

The retention of this Article is necessary for reasons which are obvious.

23. Article 365

It is necessary to retain this Article if the powers of the Union Executive under the constitution are real and not illusory; it is not to be exposed to mockery and reduced to impotence in relation to this state; if, in the absence of an effective sanction, its lawful directions are not to be flouted with if its duties and responsibilities under Article 355 are to be carried out satisfactorily; and if the government of the state is to be carried on in accordance with the provisions of the constitution.

24. Article 372

Article 372 makes mention of Article 395. This reference is inappropriate because Article 395 is proposed to be omitted.

25. Article 374 (Advisory Board)

It is proposed to amend clause (4) of Article 374 in order to provide for the abolition of the State Board of Judicial Advisers and the transfer of the appeals pending before it for disposal to the Supreme Court of India, but this is likely to make matters worse in one respect. The Board's present jurisdiction is wider than that proposed to be conferred on the Supreme Court. This will result in greater finality attaching to the decisions of the local courts because fewer appeals will lie to the Supreme Court than lie to the Board at present. Moreover, the appellate jurisdiction of the Supreme Court in relation to the Jammu & Kashmir courts will not be as wide as that which it exercises in relation to the courts of the other states. The provision contained in Chapters V and VI of Part VI read with Part VII of the Indian Constitution relating to judiciary are not being made applicable to the judiciary of this state. It cannot therefore, be pretended that the judiciary of this state including its High Court will command the same measure of confidence and prestige which the judiciary of the other states commands. If the confidence of the people in the justice administered in this state is not to be undermined, it is necessary that this state be brought up to the level of the other states by applying to it all the provisions of the Indian Constitution relating to judiciary just as they apply to the other Part 'B' states. At any rate the present position when the Advisory Board is functioning is much better than that which will result from the proposals after the Board has been abolished.

26. Article 387

This Article should be retained till a new regular Census has been completed in this state, because until then, there should be some provisions in the constitution under which authoritative estimates of its population could be made, varied from time to time, for purposes of elections. Of course, some modifications of the Article will be necessary in its application to this state, because the three-year period mentioned in it has already expired. The estimate of 44,10,000, proposed for purposes of Articles 54 and 55 cannot remain fixed figures for all time, and will have to change from time to time, but it should not be necessary to amend the constitution itself every time a correction of this figure becomes necessary.

27. Schedule VII, List I, Entry No. (3)

This entry at present applies to this state without any modification, but, it is now proposed to curtail its scope considerably. There is no apparent reason to justify this course. The expression 'administration of cantonments' is not wide enough to cover all the functions included in this entry. Evidently, the army authorities need comprehensive powers in this respect. It should not be forgotten that this state is still a war area and that the opposing armies are still facing each other on its borders.

28. Schedule VII, List I, Entry No. (9)

This entry is applicable to this state at present but it is proposed to omit it altogether, without the slightest justification. It should be retained, because its subject matter is connected with defence, foreign affairs and the security of India, which are the exclusive concern of the Union.

29. Ninth Schedule

As many as six laws of this state are proposed to be included in this Schedule. It is inequitable and unnecessary to protect some of these laws in this manner. In particular, the Distressed Debtor's Relief Act, the Alienation of Land Act and the whole of the Tenancy Act need not find a place in this Schedule.

□

Praja Parishad and Jana Sangh

PRESIDENT, ALL INDIA JANA SANGH

After the 1952-53 agitation, Pt. Prem Nath Dogra's popularity rose so high that he was elevated to the position of president of the Akhil Bharatiya Jana Sangh in the Bhopal session of the party for 1955-56. As president of an all-India party, he toured most parts of the country. Wherever he went, he was given a rousing reception. He has been the only person from Jammu hitherto to become the president of an all-India party. Hc was an instrument in merging of the Praja Parishad in the Ekta Sammelan of the party in Bharatiya Jana Sangh in 1964. He remained the president of *pradesh* unit of the Jana Sangh upto 1967. The last agitation led by Pt. Prem Nath Dogra was that for removal of regional disparities in the supply of food-grains, both in terms of rates and scales in 1967-68. Besides Panditji, thousands of party workers courted arrest.

Pt. Prem Nathji Dogra at Delhi where he was elected All India Jana Sangh president in 1955

Panditji with senior activists after his release from Jammu Jail in 1969 (food agitation)

In the wake of this agitation, a high-powered commission was appointed. This was led by a retired Chief Justice of India, P.B. Gajendragadkar.

This commission on regional imbalances indicted the state government and made several recommendations, including providing the supply of rations on an equal scale and rates.

Pt. Prem Nath Dogra's life was full of events. He remained an extremely busy man throughout his life. His zeal for serving the society as also the party could be judged that even in 1972, when he was seriously ill because of cancer, he used to take interest in the party activities and issued recorded appeals to the electorates to vote for Praja Parishad and make a success of the party candidates. He passed away on 21st March, 1972.

Pandit Dogra had only one son, who expired at the age of merely nine years.

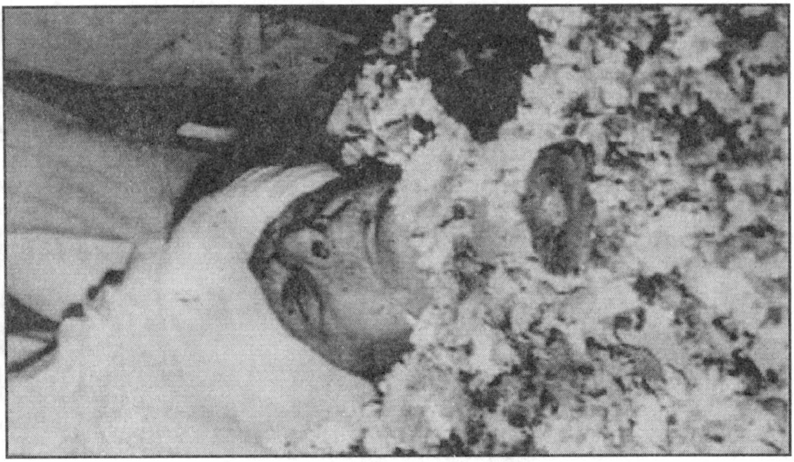

Antim darshan *of Pt. Prem Nathji*

Pt. Prem Nath's antim yatra

AT THE PEOPLE'S LEVEL

To have closer ties at the level of the masses, in 1964 the Praja Parishad was merged with the Bharatiya Jana Sangh.

Taking cue from this step, the Congress, under the leadership of Lal Bhadur Shastri asked its ruling men of the state to merge their National Conference with the Congress. And thus for the first time on 26th January, 1965, the regular unit of the Pradesh Congress came into being in this state.

Earlier, the Congressmen of this state would take shelter under the banner of a regional outfit, viz. the National Conference.

After the lead given by the PP/BJS, the then Communist Party of India and some other parties too established their *pradesh* units in J&K.

FINAL GOAL STILL AWAY

Though considerable achievements have been made because of the movement launched by Pt. Dogra, the final goal still remains to be achieved.

□

The Great Dogra and Other Activists of the Praja Parishad

Pandit Prem Nath Dogra was born in a respectable Brahmin family at village Samailpur, about 20 kms from Jammu. According to a booklet written by Sham Lal Sharma, who was a close associate of Panditji, the birth of the great soul had taken place on 24th October, 1884. His mother had expired when he was still a child and he was nourished by his maternal grandmother.

Pt. Prem Nath Dogra (24th October, 1884 – 21st March, 1972)

After his basic schooling in the village, he was taken to Lahore where his respected father, Pt. Anant Ram was posted as administrator to look after the state properties in Lahore and other places in undivided Punjab.

As Prem Nath was the only child of Anant Ram, special care was taken for his education.

Anant Ram stayed in the palace of Maharaja Dhian Singh. The young Prem Nath was admitted in the nearby Pir Mitha School of Lahore and later on to the Model School. After his matriculation in 1904, he was admitted to the Foreman Christian College.

Pt. Anant Ram, father of Pt. Prem Nath Dogra, senior officer in the Maharaja Hari Singh government

In college, the young Dogra came to be a noted figure as he excelled in various games, especially football. He was popular not only among the students but also amongst the senior teachers of the college. The booklet has also given an account about the popularity of the Dogra youth.

Upon completion of his graduation in 1908, he came back to Jammu with many distinctions and prizes. The then Settlement Commissioner of Jammu, Talbert, appointed the young Dogra as *tehsildar* of Akhnoor for training purposes in 1909.

Pt. Prem Nath Dogra upon his graduation from Lahore University

In 1910, Pt. Dogra was posted

at Udhampur as Assistant Settlement Officer and then in 1912, he was deputed at Jammu with special powers of *munsif*.

In 1913, Dogra was appointed as Secretary to the Governor of Kashmir and later as the Wazir-Wazarat (DC), Mirpur.

Sportsman

Pt. Dogra was a great sportsperson. In his college days at Lahore, he excelled in races, football and also hockey.

Pt. Prem Nath Dogra as Wazir-e-Wazarat in 1931 (DC)

Upon completion of his graduation, when the young Dogra returned to Jammu in 1907, according to the former Governor of Jammu, the late Chet Ram Chopra, Prem Nath brought a bag full of prizes and certificates.

Even after becoming an octogenarian, Panditji used to attend many functions linked with sports and took keen interest even in *kabbadi* which was common in those days, to encourage the players.

After the demise of Maharaja Pratap Singh, Pt. Prem Nath Dogra held important positions in the Revenue Department when Maharaja Hari Singh assumed the reigns of power.

In his booklet, Sharma has given an account of the popularity of Panditji even amongst the Muslims when he was posted at Muzaffarabad as Wazir-e-Wazarat (DC). In the Valley those days, the Sheikh-led Muslim Conference had created communal trouble, resulting in widespread violence.

Some senior high-ups in hierarchy of the Maharaja, feeling jealous of the popularity of Prem Nath Dogra amongst the Muslims, conspired to accuse him of being mild towards the anti-Maharaja agitators. Hence, he was prematurely retired in 1932, when he was just about 50 years of age.

PUNISHED FOR VIRTUES

Acchri Devi, wife of Pt. Prem Nath Dogra, who was known as Mataji

Durga Dass Dogra, advocate and an activist of Bharatiya Jana Sangh, has given an account of the happenings about premature retirement of Panditji.

Some high-ups, including a minister close to the Maharaja were jealous that there was no violence under the administration of Pt. Prem Nath Dogra, unlike in other parts of Kashmir. Dut to doubts created by the jealous higher-ups at the instance of the Maharaja, the then Prime Minister of the state visited Muzaffarabad, and a large number of people shouted slogans, 'Prem Nath Dogra *zindabad*'. This also irked the Prime Minister. Frivolous charges were concocted against Pt. Prem Nath to annoy the Maharaja. On the basis of the report prepared, they succeeded and Maharaja Hari Singh vide his order no. A-57/W of *Samwat Bikrami* 1988-1989 (18th July, 1932) retired Pt. Dogra prematurely. The people of Muzaffarabad loved Panditji from the core of their heart and felt angry and resentful. At Nagin Bagh, Srinagar on 6th September, 1932, a big gathering condemned this royal order and a Kashmiri poet, Abduzafar Kashmiri, gave vent to his feelings of hurt in his verses, originally in Urdu and translated in Hindi.

THE GREAT DOGRA

Prem Nath Dogra was popularly known as Panditji. He was a legend and a vintage personality.

Gopal Sachar, a veteran journalist, who had worked under the stewardship of Panditji from 1950 to 1972, in various capacites including incharge of *prakashan vibhag* of the PP/*Pradesh* BJS and editor of the official organs of the party, viz. *Jai Swadesh*, the *Swadesh* and *Deepak*, observed that Maharaja Gulab Singh had knitted the great Indian state of J&K, but it was Pt. Prem Nath Dogra who by his untiring efforts played a stellar role to make this state an integral part of India, more so in the removal of several barriers between this state and rest of the country.

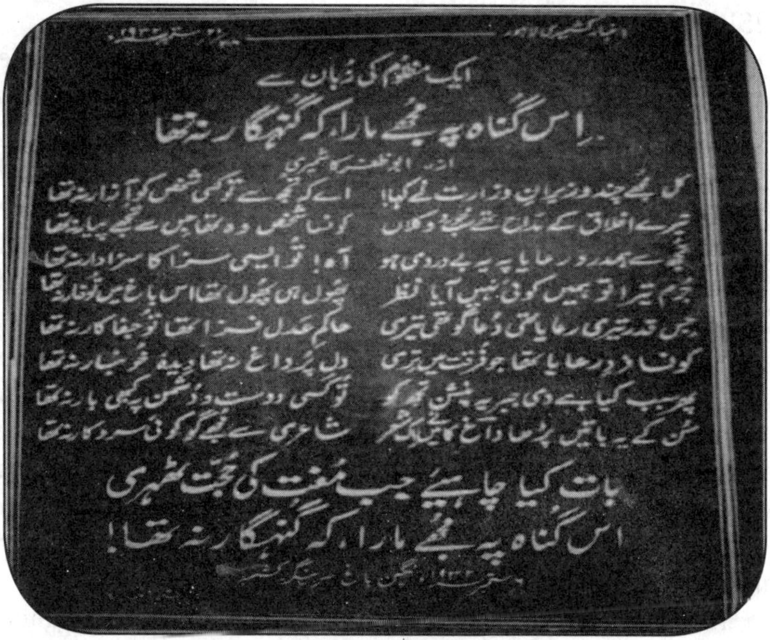
ایک مظلوم کی زبان سے
اس گناہ پہ مجھے مارا، کہ گنہگار نہ تھا
بات کیا چاہیے جب مفت کی حجت ٹھہری
اس گناہ پہ مجھے مارا، کہ گنہگار نہ تھا!

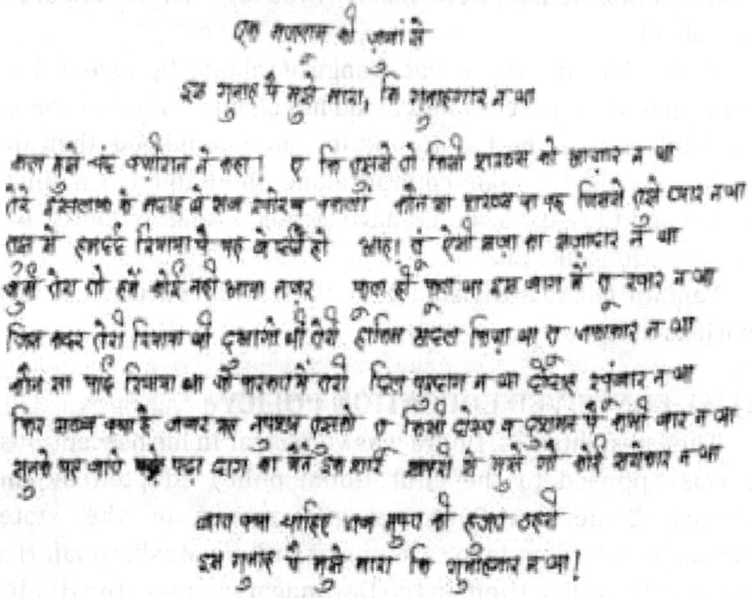
एक मज़लूम की ज़ुबां से
इस गुनाह पे मुझे मारा, कि गुनाहगार न था
इस गुनाह पे मुझे मारा कि गुनाहगार न था!

VISIONARY PANDITJI

Pt. Dogra had a great quality of taking up any public issue with arguments. He always advised his colleagues and followers to be *mudlal*, i.e., speak with arguments and reasoning.

He was opposed to any kind of division or differential treatment on basis of religion, creed or colour. He termed the two-nation theory of Mohammad Ali Jinnah as obnoxious and dangerous as it divides people on communal lines and generates ill-will amongst people with different religious faiths.

Panditji was of the view that religious faiths are ways to worship God to seek peace, prosperity and tranquillity. One can do so in a temple, mosque, church or elsewhere, but it cannot form the ground for nationhood or any other political identity. He was of the opinion that if religion is made a ground for such a division, how would India exist, as this country has numerous faiths to worship the Almighty.

He also used to assert that 'we Indians have a common culture. Our forefathers were one. We lived together and are of the same blood.'

He used to emphasise that change of religion by anyone does not mean that the past or one's blood has changed. He also argued that if religion can be the ground for any nationhood, then the Muslims should have one country alone, the Buddhists a single country and Christians should have formed a single country. But there is nothing like that.

Panditji felt that division of India was ill-conceived with a nefarious design.

(A) ILL-CONCEIVED EDUCATION POLICY

The far-sighted Pt. Dogra was very clear in his perceptions. He was opposed to the educational policy adopted by the National Conference/Congress government of the state, especially with regards to teaching of Urdu in Muslim-majority areas and Urdu-like Hindi in the Devanagari script in the Hindu-dominated areas. He visualised that this would not only lead to a communal divide but in the Hindu areas too, the younger generation would face problems in being ignorant of Urdu in Persian script and the learning of Urdu in Devanagari would prove meaningless as Urdu was the state language. Similarly, Muslims would be ignorant of Hindi, which is the national language.

Pt. Dogra had been pleading for adoption of Urdu in the prevailing Persian script as being the state language and Hindi in Devanagari in all the areas of J&K as it is the national language.

But the suggestions were ignored with the obvious results. In all goverment offices and even in police stations, the basic jobs like the posts of *patwaris, munishis* and that of *nazars* are being manned mostly by Muslims even in Hindu-dominated areas as Urdu-knowing Hindu youths were not available. The Hindu youths are facing problems even at high-level recruitment, so much so that in appearing for KAS exams and also in judiciary there is the language problem as the basic record is in Urdu.

Pt. Dogra had been pleading for adoption of both Urdu and Hindi in the entire state as both being essential for practical purposes. Unfortunately, his suggestions were overlooked. The results are obvious.

He had also been emphasising for making education job-oriented to tide over the problem of unemployment.

The only noteable suggestion which was agreed to, and that too in the late sixties, was the adoption of NCERT books. Otherwise earlier, strange kinds of books were part of the curriculum. Even *Naya Kashmir*, the manifesto of the National Conference was included in the school books and erstwhile rulers were painted as cruel and totalitarian.

(B) ECONOMIC MATTERS

Panditji had clear-cut views on various economic matters. In and outside the Assembly, he had been airing his views with reasoning.

To overcome the growing unemployment, he had been emphasising the need for special attention to develop the industrial and tourism sectors.

He had been warning that reliance on mere government services would not work to meet the challenges of unemployment.

About top-heavy administration, Pt. Dogra had been cautioning the government leaders that this would lead to increased chances of corruption and various other problems. He was of the opinion that lesser government and more governance would be ideal.

In the industrial sector, he felt that separatist policies of the ruling leaders would prove a great hurdle as this would come in the way of investment from outside the state. The lagging behind in growth of industries would cause the state to face the problem of unemployment. More so, it would come to be a consumers' state with little to deliver to come out of its morass. Because of the separatist tendencies, the state's industrial sector could not grow.

For development in various sectors, he used to stress on exploiting the vast hydel power potential which was most needed for developmental activities.

Pt. Dogra was critical of the government leaders for ignoring the development of places of tourist interest in the Jammu region due to narrow regional considerations.

According to Sachar, Pt. Prem Nath was a great Dogra, a remarkable soul and a patriot to the core of his heart. He dedicated his entire life to serve the society in various spheres of life. He was also a noted sportsman.

AN ABLE ADMINISTRATOR

Pt. Prem Nath Dogra was a social reformer, a man with a vision, who faced great hardships for the unity and integrity of the country. He did not budge from his path even when many others were giving in to coercions and different kinds of pressures, including jail in difficult conditions. He struggled hard for a cause, viz. the removal of barriers between J&K and rest of India.

FATHERLY FIGURE

The residence of Pt. Prem Nath Dogra always hummed with activity throughout his life. His place of residence was regarded by different people as their own home.

Often, certain people used to sit around him even when he was taking his meals. Several persons quite often came to get their family disputes settled. And like a head of the family, his advice was taken as a verdict to be honoured.

Several persons use to park their vehicles in the courtyard of the residence of Panditji without any objection.

Interestingly, Panditji never had his own vehicle. He mostly used to walk on foot, travel in buses and even on ponies to reach far off places to address meetings and rallies.

His routine was to have a long morning walk and several

morning walkers felt proud to be in the company of this grand old man, walking swiftly.

Generally, after his morning walk, Panditji used to sit in an open room to attend to the visitors. Sometimes, along with such persons he used to go to the Secretariat and other offices to get their problems settled. He was treated with respect by the government functionaries.

Pt. Prem Nath Dogra was a man of the masses. He not only attended to the problems of his partymen and followers but also quite often, people of opposing parties used to come to him to get their problems sorted out and he was readily available.

He took all the people as his own, although this irked the activists of the Praja Parishad/Bharatiya Jana Sangh. But he never hesitated to extend a helping hand to anyone who came to him. He was therefore treated as *ajatashatru*, i.e., having no enemy.

In this regard, Dharm Chand Parshant, a senior correspondent of the PTI news agency, in his tribute to Pt. Prem Nath Dogra had recalled that once in Srinagar, he saw many Kashmiri Muslims gathered at the gate of the room of the Badshah Hotel where Dogra was staying. He questioned them as to why they had come to this Dogra as he was an RSS man, but their reply was, "(Don't say so. He is a man of the God who takes care of everyone)."

"Yeh to Khuda ka banda hai jo sab ki sunta hai"

Pt. Dogra was indeed revered by all.

SOCIAL ASPECT

Pt. Prem Nath Dogra used to receive frequent invitations to social functions. But he had made it a point to attend personally to receive the marriage parties at the time of marriage of a girl and send congratulations to the family of a male.

He used to attend the religious gatherings not only that of Hindus and Sikhs, but also of Muslims and other communities, notwithstanding that he was the Prant Sanghchalak of the RSS. He was thus conversant with the philosophy of many religious faiths. Hence, his conviction was that no faith taught hatred but there are elements who abuse these for their petty ends.

AS LEGISLATOR

The role of Pt. Dogra as a member of the State Assembly was highly regarded even by his opponents. More than raising any noise, he used to hear the views of others with rapt attention. His presence in the House was unmatched even when he had become an octogenarian.

Pt. Dogra used to be quite critical and even sarcastic about the policies and drawbacks of the government, but never attacked any individual. He mostly talked about policies with suggestions to rectify the wrongs.

AS THE LEADER OF OPPOSITION

Once, at the end of a session, the then chief Minister G.M. Sadiq observed that if anyone had to learn about the role of a leader of Opposition, he should follow Dogra Sahib.

Pt. Dogra was nominated and elected two times to the Praja Sabha (then State Assembly) in 1936 and 1942. He was also elected to the State Assembly in the General Elections of 1957, 1962 and 1967.

RELIEF WORKS FOR REFUGEES

Being a multi-faceted personality, Panditji and his colleagues played an important role in arranging relief for the uprooted people coming in as refugees from adjoining newly-created theocratic state of Pakistan as also displaced persons from Pakistan-occupied Kashmir in the 1947, 1965 and 1971 invasions by the enemy.

Pt. Dogra also gave a helping hand to the security forces whenever they sought. The RSS activists under guidance of Panditji played an important role in raising an airstrip at Jammu for landing of Indian warplanes in 1947, when Pakistan had launched a massive invasion to grab this state by use of force. He readily made available any help that was sought by Indian forces.

In times of natural calamities, Panditji was always eager to that the needy obtain a helping hand.

EVIL OF UNTOUCHABILITY

The far-sighted Panditji, unlike many others, was of the view that untouchability is a curse against mankind. In 1932, when Maharaja Hari Singh announced reforms, including the opening of gates of temples for all castes, Pt. Dogra felt the mere declaration would not work; the malady was deep-rooted. He organised the Brahmin Mukhia Mandal and also gained entry to the Sanatan Dharma Sabha, which was not very supportive of the eradication of this evil. At the same time, he devolped friendly relations with the Arya Samajis and Harijan activists (Pracharaks) to ensure that the objective was achieved without tension.

By this approach, Panditji made the contentious task easier into eradicate the long-practiced malady and many remember him for his administrative skill to sort out contentious issues in a cordial manner.

The Maharaja, impressed by the approach of this great Dogra, also made it a ground for his nomination as a member to the first Praja Sabha in 1934. The Sabha was in a way the first Assembly of the state.

LIQUOR THE WORST EVIL

Panditji used to term the abuse of drugs, above all, liquor, as a big evil. In the course of his speeches, especially in the rural areas of Jammu, he made it a point to ask the people to refrain from consuming liquor. Along with this advice, he used to explain the ill-effects of such narcotics.

In the early fifties, Panditji had a strange experience. He was going on a pony to Plawanwalla in the Akhnoor *tehsil*. At Padli, a small locality near Plawanwalla, some elderly persons were waiting for Panditji. They stopped the pony and requested Panditji to take 'cold', of which the bottles were kept in the cold waters of the tributary.

After his initial surprise, Panditji smiled and asked these 'hosts' to reach Plawanwalla and on return take the 'cold'.

To the surprise of many, Panditji in his over 30 minutes' speech, talked only against the evil of liquor and reminded the people how the brave Dogras had made this big state of J&K and what responsibilities of their generations, to defend this state as a part of India, were.

This speech of Panditji had a great impact upon the people of this entire Dogra-dominated area. Most of the people left this 'cold' drinking and during the 1952-53 agitation for full integration of the state with India, the largest number of *satyagrahis* came out from this belt of the state to take part in the movement. And as many as eight people were from this area alone, out of 16, were martyred in that huge agitation of 1952-53.

PROHIBITION

Pt. Prem Nath Dogra almost in every session of the Assembly had been voicing for prohibition and listing the ills caused by the increased consumption of liquor and other narcotics.

Once in the late fifties, the then Prime Minister Bakshi Ghulam Mohammad in the State Assembly rejected the demand for prohibition on the plea that this state was a place of tourists. Pt. Dogra retorted, "You do offer liquor to visitors but in Jammu, pilgrims come to Vaishno Devi; they do not come for taking liquor."

He felt that booze was spoiling the people, more so that of Jammu on many accounts. It is surprising that this ill still persists and is harming many aspects of life due to erroneous reasons.

CARING FOR THE POOR AND AGED

Panditji used to take care of the aged and handicapped also. He managed to rope in some retired officers and others to raise a *vriddhashram* at Ved Mandir, Jammu.

Towards this end, he had the dedicated services of Dr. Prabhkar, Ishwar Dass Mengi (who was popularly known as Masterji as he was from the Education Department) as also that of some others, including one retired DFO named Khosla.

Panditji was also a trustee of some important trusts including one that was known as Narad Muni Trust. Besides some places in Jammu, the Hanuman Mandir at Srinagar was also under this Trust.

Pt. Dogra with senior leaders at his residence, Kachi Chawni after a meeting

THE GREATNESS OF PANDITJI

The greatness of Pt. Prem Nath Dogra can be judged from the fact that he never hankered after amassing any wealth or property despite holding several important positions in and outside the government. His ancestral place, known as *Panditji ki Kothi* remained open for all, throughout his lifetime. Significantly, even after 45 years of his death, this historic place still houses the office of BJP, which reminds of the greatness of the man who could be the torchbearer for those who want to serve the society and the nation in various capacities in a selfless manner.

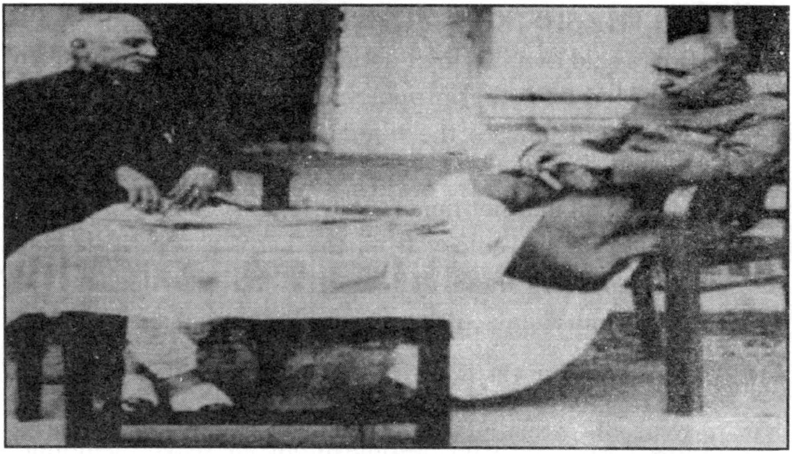

G.M. Karra, a senior Kashmiri Muslim leader, discusses a point with Prem Nath Dogra when he called upon the latter at his residence in Jammu

This place also reminds the visitors of how great he was. At the time of first death anniversary of Panditji in 1973, RSS leader Madhav Rao Muley in his tribute to Panditji had stated this.

FAULTY LAND REFORMS

In 1950, the Sheikh Abdullah-led National Conference government under parochial considerations snatched the lands of the farmers and *jagirdars* with the attractive slogan of 'Land to the tiller'.

These lands were mostly gifted during Maharaja Gulab Singh's time to those who had displayed bravery in action in his campaign to knit together the big state of J&K. He also gave away lands as *jagirs* to the heads of principalities who had surrendered before him and given up their sovereignty.

It is notable that before the creation of this state, there were as many as 22 principalities in Jammu region alone. As the Dogra saying goes: *'Bai Raj pahar dae, wich Jammu Sardar'* (there were 22 small states in this region and Jammu was the bigger one.)

OPPOSED THE SHEIKH'S MOVES

Pt. Dogra said that it is high-handedness to deprive anyone of their ancestral or any other property, without any compensation. If the principle of land to the tiller is to be applied, then why shouldn't the bus and a truck go to the driver and a factory to the workers and so on in other fields?

But riding on the eulogy from the Leftists, the NC leaders and the time-servers dubbed Pt. Dogra and his colleagues as reactionaries and agents of landlords, communalists and what not.

Undeterred, Pt. Dogra came out with alternate suggestions that instead of resorting to unlawful acts and perpetrating anarchy, the government should set up industrial units, develop tourist resorts and create various jobs. But the new rulers did not bother and continued to divide the people on communal, caste and other lines.

Pt. Dogra also opposed the much-acclaimed land reforms of the 'progressives' by observing that the measures adopted lacked farsightedness as the government had first fixed the landholding limit at 182 *kannals* and then reduced it to just 100 *kannals*.

The situation thus created indicates how visionary was Pt. Dogra as with the passage of time, the landholdings have been divided into small pieces because of the bifurcation of families.

Even the government's own survey today reveals that over 95 per cent farmers in this state have come to be known as 'marginal', which is an uneconomic unit. This not only adversely affects the economic condition of farmers but also the entire agricultural pursuits.

It is evident from the fact that food-grain imports which stood at 40 thousand metric tonnes in 1950, have now gone up to 10 lakh tonnes. In addition, over 15 lakh sheep and goats, hens and other food items have been imported to meet the people's requirement, notwithstanding the slogans of self-sufficiency for which thousands of crores of rupees have been spent.

THE SHEIKH'S ANTICS

In 1949, the dispensation of Sheikh Abdullah arrested and jailed Pt. Prem Nath Dogra. The frivolous charge was that he was against Muslims because many of them had left for Pakistan from Jammu areas. Hence, he was not only arrested but was detained without any trial. Not only this, he was shifted to Srinagar Jail to face the vagaries of a severe winter.

But the travesty of the happenings was that in 1938, when Sheikh Mohammad Abdullah came to Jammu and at a gathering of the Dogra Sadar Sabha, he praised Pt. Prem Nath Dogra saying that he was a great secular officer. He handled the situation without resorting to any kind of repression as Wazir-e-Wazarat at Muzaffarabad in 1931, when there was great oppression in other parts of Kashmir (Jammu & Kashmir).

But after the end of monarchy in the state, the same Sheikh acted in a more despotic manner. Any adversary of the ruling *junta* was taken as an 'enemy agent' and very cruel treatment was meted out in the jails.

The charge against Pt. Prem Nath Dogra was an obvious design of generating ill-will between the Hindus and Muslims of Jammu and divide Jammuites on communal lines as also generate hatred against the Praja Parishad in the Valley of Kashmir.

□

Tribute from Madhav Rao Muley (RSS)

पंडितजी, एक अलौकिक व्यक्तित्व

श्रद्धेय पंडित प्रेमनाथ डोगराजी का जीवन आपके युग में एक अनोखा व्यक्तित्व है। जिस काल में स्वार्थ, लूट-खसोट, भ्रष्टाचार, धोखाधड़ी आदि बुराइयों को ही समाज में प्रतिष्ठा प्राप्त हो, उस काल में निस्स्वार्थ, सहृदय, परोपकारी तथा राष्ट्रभक्ति के भाव से भरा हुआ पवित्र व्यक्तित्व क्या असामान्य वस्तु नहीं? ऐसे श्रेष्ठ ध्येयवादी जीवनादर्श ही आज की पीढ़ी को कर्तव्यपरायणता तथा देशभक्ति के संस्कार देने की क्षमता रखते हैं।

Tribute in Hindi from RSS Madhav Rao Muley to Panditji

पंडित प्रेमनाथ डोगराजी ने उच्च पदों पर कार्य किया—अनेक वर्षों तक नगरपालिका के अध्यक्ष रहे, अनेक सामाजिक, धार्मिक तथा राजनीतिक संस्थाओं में कार्य किया, किंतु उनके इस विविध समाज-सेवा के कार्यों में विशेषता यह रही कि उन्होंने यत्किंचित भी स्वार्थ साधन नहीं किया, नाम की चाह नहीं रखी। वे एक अखंड कर्मयोगी थे। उनका घर मानों समाज-सेवा का कार्यालय ही था। सभी जातियों, सभी वर्णों, सभी वर्गों तथा हर स्तर के लोग अपनी-अपनी सभी प्रकार की समस्याएँ सुलझाने के लिए पंडितजी के पास दिन भर आते रहते थे। पंडित प्रेमनाथ डोगराजी सहृदयतापूर्वक सभी की बात सुनकर उनको यथोचित सलाह एवं सहायता देते थे। इस तरह उनका व्यक्तित्व संपूर्ण जम्मू-कश्मीर में उनकी मृत्यु तक छाया रहा। मुझे उनके व्यक्तित्व की झलक तब मिली, जब मैं राष्ट्रीय स्वयंसेवक संघ के

कार्य के निमित्त जम्मू गया तथा मेरे आग्रह पर उन्होंने उधर के कार्य का नेतृत्व ग्रहण किया। जहाँ उनका व्यक्तित्व अत्यंत तेजस्वी एवं प्रखर था, वहाँ वे दीन-दुखियों के लिए जीवनाधार थे। कठिन-से-कठिन प्रसंग में भी वे अपना संतुलन बनाए रखने में सिद्धहस्त थे। अपनी वृद्धावस्था में भी तरुणों को मात देने वाली तरुणाई उनमें मौजूद थी। ऐसा अलौकिक व्यक्तित्व था पंडितजी का।

पंडित प्रेमनाथ डोगराजी के जीवन के संबंध में यह छोटी पुस्तिका लिखी गई है, यह तो ठीक है, किंतु इससे संतोष नहीं हो सकता। वास्तव में पंडितजी का समग्र जीवनवृत्त प्रकाशित होना आवश्यक है। मैं आशा करता हूँ कि प्रकाशक इस दिशा में अवश्य सोचेंगे।

—माधव राव मुल्ये

सरकार्यवाह

राष्ट्रीय स्वयंसेवक संघ, प्रधान कार्यालय, नागपुर

(Ref: Dogra, Prem Nath, Prem Nath Dogra (बहुआयामी) Vyakitatva, *Hindi edition)*

STORY OF THE STATUE

Like his life which was full of struggle, the statue of this great Dogra also reveals the innumerable problems created by ruling leaders of the Congress-National Conference.

The Jana Sangh had contested the civic elections in the capital city of Jammu with several promises in its manifesto. One of these was also to install the statue of Pt. Prem Nath Dogra near the Jammu-Tawi Bridge.

In the wake of 1972 elections, Vaid Vaishno Dutt was elected president of the Municipal Council. In accordance with the manifesto, a life-sized statue of Pt. Prem Nath Dogra was prepared, but first the ruling leaders of the Congress and later on the Sheikh Abdullah-led National Conference created hurdles over the place of its installation.

While this struggle was still going on, there came the Emergency on the night of 25 June, 1975. The National Conference, talking about autonomy of the state, did not wait even for two hours and indiscriminate arrests were made. The Municipal Council was superseded and its president and some others were arrested and jailed. The statue was placed under the staircase, where it remained for about a decade in a neglected position.

In 1980, the Municipal Council elections were held and Ved Bajaj was again elected as president of the JMC.

In the meantime, the Congress-National Conference unity fell apart. The Farooq Abdullah-led National Conference government was defeated by the rebels of National Conference led by his brother-in-law, G.M. Shah, who became the Chief Minister with the support of Congress.

In 1983-84, when G.M. Bhaderwahi was a minister in the Cabinet of Shah, Bajaj got the opportunity to install the statue of Panditji at the promised site near Tawi Bridge.

In the function, G.M. Bhaderwahi also participated and paid tributes to Pt. Dogra, recalling the services and popularity of Panditji among the people as an administrator of Bhaderwahi *jagir* of the Maharaja.

It was in 2016 that the BJP MLA of Jammu East, Rajesh Gupta, by spending a few lakhs of rupees from his Constituency Development Fund renovated the place around the statue. This has given a charming look to the place and also to the statue.

The multifaceted Pt. Prem Nath Dogra was a great sportsman as well. He was a noted player of football during his college days at Lahore. To keep the memory of this sportsperson alive, the Pt. Prem Nath Dogra Football Memorial Club headed by Rajesh Gupta, MLA, organised a big football tournament and officially the mini-stadium of Parade Ground, Jammu, was named as the Prem Nath Dogra Stadium.

□

Speeches of Pt. Prem Nath Dogra

J&K LEGISLATIVE ASSEMBLY DEBATE, 1958

Prem Nath Dogra: Sir, the Sadar-i-Riyasat's address is under discussion for the last two days and many of the hon'ble members have expressed their views. I too want to express my views on it. I have carefully studied the address and reached the conclusion that the address, instead of making mention of achievements made by the government and problems facing the people, has given a faded picture of last year's activities of the government and which are published either through press notes or newspapers, etc. The address does not make any mention of the problems, like unemployment, corruption and other anti-national activities being faced by the people. In the address, a mention has been made about national integrity and solidarity. It also says something about the danger of conflicts on our borders we are facing from Pakistan and China...

Mr. Speaker: The areas touching China and Pakistan are matters of defence and foreign affairs. Therefore, these cannot be discussed in this House.

Bakshi Ghulam Mohammad: Sir, since the hon'ble member belongs to the second biggest party, he may be allowed to speak on this too, so that we would be able to know his views. No doubt, we cannot raise any matter relating to defence in this House. Since the Sadar-i-Riyasat's address makes reference to a danger on the borders, therefore, he may be allowed to express his views.

Mr. Speaker: No restriction has been imposed to discuss this question. I have said that the scope of discussion on this question is limited.

Prem Nath Dogra: Sir, so far as our borders are concerned, we are facing danger from two countries, i.e., Pakistan and China. A vast area of our state is under the occupation of Pakistan, which entered the state territory and besides committing murders, the infiltrators abducted the cattle of the people. No action has been taken against them. The victims have not been paid any compensation. What safety measures are being taken by the government against this danger has not been mentioned in the Sadar-i-Riyasat's address. Similarly, nothing has been said about the danger posed by China as an aggressor. However, this danger has been existing for the last so many years. The address says that we apprehend danger from China in 1959. I regret to say that it is not correct. The aggression from their side is being repeated for the last five years and this has not been made known to the people. In the last session, I raised the question in this regard and the Hon'ble Minister for Ladakh Affairs had in his reply stated that the government was aware of this aggressive activity from the year 1954-55. The subsequent statements made by Pandit Nehru in the Parliament and the official documents also reveal that China had started constructing a road in our territory during the year 1954-55. It is a very important matter, which is being concealed by the government. I want to know whether our administration was working there and since a minister was made incharge of this particular *ilaqa*, then why we were not made aware of this danger in time? This is most regrettable. The territory of our state extends over 84 thousand square miles. Our government should at least know the boundaries of our state. Such a failure on the part of the administration shows its inefficiency. That is why our government could not know the activities of the Chinese government in our territory from the year 1954 to 1959. Now China has occupied about 12.5 thousand square-miled area of our country. The Sadar-i-Riyasat's address does not indicate the steps intended to be taken to get back this *ilaqa*. Thank God, they have taken some steps to check the onward march of the Chinese. Secondly, a mention has been made in the address about the solidarity of our country. But it does not indicate as to how you want to maintain the solidarity; whether the extension in the Cabinet will maintain national integrity. Earlier, there were five ministers, then their numbers started increasing and now there are 16 ministers, but it is not known what benefits the people of the state are deriving from this increased number of ministers. These ministers are paid towards this fact. The important question relating to national solidarity is that we should be represented properly in the Lok Sabha and the people of the state should be given a right to elect their representatives. At present, the ruling party has nominated some six persons for the Lok Sabha and they too have been directed to sit in the Lok Sabha with the Congress party. Thereby, they will be under the discipline of that party. Are they our real representatives? I feel they are not. Sir, the true solidarity can be possible only when the people of the state enjoy those privileges which are enjoyed by the people in other parts of the country. In this connection the most important thing is that the people of the state should be given the right to return their true representatives to the Lok Sabha so that they could play their right role in solving the problems faced by the country. I feel pleasure at extending the jurisdiction of the Supreme Court and the Election Commission over the state to some extent. But I fail to understand as to why you are afraid of sending representatives to the Lok Sabha through direct election. Complete accession of the state with India is necessary for national integrity. The 6th of February is observed as Day of Accession. Due to heavy rains, you could not celebrate this occasion during the current year. Contribution is made by the people. I want to tell you that the accession of the state with the Union of India was made by the Maharaja on 22nd October. I don't know how you observe this day on the 6th of February. Sir, the hon'ble members who used to sit with us have now crossed over to the Treasury benches. More than once, I have stated that all of you are chips of the same block. There was some annoyance among you which has not been removed. Sadiq Sahib, while sitting on the Opposition benches for four years, has experienced the difficulties of the Opposition. He often used to talk about these in the House. I would request him (Sadiq Sahib) that he should help us because he has himself experienced our difficulties, provided he remembers whatever he has gained during this long period. We have some basic differences but we will always extend our full support to you in any effort made by the government to defend the borders. I assure you that though I am too old, I am still prepared to go to the border and give my life in defence of the country.

Sir, the government has framed rules for conducting elections to the Panchayats. Before conducting these elections, it was decided that leaving apart the party politics, only such persons who enjoy confidence of the people and have good reputation should be allowed to be elected as members of the Panchayats. I felt very happy that the Hon'ble Prime Minister issued directions in this behalf, but I regret to say that it did not actually happen. The directions issued by the Prime Minister would not be implemented with the result that grave irregularities were committed during these elections. So much so, the ballot papers while counting were exchanged.

Bakshi Ghulam Mohammad: Will you please give me the name of a person, place and *tehsil*, so that I could give you a reply tomorrow?

Pt. Prem Nath Dogra: It happened in *tehsil* Samba.

Bakshi Ghulam Mohammad: What is the name of that person?

Pt. Prem Nath Dogra: I don't know. However, I will tell you today after making an enquiry.

The persons elected as the members of Panchayats are illiterate and any educated or reputed person is not permitted to be elected. Unfortunately, junior officers are appointed as election officers who can come under influence and are forced to omit irregularities. It might have come to the notice of the Hon'ble Prime Minister that elections are not contested on party basis but the local officers know everybody. They know the persons having affiliation with the Praja Parishad, National Conference and the Democratic National Conference. Therefore, efforts are made to get the person belonging to the ruling party returned. This should not happen. I can say with confidence that the quantum of the irregularities committed during the recent elections is much higher as compared to the previous elections. It was announced in this House that only persons belonging to such communities which do not have representation in the Panchayats would be nominated. A press note regarding these nominations was also released but the names of persons nominated have not so far been announced, I will be in a position to tell you whether genuine persons have been nominated after the nominations are made. Huge amounts are being obtained from the Central Government for the developmental plans. Much has been said about planning, but we have to see as to how much benefit has been derived by the people from these huge expenditures. It has been claimed that national income has increased to a considerable extent. But there seems no increase in the national income in the face of the price rise. I had stated during the last session too that only a few persons have been benefitted and who have become rich. Their conditions have definitely changed. A commission should be set up to find out the increase registered in the national income. This has been done by the Central Government and I feel that the commission has started functioning.

Now I would like to say something about corruption. A law has been passed for its prevention. While passing this law, it was thought that it would lessen corruption but on the contrary, this evil has furthered increased. Some drastic steps are required to be taken in this behalf, but I regret to say that it is not being implemented. It is now being said that a complaint should be lodged with the commission. Lodge a complaint supported by witnesses is not so easy for an ordinary man. The people are not yet prepared to encounter this evil.

Bakshi Ghulam Mohammad: Can you suggest some measures in this regard?

Pt. Prem Nath Dogra: You have close contact with the people. Therefore, it is not difficult for you to get information in this regard.

Bakshi Ghulam Mohammad: Sometimes I also get information but you should give your suggestions.

Pt. Prem Nath Dogra: My submission is that you say much about eradicating corruption, but practically do nothing in this behalf with the result, that the people get encouraged day by day.

Much has been said about agriculture and great emphasis paid on the increase made in agriculture production by implementing various schemes. I would like to know the extent of increase so made and the place where it is said that double cropping will be introduced? But I want to know whether the resources required for this are available with us or not? Sardar Kulbir Singh has stated that an area of 14,480 *kannals* has been brought under double cropping and this experiment has proved successful.

(*Note*: Some members were busy talking to each other.)

Mr. Speaker: I will be forced to change the seating arrangement if the hon'ble members do not desist from gossiping.

Pt. Prem Nath Dogra: I am not prepared to accept this; the nature of soil differs from field to field. The soil of 10 fields can be better than the others in the same area. So far as I know, all the people are not enjoying the same facilities. A pamphlet has been released about the agricultural activities, indicating the methods of double cropping. The pamphlet says that 30 maunds of cowdung and 12 kgs of ammonia sulphate are required for one acre of land yielding double crop. Maybe the Director, Agriculture, might have obtained this much quantity of cowdung for experimental purposes but all the people cannot have this quantity of cowdung. You know that the people of this *ilaqa* where this experiment is being done have a very small number of cattle, because they do not have sufficient number of pastures. When there are no cattle, wherefrom you can obtain cowdung? In these circumstances, I am forced to say that these things are mere propaganda and nothing practical is done in this behalf. Necessary steps are required to be taken for providing irrigational facilities.

Besides this, a law relating to the consolidation of holdings was passed but there is no staff to implement the same. Before passing this law, some persons should have been trained for this purpose. I have come to know that some officers from Uttar Pradesh are being imported. This shows the inefficiency in the administration. There are so many officers working in the concerned department and a few of them should have been deputed for training.

We are receiving considerable funds from the Centre for opening new schools, but it has been found that most of the schools face difficulties due to inadequate staff and equipment. It will be useless due to inadequate staff and equipment. It will be useless to open Higher Secondary schools if trained teachers are not deputed there for teaching purposes.

Prices are shooting up day by day and no efforts are being made to check them. It is no argument to say that people living in India are also affected due to rising prices. The low-paid employees have been hit by the spiralting prices. The government sanctioned Rs. 5 as dearness allowance in their favour but this is insufficient, keeping in view their meagre income and the rising prices. Much attention is needed to better the condition of these poor employees.

Tall talks are made about socialism, but I can not comprehend what it actually means.

Mohammad Ayub Khan: It is our ill luck...

Pt. Prem Nath Dogra: The Congress, Praja Socialist and the National Conference parties make tail claims of building a socialistic pattern of society, while the fact is that nobody adheres to this ideology. We have to revive our own ideology and not toe that of the foreign countries.

Mr. Speaker: Your time is over; you please conclude your speech.

Pt. Prem Nath Dogra: Yesterday, some members evoked regional feelings. It surprises me to see the hon'ble members giving rapt attention to Mr. Goni or some other members when he discusses the backwardness of his constituency, but when we talk of Jammu province, we are accused of raising regional feelings. We were faced with the same attitude during the autocratic regime. Little attention is being paid to the development of Jammu. Since the Centre has accommodated the government with adequate funds, I would request that more attention should be paid to the development of the Jammu region.

Tourism also figured in the discussion yesterday. Ayub Khan, in his speech, revealed that 50 per cent of the funds are utilised for developing tourism in Jammu. To me this argument has not struck as sound. Works which are carried out in Banihal or Kud are included in the developmental works of Jammu. If the government is serious in developing Jammu, it should make efforts to promote tourism.

Pt. Prem Nath Dogra: Sir, on a point of order, unfortunately the allotment of time for various members is such as to not allow us to express our views fully. My submission is that one or two points are raised here and deem it necessary to answer them; otherwise, I fear that if the misunderstanding is not removed, the people may have a different opinion of our party.

Mr. Qasim and other friends criticised some of the actions during the general elections. Since the time at my disposal is too short, I cannot cover all the aspects, yet I shall try to refer to some of the important points while replying to their criticism. Although I feel that I may get the right occasion to dispel the doubts related in the House, I still fear I may not be able to answer their criticism point by point because we are always handicapped by a shortage of time. As such, I would request the Chair to fix at least half an hour for disseminating these points so that we may get an ample opportunity to make our stand clear. How strange it is that in this, those against whom the tirade is made are not given the opportunity to make their position clear. It is said that in case the election problem of Kashmir is discussed and thrashed out, the country will lose Kashmir. I wonder how this will happen.

Voices: Kashmir will never secede.

Pt. Prem Nath Dogra: Sir, this is what they say. All of you know that the elections were not fair.

Ghulam Ahmad Mir: Sir, is he making a speech or raising a point of order?

Pt. Prem Nath Dogra: Sir, my intention is to draw the attention of the Hon'ble Speaker towards the fact that we should be given enough time to answer the criticism directed against us. Here a queer procedure is in vogue, i.e., whatever a man wants to speak, he goes on speaking caring least whether it has any relevance to the occasion or not. I have no objection if the criticism is made against my person but I will never put up with what is said about my party to discredit it in the eyes of others. We are in the field and our main objective is to fight for the cause of the country. I warn them to refrain from making uncalled for remarks against our party.

J&K LEGISLATIVE ASSEMBLY DEBATE, 15TH FEBRUARY, 1960

Pt. Prem Nath Dogra: Sir, I intend to say many things about the address of Sadar-i-Riyasat but very little time is at my disposal, so I would try to place a few things before the House. I hope to get some more opportunities during the discussion on the Budget, etc., and then I can go into details. At present, I will confine myself to the address. It has been mentioned in the address of the Sadar-i-Riyasat that the state's emotional integration with India has been completed. I admit that during the last few years, much has been done to complete the emotional integration of the state with India but to say that it has been completed is far from the truth. A few things have been done in this behalf which our party desired. Our party right from the beginning has been requesting the government not to curb the rights of the people. We have all along maintained that one constitution, one flag and one President of the country is essential for the complete emotional integration of the state with India. Unless this is done, integration cannot be complete. I am not prepared to accept this. One important thing to which I would like to refer at some length is about the right of citizenship. This question at present is one of the biggest hurdles in the complete integration of the state with the rest of the country. We enjoy Indian citizenship and thus we can join Indian services, we can purchase property and can cast votes in India but those

Indians who were living in this state since long are not allowed to purchase land or any other property here nor do they enjoy the right to vote. This is the greatest hindrance to our integration with the rest of India. My second point is that the Lok Sabha is the highest democratic institution of the Union and is a sovereign body. To it, our state representatives are sent by indirect elections. This is another great hurdle in our emotional integration with the rest of the country. The representatives nominated by the government cannot accurately represent the cause of the people of this state because they cannot exercise their independent judgement regarding any question. It is therefore, necessary that the representatives of this state to the Lok Sabha should not be nominated. As regards the flag, it may be said that Indian flags are hoisted on the rooftops of the both the Houses, which is in contravention to the basic principles of the constitution of the land.

Hon'ble Prime Minister: This is our state flag.

Pt. Prem Nath Dogra: Normally every country has only one flag and this flag is also the flag of the ruling party.

The jurisdiction of the Supreme Court has been extended to this state but the appointment of the judges of the High Court has been left in the hands of the Sadar-i-Riyasat according to the constitution. His position is not similar to that of the Governor of the state. He is elected on party lines, so he is not an independent functionary. He cannot act against the wishes of the party in power. So long he is elected to his office by the majority party, he cannot function independently. Similarly, the judiciary too will not remain independent. The definition of a permanent member of the state in the constitution makes discrimination between rest of this state and citizens of the rest of India. There is a big obstacle in the way of complete integration of the state with the rest of India. For complete integration, one flag, one constitution and one President are essential. Another thing which is very important and which I consider should have been mentioned in the address is the Chinese aggression. During the last session too, we tried to raise this question but we were not allowed to do on the plea that it is a Central subject. Now the question has been touched in the address, so I take this opportunity to ask the Hon'ble Prime Minister as to when the Chinese committed this aggression and was this fact brought to his knowledge? So far as my information goes, China was constructing a road in that *ilaqa* since 1954, which they completed after two years. I want to know if the government was aware of this fact. There is a DC, a special Minister for Ladakh Affairs and one advisor from the Government of India, who generally goes to Delhi after every fourth day. Now I want to know that in spite of the presence of such a large number of officers, why was the government not kept informed about the Chinese manoeuvre during these four years? Was this fact concealed from us? Yesterday, I was going through the speech of the minister-in-charge which he delivered in the session of the National Conference. In that speech he has stated that he had come to know about the construction of road by the Chinese as far back as 1954. Had our state government informed the Central Government about it or else they are giving us wrong information about it by saying it was the end of 1957 or the beginning of 1958 on looking at a Chinese map? From the map they realised that the Chinese are creating trouble on the Ladakh border and have actually occupied our territory. Some areas where our government was sleeping over this matter for such a long time makes us wonder what they were doing in Leh! During autocracy there used to be a large portion of Ladakh that is barren, but our grazers used to go to pastures as far as Aksai Chin to graze their cattle. They had informed the government about the Chinese manoeuvres on the border. Why did the government conceal this information? You have been constructing a road from Kargil to Leh for the last four years. Lakhs of rupees have been spent on it but it has not been completed so far. What has the government been doing there? Now they say that China has deceived us on our trust. When the Chinese found our border unprotected, they could not resist the temptation of incursion into our territory. These *ilaqas* became part of our state under a treaty signed in 1842 and the border between the two countries was settled under the Simla Convention of 1914. My information is that the British were in search of routes as far back as 1858 to defend this area from foreign aggression. The officers posted to this *ilaqa* used to tour for 20 days at a time, the border areas during the autocracy and were properly looking after our border defences. No one wants to go to the forward areas after 1947. So far as I know, the government informed in 1955 that people with communist leanings have entered into Ladakh and are carrying on propaganda in favour of their ideology. Sometime back, the general secretary of the Praja Parishad went to Kishtwar. There he was informed by some sheep grazers that some communists had also entered Paddar. The prime occupation of these people is sheep and goat rearing and drawing water from the then Padar Salt Lake. They said that this year they were neither allowed to graze their sheep and goats nor to make any movement. The government was quick in refuting this statement. A bridge between Kargil and Leh was set on fire which clearly show that there exist some elements who favour the Chinese advance into the state. There exists also a party in India which openly sides with China. The government has posted some officials to the post offices in the state and whose function is to censor lectures addressed by me. From where has our government got such a large number of secret agents? Is it a part of their strategy that for a considerable period of time they could not unearth the Chinese aggression? China has occupied 8,500 square miles of Ladakh at present.

Sir, I was delighted to hear from the hon'ble members of the House that they are prepared to make any kind of sacrifice for the defence of their country. Sir, it is easy to talk about making sacrifices, but it is quite a different and difficult thing to do something practically. I admit that the people are prepared to give any amount of sacrifice because they have a great sense of patriotism. However, we have to prepare our country to face any eventuality. How can that be done?

We have got a large number of ex-servicemen. Some of them are, of course, old but those who are healthy can prove of great help in strengthening our border defence after a little training. It is for this government to pay special attention towards this. Recently, I read in a newspaper that the Government of India is going to give military training to 50 thousand girls. The conditions obtaining in our country are such that instead of young men, young girls are being asked to go to forward areas to defend our borders.

Major Piara Singh: Women forces are meant to maintain the internal security of the country.

Mr. Speaker: Panditji is referring to women, but there is no woman representative in this House who could have given a reply to him.

Hon'ble Prime Minister: No interference; let him continue.

Pt. Prem Nath Dogra: Sir, this in itself is not sufficient. Each and every citizen should be given proper military training.

Hon'ble Prime Minister: Panditji was talking about some bridge which was set on fire. Where is it situated?

Pt. Prem Nath Dogra: I had referred to the Chagla Bridge which is on the Indus. I have read in some paper that this bridge was set on fire.

Mr. Speaker: There are only five minutes left of your time.

Pt. Prem Nath Dogra: Sir, I bow to your ruling but permit me to say that in five minutes, I cannot do justice to the matter under discussion. No doubt, the government has enhanced the rate of dearness allowance of the government servants, but this is nothing in comparison to the ever-increasing dearness allowance with their basic pay, so that their pension benefits would also be enhanced. We have already suggested that a committee be set up to check the soaring prices in the state. In a meeting held at Srinagar, we placed a few suggestions before the Hon'ble Prime Minister in this regard. Increased dearness allowance has been granted to the government employees in active service but the pensioners have not been given any benefit at all. Their allowances were enhanced from Rs. 1 to Rs. 1.50. Such an increase in their dearness allowance was made, but they not only had to submit recommendations about the dearness allowance but also had to make recommendations regarding many other matters. Unfortunately, the detailed report of this commission has not been placed before this House. I hope the government would place the report before this House. We can offer our suggestions only after studying the complete report of the Pay Commission.

As regards floods, Kashmir Valley was hit by floods only once during July 1959. After that date, a number of floods following heavy rains visited Jammu and a number of villages were completely washed away by that flood. The government distributed relief among the July 1959 flood victims but those who suffered loss after the July floods were given no aid or relief, although justice demands that those victims should have also been given some relief.

Hon'ble Prime Minister: Sir, we have given relief only to the flood victims, but the case of those who sustained some losses due to rains are under consideration of the government.

Pt. Prem Nath Dogra: Sir, I would again submit that the losses sustained by the people of Jammu province due to rains cannot be adequately compensated. It is right that those who suffered due to floods should get some relief. The government is framing a master plan in this behalf for which experts have been requested to scrutinise the schemes of flood control, but my submission is that it will take time to implement the master plan. I would request that immediate steps be taken to save those villages which are in imminent danger of floods.

Mr. Speaker: Your time is up.

Pt. Prem Nath Dogra: Sir, I would place my views before the House on various other occasions.

(*Note*: The hon'ble member then resumed his seat.)

LEGISLATIVE ASSEMBLY DEBATE, 1967

Mr. Speaker: There remain only four minutes.

Mr. Ali Mohammad Naik: Some aspects hold good with regard to the condition of hospitals in rural areas. There the government at present is sanctioning three-and-a-half thousand rupees for one hospital covering an area with a population of 40 thousand people. Therefore, I would request that this amount be enhanced so that the people are benefitted. A mention of government employees is there in the Governor's address. The government should try to raise the standard of their living by increasing their salaries. This will enable the employees to discharge their duty honestly.

It would also check corruption. It has been observed that our state government appoints officers to higher posts, but not a single officer from our state is deputed outside the state. I am at a loss to understand the reason. This demoralises the government employees. With these words, I conclude my speech.

Pt. Prem Nath Dogra: Sir, I had no intention to express my viewpoints but since no member rose to speak and the present situation obviously demands that I should say a few words regarding this matter, I therefore rise to speak. I shall also continue my speech tomorrow. The Governor's address is at present under discussion in the House. These addresses are usually discussed every year. This year, this address was read out twice in the House, i.e., in Jammu, when the session was called for a few days. The address read out at that time and the present address is almost of a similar nature.

Actually the address is drafted by the high officials and the Governor, thereafter, reads it out. The address is designed to appreciate the policies of the government. This appreciation is of the nature which a milkwoman would give to her milk saying that it is never sour. While this address was read out in the House, I tried to gauge the reaction by reading the faces of those who sit on Treasury Benches and in the public gallery as well. The members sitting on the Treasury Benches listened to the address with a sympathetic heart as there was no mention of the promises which they had held out to the common people. It pinches me to say that the government deserves no appreciation in this behalf. The members sitting on the Treasury Benches did not seem to be pleased with this address, which is regrettable.

These members will always support your viewpoint as you have provided them a chance to enter this House from the back door without any contest. I will appreciate the good work of the government and criticise its bad policies. It has often been observed here that problems are discussed but the decisions taken are never implemented. I would request Mr. Sadiq to get these problems solved.

The first problem we face is regarding the elections. The government should have provided an opportunity to the representatives of the people to enter this House. But all unconstitutional methods were adopted during the course of the elections. Almost one-third of the total members here have been elected untested. This procedure is being adopted since 1947. All of you know that at the formation of the first Constituent Assembly, the ruling party took all the 75 members from the National Conference party and no member from the Opposition was included. It is in this context that at present we are facing numerous difficulties and we have not been able to check it. It would not have been so, had the government nipped the evil in the bud.

We had many aspirations from Mr. Sadiq—that he would take the state on the path of progress but this dream never did come true. The government frames rules and regulations for the betterment of the people but if the government itself violates these laws, who is to be blamed for that? I can quote hundreds of such examples. You can very well see these violations in the *tehsils.* I personally feel that these irregularities are not brought to the notice of the Hon'ble Chief Minister and if he is in the know of these things, then action is not taken against the responsible authorities. I can personally expose several such scandals.

The government is thus creating obstacles in the way of smooth administration. The miserable condition of the poor refugees of Poonch has already been clarified by Mr. Sahib. I would say in this connection that 60 to 70 thousand persons went to Pakistan, where they were given training guerrilla warfare. It clearly indicates that in the near future, the Pakistan government-trained guerrillas will be found within the state. When the said persons were allowed by our state government to return to their houses, it was severely criticised. The ministers at that time assured us that these people will be allowed to return under some set procedure.

But this assurance was never implemented. Nobody cared to see whether they are coming back with any good or bad intention. Instead, they are presently the favourities of the government. Nobody dares to raise a voice against them; instead, poor innocent people are victimised under D.I.R. etc., as they have no voice and cannot stand against the pets of the government. If these things continue, then it will not be possible for us to bring stability in our political setup. This state has been turned into a police state and policemen are visible everywhere. May I ask the government as to where our police force was and where was law and order on 7th June, which brought a bad name to our state?

It was a day when riots broke out in the city, unchecked.

This issue was also discussed in Parliament. Christians all over the country have stood against these riots. It is a fact that the government has granted 1 to 2 lakh rupees to them to reconstruct their churches. But I may say that they are not satisfied with the role of the government in this connection. It was argued that the police was demoralised when this situation arose. I would say that if our police is not capable to check such happenings, then it is regrettable.

The police should not get demoralised by the mere decision of a commission. Pakistan is busy in purchasing arms and ammunition which pose a severe threat to our sovereignty. It will have an ultimate effect on our people. It is our duty and the duty of our government as well, to be faithful to our duties. We should convince the people in general that there is nothing to worry. It will enable us to go on with our usual business.

The present ministers compel the *tehsildar* and Deputy Commissioners to indulge in irregularities for petty matters. The services of low-paid employees are misused by the higher authorities. Non-influential persons always become victims and thus never get justice. I will quote an instance of a particular person who was allotted some plot of land. Another piece of land was also allotted to some second person for residential purposes near the border area, but he refused to take possession as he did not deem it fit for the said purpose. The first person in whose favour allotment was made was then asked to give some of its portion to the person who had refused. When the concerned officer submits the papers for allotment with the remarks that the land can not be allotted to such a person under rules, the minister exhibiting extra magnanimity relaxes the rules and issues the order accordingly.

But now the case is resubmitted to the custodian. Generally, he gives his verdict that the minister has no authority to lease the land and if he has done so, he has adopted a wrong procedure. As such, many cases are spoiled. As a matter of fact, the Custodian General asks the concerned *tehsildar* to carry out on-the-spot inspection of the case but he refuses, since the Deputy Minister compels him not to go there. When cases are dealt with in such a manner, disputes are bound to arise. These disputes culminate in litigation and cases multiply. Consequently, some get injured and have to be taken to hospitals where doctors are requested to issue injury certificates, which are issued only after paying them. Such cases are innumerable and this state of affairs is highly condemnable.

Note: At this stage, the time bell rang and the hon'ble member resumed his seat.

Mr. Speaker: With this our business for today comes to an end. We will meet here tomorrow on Tuesday at 9 a.m.

Note: The House then adjourned till 9 a.m. on Tuesday, 8th August, 1967.

□

Pt. Prem Nath Dogra's Last Speech before Death

एकता में बल, फूट में तबाही
(पं. प्रेमनाथ डोगरा का मृत्यु से पूर्व एक भाषण)

'एकता में बल है और फूट विनाश लाती है'—इस सिद्धांत पर कोई दो मत नहीं हो सकता। भारत का इतिहास इस बात का साक्षी है। जब-जब देश में एकता निर्बल हुई और फूट ने जन्म लिया, तभी देश के शत्रुओं को आक्रमण करने का अवसर मिला तथा इन आक्रमणों के कारण ही देश को तबाही का सामना करना पड़ा, और अंत में फूट का ही यह परिणाम था कि देश को सैकड़ों वर्षों तक गैर-मुल्कों की दासता का मुँह देखना पड़ा।

अतीत के कठोर तथ्यों को भुलाया नहीं जा सकता। 'देश की स्वतंत्रता की रक्षा हो। फूट जन्म न ले पाए। देशभक्ति की जड़ें दृढ़ हों और देश समृद्धि की ओर अग्रसर हो।' यह ध्यान में रख आज राष्ट्रीय एकता की देशव्यापी चर्चा हो रही है। मूल रूप से इस प्रश्न पर विचार-विमर्श करना आवश्यक है। परंतु विचार-विमर्श के साथ ही यह आवश्यक है कि राष्ट्रीय एकता को दृढ़ करने के लिए ठोस कार्य किया जाए। यह ठोस कार्य करने में सामाजिक संस्थाएँ कैसे और कहाँ तक सहयोग दे सकती हैं! इस बात पर विचार करने से पूर्व आवश्यक है कि राष्ट्रीय एकता के लिए उन सारभूत तथ्यों को समझ लिया जाए, जो किसी भी राष्ट्र को राष्ट्र का दर्जा देती हैं और जिन्हें अपनाने से राष्ट्रीय एकता स्थिर बन सकती है।

राष्ट्रीय एकता कोई बनावटी वस्तु नहीं। यह एक भावना है, जो समय की आँधियों और समय के घटनाचक्र के होते हुए भी देशवासियों को एक-दूसरे से जुदा नहीं होने देता। यह भावना कुछेक सामूहिक आधारों पर निर्भर है। यह आधार हमारी

संस्कृति, हमारे पूर्वज, हमारा एकमात्र इतिहास और हमारी मर्यादाएँ हैं। सहस्रों वर्षों से भारत, कन्याकुमारी से लेकर कश्मीर तक, एक देश के रूप में चला आया है। यदि समय के चक्र ने कुछ समय के लिए इसका विभाजन भी कर दिया और राजनैतिक दीवारें हमारी एकता की राह में खड़ी की गई तो भी स्वभाव से हम एक-दूसरे से अलग न हो सके तथा समय परिवर्तन के साथ पृथकता और विभाजन की रेखाएँ स्वयं ही लुप्त हो गईं।

फूट के परिणाम देशवासियों ने कई बार भुगते हैं। जब कभी फूट और पृथकता के चिह्न उभरने लगते हैं तो प्रकृतिवश देशभक्त परेशान होता है कि देश की एकता खंडित न हो, राष्ट्रीय एकता दृढ़ हो और देश के शत्रु देश की स्वतंत्रता के लिए खतरा न बन जाएँ, इस उच्च उद्देश्य को लेकर सभी अपने-अपने स्तर पर विचार करते हैं। आज जब देश में राष्ट्रीय एकता पर विचार हो रहा है तो सभी का मत है कि सामाजिक संस्थाओं को इस महान् उद्देश्य के लिए महान् कार्य करना है। इस राष्ट्रीय एकता की दृढ़ता के लिए हमारी शिक्षण संस्थाएँ सबसे अधिक लाभदायक सिद्ध हो सकती हैं, कारण कि देश के भविष्य का निर्माण इन्हीं शिक्षण संस्थाओं में होता है। आनेवाले नागरिक इन्हीं संस्थानों में निर्मित होते हैं। उनकी बुद्धि को हम जिस साँचे में चाहें ढाल सकते हैं। यदि प्रारंभ में ही राष्ट्रीय एकता की भावना इनमें जाग्रत् कर दी जाए और विद्यालयों को उनकी देश के प्रति जिम्मेदारियों से परिचित करवा दिए जाएँ तो फूट के विचार अपनी मृत्यु स्वयं ही मर जाएँगे। आज इस बात की बड़ी आवश्यकता है कि शिक्षण संस्थानों में प्रारंभ से ही उन आधारभूत मर्यादाओं से परिचित करवाया जाए जिन पर सहस्रों वर्षों से यह देश खड़ा रहा है तथा देश की स्वतंत्रता व एकता के लिए इन बुनियादों को अधिक-से-अधिक दृढ़ बनाना हरेक देशवासी का महान् कर्तव्य है।

शिक्षण संस्थानों के अतिरिक्त नगरपालिकाएँ, पंचायतें और अन्य लोकसेवा विभाग भी इस राष्ट्रीय एकता की दृढ़ता हेतु महान् कार्य कर सकते हैं तथा इन संस्थाओं द्वारा हमारी स्वतंत्रता व एकता के शत्रुओं के कुत्सित प्रयासों से भी जनता को अवगत कराया जा सकता है।

देश में कितनी ऐसी संस्थाएँ हैं, जो देशभक्ति की भावना से ओतप्रोत हो अपने कार्य में जुटी हैं, कितनी सांस्कृतिक संस्थाएँ हैं, जो इस देश की उन्नति के लिए कटिबद्ध हैं और फिर अनगिनत धार्मिक और सांप्रदायिक संस्थाएँ भी हैं, जो अपने-

अपने ढंग से अलग-अलग स्तरों पर समाज की भलाई और कल्याण के कार्य में कटिबद्ध होकर लगी हैं।

आदिकाल से ही भारत की महानता रही है। इतने भिन्न विचार रखने और ईश्वर को मानने के अलग-अलग ढंग होने पर भी, इन सबको ही समाज का अंग माना है। अनिवार्यता केवल इस बात की है कि सभी संस्थाओं को इस प्रकार इकट्ठा किया जाए और ऐसी जागृति लाई जाए कि सभी सबसे पहले देश को प्रथम मानें और तदनंतर अन्य किसी बात को।

देश में कुछ लोग ऐसे भी होते हैं, जो कुछ ऐसी शक्तियों के हाथों की कठपुतली बने हैं, जो इस देश का कल्याण नहीं चाहतीं। करोड़ों लोगों के इस देश में इन लोगों की संख्या शून्य मात्र है। यदि देशवासियों में एकता की भावना जाग्रत् रहेगी तो कोई भी बाह्या या भीतरी सत्ता हमारी स्वतंत्रता के लिए खतरा नहीं बन सकती और देश समृद्धि के मार्ग पर स्वयं ही अग्रसर होने लगेगा, आगे पग बढ़ाता चला जाएगा।

राष्ट्रीय एकता का कार्य भले ही आज कठिन दिखाई पड़ रहा है, परंतु आधार की दृष्टि से देश की स्वतंत्रता को जीवित रखने के लिए विकलता आज भी तना ही संकल्पबद्ध है, जितनी आजादी से पूर्व थी। 1962 में हमने देखा है कि जब चीन ने इस देश की सीमाओं पर आक्रमण किया तो सारा देश अपने आपसी मतभेद भूलकर देश रक्षा के लिए एक होकर डट गया, किसी ने शत्रु का पक्ष लेने का साहस तक नहीं किया। इसी प्रकार 1965 में, जब पाकिस्तान ने जम्मू-कश्मीर को हड़पने के लिए सशस्त्र घुसपैठिए भेजे और बलपूर्वक भारत के इस भाग को हथियाना चाहा तो देश के सभी राजनैतिक, धार्मिक तथा अन्य संस्थाएँ अपने आपसी मतभेद भूलकर एक सुदृढ़ राष्ट्र के रूप में सामने आ डटीं।

कठिनाइयों और कठिन परीक्षाओं के इस दौर में सामाजिक संस्थाओं ने कितना भाग लिया, इसे भी भुलाया नहीं जा सकता, अतः राष्ट्रीय एकता को अधिकाधिक सुदृढ़ बनाने के लिए जहाँ कई उपाय प्रयोग में लाए जा सकते हैं, वहाँ सामाजिक संस्थाओं के कार्य-क्षेत्र को भी दृष्टि से ओझल नहीं किया जा सकता।

□

Organisation Presidents of the Praja Parishad

Hari Wazir, born in May, 1927 became the first president of the Praja Parishad when it was formed in November, 1947. Six months after his appointment as Praja Parishad president, he got selected for the Short Service Commission in Indian Army. As such, he worked in the capacity of the Praja Parishad president for a period of six months.

Hari Wazir

Hari Wazir met his fatal end in a bear-hunting expedition 3rd July, 1953 in a forest near Ganderbal, Kashmir.

Lala Roop Chand Nanda was a leading lawyer and used to play an important role in public activities. He gained significance in 1943, when in the food agitation on September 24, nine people were killed in police firing and the Maharaja appointed an Enquiry Commission, which was headed by a Justice of Bombay High Court.

Roop Chand Nanda, Reasi

Advocate Nanda along with Dr. Saif-ud-Din Kitchloo of Punjab and some other lawyers appeared before the commission to plead the public cause.

On the basis of findings of this commission, two police officials were dismissed from service and the then Prime Minister Haksar had to lose his job.

The rationing system was

introduced. All this enhanced the stature of advocate Nanda.

Because of his services to the public cause in early 1949, Nanda was entrusted with the task of leading the Praja Parishad in a difficult situation as Pt. Dogra and some others were arrested and interned in Srinagar Jail.

Madhav Lal Nanda (Advocate) 28th December, 1928 to 1st June, 1999

Section 50 was imposed in the city to prevent the Praja Parishad from holding a meeting. Keeping in view this ban, a big public meeting was organised at Ragoora, in the Jammu-Tawi region. This meeting was presided over by Ch. Mir Baksh.

This successful gathering caused alarm in the hierarchy of the new rulers.

In 1949, the *satyagraha* movement sought release of detained leader Madhav Lal Nanda who was tortured. Excesses were commited to terrorise the Praja Parishad activists. The government leaders as a tactic released Nanda amidst several rumours, but to clear the air and keep up the morale of the agitators, Nanda's elder son, Madhav Lal took out a procession, defying the prohibitory orders and courted arrest the same day and suffered in jail due to terrible conditions. Madhav Nanda remained in jail till Pt. Dogra and others were released.

Ruddar Mani Sangra of Kootaha, Teh. Hiranagar along with Pt. Prem Nath Dogra

Besides his legal practice, Roop Chand Nanda, prior to 1947, had acted as head of a few social and political bodies, including the Hindu Mahasabha, and had contested elections.

Ruddar Mani Sangra, a

veteran social activist, belonged to village Kootaha, *tehsil* Hiranagar, district Kathua. He was appointed as president of the J&K Praja Parishad in middle of the 1949 *satyagraha* movement when Sheikh Abdullah, supported by Jawaharlal Nehru, had let loose a reign of terror. The then Praja Parishad president was forced to resign.

After Ruddar Mani was appointed president, he was arrested alongwith his colleague, Thakur Baldev Singh, an advocate. They were jailed under Section 3, which was notoriously called *'Dafa Tun'* as many were jailed without trial. Thakur was lodged in the solitary Cell No. 1 and Sangra in Cell No. 2. The entire family of Sangra took active part in all the movements of the Praja Parishad and the Bharatiya Jana Sangh. They faced cruelties and harassment with great courage. In the photo Ruddar Mani is seen with Pt. Prem Nath Dogra in October 1949, after Panditji was released from jail.

□

The Young Editor of *Jai Swadesh*

Gopal Sachar, when he was released from jail in 1949

Gopal Sachar was born on 17th July, 1927. He came in contact with senior Praja Parishad leaders at Raghunath Pura, Jammu in early 1949. They used his residence in Jammu as a hideout. He was given the task of preparing handwritten cyclostyled wall posters which were titled, *Lok Bani* and *Akash Bani*.

Gopal Sachar was arrested thrice and jailed but in the 1949 *satyagraha,* he was badly beaten. Then, to terrorise him further, he was lodged in Central Jail, Jammu in a solitary cell meant for convicts given death sentence. He endured horrible conditions for over three months. At the end of the agitation in early October, 1949, he was released but lost his government job.

Again, in the 1952-53 agitation, Gopal Sachar was entrusted with the task of handling publicity matter by remaining underground for over six months. Sachar was declared an offender besides three others. In February, 1953, he was arrested from a hideout and lodged in a solitary room overlooking the Jogigate Shamshan Ghat. The then Police Lines were located near Jogigate, Jammu.

After about a week, attempts were made to shift Sachar to Srinagar by air along with three others, but because of his resistance for two days despite being handcuffed behind the back, the pilot of the Dakota plane refused to air lift this 'dangerous' passenger to Srinagar. At this, the angry policemen lodged him in a dirty lock-up of the police station, Sadar, located near Gummat Gate, Jammu. But because of the rumour spread that the young boy had jumped out of the plane, many people began to gather to see him.

After some hours in the police station, he was again shifted to the solitary room of the Police Lines where Gopal Sachar was kept earlier.

Upon opening of the land route to Srinagar, Gopal Sachar was taken to Srinagar Jail in the third week of April in a heavily guarded jeep. On nearing Srinagar, both his hands were handcuffed behind his back.

जनता के हृदय सम्राट

पंडित प्रेम नाथ जी डोगरा

The front page of the first issue of Jai Swadesh, *the official organ of the Praja Parishad, 13th September, 1955*

In Srinagar Jail, Sachar was lodged in Kukerkhana, adjacent to the main iron gate of the jail where senior Praja Parishad leader Rishi Kumar Koushal and his colleague Faquir Chand of Katra Vaishno Devi were already lodged. (This Kukerkhana was meant for rearing hens and cocks of the jail officers, but this was considered a better place than the conditions inside the jail). This was obviously done to keep them away from other activists and avoid trouble inside the jail.

On 12th May, 1953, after the arrest Dr. S.P. Mookerjee and shifting him to Srinagar, all the three were shifted to the Zenan Khana, the place for lodging women who were arrested and convicted.

Already about 25 other Praja Parishad activists had been interned in this place.

All the *satyagrahis* and other activists were brought back to Jammu and released in the first week of July at the end of the agitation.

Gopal Sachar now faced the problem of unemployment but at the suggestion of Panditji, he was entrusted various duties in the party office, especially for publicity matters. He worked in various capacities, including as the editor of the party organs, viz. *Jai Swadesh*, *Swadesh* and the *Deepak*—all Urdu/Hindi weeklies.

But some months after the demise of Pandit Prem Nath Dogra in 1972, Gopal Sachar left party work and began to work as an independent journalist for many newspapers as also for two news agencies, including the *Hindustan Samachar* (Yugvarta) and also as a helper for the UNI from 1984-2001. He is still associated with some papers and writes for them, even at the age of 90 plus.

Notwithstanding the commitments pledged in the National Conference bible, the *Naya Kashmir*, to ensure freedom of speech and that of the Press, it was very difficult to publish a paper. The editor of *Jai Swadesh* listed some details in its first editorial of the weekly, dated 13th September, 1955, saying how long it took to obtain the permission for its publication. He even had to take recourse to the court.

MESSAGE OF PANDITJI

At the time of launching the party organ, the Urdu weekly *Jai Swadesh*, the following observations were made by Pt. Prem Nath Dogra as president of the Praja Parishad:

"The path of true nationalism, which we have adopted, is no doubt lengthy and cumbersome, but ultimate victory would be ours."

Ridiculing the charge of the Leftists that the Praja Parishad is trying to exploit the working classes, Panditji maintained:

"We want to give people both Ram and *roti* and see that they should act as per their faith for peace and also its work to earn a prosperous life."

In 1957, when the elections to the first Legislative Assembly were held, the Praja Parishad captured five seats. The election results provoked angry protests from the party as the National Conference had rigged the elections and manipulated the results so that it could get a majority. Pt. Dogra charged the government with unfairness, bungling and mismanagement. Similar problems were always created when holding meetings and rallies.

In 1959, the Praja Parishad held its annual meet on 2, 3 and 4th April, but for seeking permission to use the loudspeaker and that of the ration, the chief of the organising committee, Shyam Lal Sharma had to repeatedly meet the then Premier Bakshi Ghulam Mohammad. In 1962, the Praja Parishad captured three seats of the state Legislative Assembly and in 1964, the party merged with the Bharatiya Jana Sangh.

□

The Nationalist Khan

Col. Peer Mohammad Khan, 9th September, 1892 to 23rd January, 1982

Col. Peer Mohammad Khan was a nationalist to the core of his heart. In 1947, after the evil division of India, the theocratic state of Pakistan came up in the neighbourhood of J&K. The virus of communal frenzy began causing problems. To grab the state by force, Pakistan launched a massive invasion through armed tribesmen supported by its army.

In the communal frenzy thus caused, many soldiers of the state's army and police betrayed the Maharaja by joining hands with the enemy. But Col. Peer Mohammad Khan and others stood like a rock to check the advancing invaders.

In the wake of the signing of the Instrument of Accession and the landing of the Indian troops in the state, an emergency dispensation led by Sheikh Abdullah was formed. Col. Khan was entrusted with the task, which also included that of re-organising the security setup. He did a commendable job and organised the J&K militia and cadet corps to extend a helping hand to the Indian forces in guarding vital installations.

Col. Khan was an associate of Pt. Prem Nath Dogra after his term in the government.

In 1972, after the death of Panditji, a serious situation arose in the *pradesh* Bharatiya Jana Sangh, as certain prominent activists of the party fell prey to the machinations of the Jana Sangh's adversaries. Many party leaders approached Col. Khan to head the *pradesh* unit. He was thus elected president of the BJS in this state. He held this office for about three years and worked to strengthen the party.

□

Heroes of the Movement

Shyam Lal Sharma, vice president of Praja Parishad

In addition to suffering imprisonment for several months along with Pt. Prem Nath Dogra, Shyam Lal Sharma served the Praja Parishad/Bharatiya Jana Sangh in various capacities, including as the vice-president of the *pradesh* Bharatiya Jana Sangh and earlier chief organiser of the Praja Parishad.

Basically an educationist, Shyam Lal Sharma also as headmaster of the SD Sabha High School, Jammu. Being a literary figure, he worked for promotion of Dogri and took keen interest in compiling the dictionary of the Dogri language.

His wife, Shakti Sharma was also an educationist. She served in the college for women as professor and then as principal. She played an important role in looking after the families of the arrested and jailed persons during the Praja Parishad movement.

Durga Das Verma, general secretary J&K Praja Parishad (underground hero of the movement 1952-53), 28th February, 1919 to 9th February, 2000

Durga Dass Verma was the most important individual during the Praja Parishad agitations. He was in-charge, viz., dictator during the 1952-53 agitation. He topped the list of first four Praja Parishad activists who were declared offenders and special police teams were deputed to arrest him. Durga Dass Verma remained general secretary of the Praja Parishad from 1949-1954. He earned a big name during this period.

Bhagwat Swaroop

Hailing from Rahon in Punjab, Bhagwat Swaroop came to Jammu after his graduation as an RSS Pracharak in the mid 1940s and served in various capacities, mostly as organising secretary in the Praja Parishad/ Bharatiya Jana Sangh and then in the BJP.

His dedicated services were the longest for over 60 years, and that too without any political ambition of getting elected to any constitutional or government body. For this selfless service, Bhagwat enjoyed immense respect amongst the activists.

Dr. Om Parkash Mengi, 16th January, 1918 to 14th November, 2009

Bhagwat's services in the Praja Parishad/Bharatiya Jana Sangh/Bharatiya Janata Party were unmatched as a humble worker with great dedication, beginning from the early forties till the early years of the new century. He was a person who always tried to keep party activists united whenever and whereever there were fissures. He played a creative role in building the organisation of nationalists and was arrested in 1952-53 in a police raid at a hideout and was subject to interrogation for months.

Dr. Om Parkash Mengi was a noble soul. He was devoted to the cause and philosophy of RSS and worked for it even in last days of his life. He was appointed as general secretary of the Praja Parishad in 1955, when some important functionaries were going astray because of corrupt and other tactics employed by the ruling National Conference leaders to weaken the Opposition, especially the nationalists. Dr. Mengi played an important role in stemming the rot.

Late Mulkh Raj Pargal, State Secretary of Praja Parisad, died on 4th February, 2017 at the age of 92

His wife, Sudesh played an important role in organising women teams to visit New Delhi and other places in the country to apprise the countrymen of the kind of cruelties being inflicted upon the *satyagrahis* after their arrest.

Being an expert in matters of law and a gentleman, originally in the Praja Parishad, Mulkh Raj Pargal came out as a frontline activist in Samba and was elected chairman of the town committee. He was also the member of the *pradesh* executive.

Pargal was an important functionary of the RSS and also a leading member of Pt. Prem Nath Dogra Memorial Trust.

Born in the border village of Mule Chak of R.S. Pura *tehsil* in district Jammu, on 14th November, 1922, Roop Lal Rohmetra came from a respectable family. His father Sukh Ram was a well-known figure of the area.

Roop Lal completed his graduation (B.Sc.) from the Prince of Wales College, Jammu and joined the RSS as a Pracharak in the early forties. He looked after the RSS activities in Reasi and Udhampur areas.

Roop Lal Rohmetra

Along with other prominent activists, Roop Lal played his role in providing relief to the refugees from adjoining Punjab and Pakistan-occupied Kashmir under the leadership of Pandit Prem Nath Dogra. He was amongst the founder-members of the Praja Parishad and was also arrested in the 1949 *satyagraha* movement of the party.

He participated in the 1952 students'

agitation on the issue of the flag and also during the movement of 1952-53. He suffered imprisonment in difficult conditions for months.

Roop Lal Rohmetra shifted to Delhi in 1958 and settled there with his family. He worked there in various capacities in the RSS with his family supporting him in nationalistic activities. His children are playing their role in various capacities to serve the society.

□

First Elections of Legislative Assembly Contested by the Praja Parishad in 1957

The Praja Parishad boycotted the Assembly Election in 1951 by Giving the Reason through Memorandium to the President of India on 8th October, 1951.

But in 1957, the party decided to contest the elections to the Legislative Assembly and contested on 20 Assembly seats in the Jammu province, wherein five candidates were elected as under:

1. Mahesh Chander from the Basholi constituency, securing 9,085 votes, defeated his rival Mahant Ram of NC who secured 5,846 votes out of a total electorate of 28,642 votes.
2. Pt. Prem Nath Dogra from the Jammu constituency secured 9,961 votes, defeating his rival Krishan Dutt Raina of NC who secured 4,746 votes out of a total electorate of 22,277 votes.
3. Thakur Sachdev Singh from the Akhnoor-Chhamb constituency, securing 12,782 votes, defeated his rival Ram Lal of NC who secured 12,745 votes out of a total electorate of 48,694 votes.
4. Sat Dev of a reserved seat from Akhnoor double-member constituency secured 13,500 votes and defeated his rival Shiv Ram of the NC, who secured 12,251 votes out of a total electorate of 29,181 votes.
5. Rajinder Singh from Jammu *tehsil* constituency secured 10,162 votes and defeated his rival Ram Saran Dass of

NC, who secured 9,864 votes out of a total electorate of 43,884 votes.

Candidates who Secured the Second Position

1. Dhian Singh from Billawar constituency secured 4,376 votes and Ram Chand Khajuria was elected by securing 8,624 votes out of the total electorate of 24,187 votes.
2. Chaggar Singh from Kathua constituency secured 4,628 votes and Major Piar Singh was elected by securing 10,993 votes out of a total electorate of 22,312 votes.
3. Thakur Baldev Singh from Jasmergarh (Hiranagar) constituency secured 5,250 votes and Girdhari Lal Dogra was elected by securing 15,319 votes out of a total electorate of 28,338 votes.
4. Dhian Singh from Samba constituency secured 5,979 votes and Sagra Singh of NC was elected for securing 9,414 votes out of the total electorate of 25,862 votes.
5. Shiv Das from Nowshera constituency secured 4,795 votes and Krishan Dev Sethi of NC was elected by securing 15,747 votes out of a total electorate of 29,616 votes.
6. Hans Raj from Ram Nagar constituency secured 717 votes and Hem Raj of NC was elected by securing 4,965 votes out of a total electorate of 26,444 votes.
7. Parasram from Udhampur constituency secured 6,876 votes and Amar Nath of the NC was elected by securing 7,183 votes out of a total electorate of 24,556 votes.
8. Shiv Charan Singh from Lander Tikri constituency secured 7,621 votes and Moti Ram Baigra of the NC was elected by securing 7,880 votes out of a total electorate of 24,266 votes.
9. Kashmiroo Ram from reserved constituency (double-member constituency) secured 4,130 votes and Milkhi Ram of HM was elected for securing 11,077 votes out of a total electorate of 24,768 votes.

10. Raghunath Singh from Bishnah Samba constituency secured 11,164 votes and Ram Piara of the NC was elected for securing 18,695 votes out of a total electorate of 40,196 votes.
11. Swami Raj of Bhaderwah constituency secured 4,537 votes and Chuni Lal of the NC was elected for securing 10,524 votes out of a total electorate of 25,447 votes.
12. Abdul Rehman from Bhallesa-Bunjawah constituency secured 2,712 votes and Goni of the NC was elected for securing 10,057 votes out of a total of 20,944 votes.
13. Labhu Ram from Ramban constituency secured 1,443 votes and Assadullah Mir of the NC was elected for securing 19,664 votes out of a total electorate of 24,026 votes.

This history shows the extent of the contribution of the Praja Parishad at that time.

□

MLAs of the Praja Parishad/Jana Sangh

Rishi Kumar Koushal (1926-2017)

Rishi Kumar Koushal was known for his good oratory skill and ability to win mass contact to serve the people. By virtue of his qualities of leadership, Koushal was elected thrice to the State Assembly from Reasi constituency despite heavy odds.

His life-sketch makes interesting reading. Koushal quit college in 1945 to become a whole-time worker (Pracharak) of the RSS. He served in the RSS for about eight years during 1947 and worked for rehabilitating and providing relief to uprooted persons of Rajouri and Reasi *tehsils*. He was a founder-member of the Praja Parishad in 1947; general secretary of the organisation in 1958-67; president, Beopar Mandal, Reasi in 1951-53; elected chairman, T.A.C., Reasi in 1954-61; member, G.C., All India Jana Sangh; elected first-time member of the Legislative Assembly in 1962; and whip of the Jana Sangh legislature group for 1962-67.

Thakur Sahdev Singh ex-MLA Praja Parishad (1957) (22nd December, 1922 to 7th May, 2016)

Rishi Kumar Koushal was a member of the Assurance Committee; member, Land Commission, 1962-68; member, Transport Committee, 1964; *pradesh* seneral secretary, Jana

Sangh, 1969-72; and closely associated with the provinicial and local Sanatan Dharma Sabha activities.

Sat Dev, MLA Praja Parisad, J&K (1957-62)

Sahdev Singh was a dedicated worker of the RSS since he was a student of the Prince of Wales College, Jammu. Belonging to Dadora village near Joudian in Jammu district, Thakur Sahdev Singh led a very simple life although he belonged to a well-to-do family.

He played a significant role in organising people to take part in the Praja Parishad agitation of 1952-53. His areas of activities were mostly Sunderbani and Naushera in addition to Joudian-Akhnoor. He was elected to the State Assembly in the 1957 elections from Akhnoor-Joudian, the then double-member constituency. Along with Sat Dev, he served the people with devotion.

Sat Dev was elected to the State Assembly from the Akhnoor double-member constituency along with Sahdev Singh in the 1957 elections. As a noble activist of the Praja Parishad, he served the people with great zeal and in a selfless manner.

Rajinder Singh Jamwal, ex-MLA, Praja Parishad (1957)

Sat Dev also took keen interest in raising the problems facing the people, especially those of Kandi and the backward areas in the Assembly.

Rajinder Singh was a dedicated activist of the RSS and a founder member of the Praja Parishad. Belonging to Jindrah village in the Jammu *tehsil*, he played a great role in organising the party units in the entire belt and took keen interest in recruiting *satyagrahis* and remained underground for several months to avoid arrest in accordance with instructions from the dictator of the agitation.

During the 1959 Assembly elections, Rajinder Singh was

Lt. Thakur Baldev Singh, senior leader of Praja Parishad, elected MLA and Member of Parliament in 1977

elected MLA from the double-member constituency of Jammu *tehsil*. He was quite a popular activist.

Later in the seventies, he shifted from Jindrah to Mishriwala in the same *tehsil*. He remained dedicated to the cause of nationalism and also worked in the non-cooperation movement.

A prominent lawyer by profession, Thakur Baldev Singh was seen as a strong person in public dealings.

Born in the border village of Snoora in *tehsil* Jasmergarh (Hiranagar) in Kathua district, his elders were known as great warriors and faced difficult days after the creation of a hostile neighbour, Pakistan. The villagers led by the members of this family defeated every attack of raiders even during the wars of 1965 and 1971.

Baldev Singh was arrested several times during the Praja Parishad/Bharatiya Jana Sangh movements and was lodged in jail. He was a close associate of Pt. Prem Nath Dogra and held important positions in the Praja Parishad/Bharatiya Jana Sangh/Bharatiya Janata Party.

In the 1977 Lok Sabha elections, the Janata Party gave its mandate to a discredited person. Many activists were annoyed. At their behest, Thakur Baldev Singh contested the Jammu-Poonch Lok Sabha seat as an independent candidate and defeated the candidates of the National Conference, Janata Party and others with a thumping majority. His election campaign was spearheaded single-handedly by the veteran Lala Jagat Narayan of Punjab and who was the head of the *Punjab Kesri/Hind Samachar* group of newspapers.

Baldev Singh was a protagonist for the abrogation of Article 370 which granted separate status to J&K. He also represented the Hiranagar constituency in the State Assembly during 1987-1990.

Ram Nath Balgotra, ex-MLA

Ram Nath Balgotra become an advocate after completing his law graduation and held important positions in the Praja Parishad and Bharatiya Jana Sangh. He was in-charge of publicity matters outside the state during the 1952-53 agitation and was arrested at Hyderabad but was released under a Madras High Court order after remaining in detention for about two months.

Balgotra was also linked with some social organisations and was elected twice to the State Legislative Assembly from Jammu city in 1967 and 1977. He also got elected as Councillor to the then MC, Jammu from ward No.1 in 1956 civic elections.

Master Dhian Singh, belonging to Guraha Slathian *tehsil* Samba was primarily a teacher and closely associated with the RSS/Praja Parishad/Bharatiya Jana Sangh. Dhian Singh, MLA, became popular amongst the people when he resigned from the government job along with his esteemed colleagues Jerman Singh, Jagdish Raj Sharma and Surinder Nath Khajuria, who jumped into the fray by offering their resignations during the great movement of the Praja Parishad. The people rolled up their sleeves and in a jiffy the whole village was transformed into a battlefield and came to be known as 'Chittorgarh'.

Master Dhian Singh

In the 1977 elections, as the newly formed Janata Party gave its ticket to certain persons who were not to the liking of the activists, Master Dhian Singh contested the Samba Assembly seat as a candidate of the Janata Front and won the election with a huge margin. He took keen interest in development works.

Udhampur had a strong unit of the Praja Parishad and

played an important role during all the agitations, including that of 1952-53. There were several leading lights who were arrested and shifted to Srinagar where they were lodged in difficult conditions, including the Zenan Khana.

Lala Shiv Charan Gupta, senior leader of Praja Parishad from Udhampur (2nd March, 1925 to 15th March, 2008)

They also included Dina Nath, Paras Ram Pichiala and others from Udhampur and other places of the district. During the agitation and afterwards, Shiv Charan Gupta played an important role. Born in March, 1925, Shiv Charan Gupta was a dominant personality and was popularly known as Thakur amongst his admirers.

Prof. Chaman Lal Gupta from Jammu, leader of Praja Parishad, Jana Sangh and Bharatiya Janata Party

He held various positions in the party. He was elected thrice to the Legislative Assembly from the Udhampur area and remained BJP group leader too. He took keen interest in developmental works of Udhampur and other areas. Shiv Charan played his role in various social and traders' bodies.

Prof. Chaman Lal Gupta was born on 13th April, 1934 in village Kaleeth, *tehsil* Akhnoor district in Jammu in a well-to-do family. He had his formal education in Jammu and Allahabad. Having completed his postgraduation in Physics from the University of Allahabad in 1958, he spent four years in Gujarat as a Pracharak of the RSS. In 1962, he was appointed lecturer in the Gandhi Memorial College, Jammu. Due to his political inclination and commitments, he was transferred frequently: first to Sopor College in 1969 and then to Degree College, Udhampur in 1971, where he resigned from the post of professor to join active politics in 1972.

He was elected the same year to the Legislative Assembly, J&K. Between 1973 to 1980, he remained general secretary of the *pradesh* unit of the Bharatiya Jana Sangh in J&K. He was also state general secretary of the BJP during 1980-1989. In 1987, he was elected to the Legislative Assembly for the second time. He also remained the state president of the BJP for two terms between 1990-95. In 1975, during the days of the Emergency, he remained underground and after his arrest, he was imprisoned along with other leaders of the Jana Sangh.

Prof. Gupta all along played a significant role in the rehabilitation of refugees. In Kashmir, as a consequence of terrorist activities, thousands of families migrated from the Kashmir Valley. Similarly in the terrorist-hit Doda district, Prof. Gupta played an active role in providing relief to the militancy-hit victims. Prof. Gupta, at this juncture, launched the *Doda Bachao Andolan* to counter the evil designs of terrorists. Over 50,000 *satyagrahis* and several national leaders actively participated in this *andolan*, after which Doda was handed over to the army and about 2,000 Village Defence Committees were formed to fight the terrorists.

Dhayan Singh, senior activist of Praja Parishad/BJS (2nd October, 1924 to 29th November, 2012)

Prof. Gupta is a widely travelled person. He is interested in reading and writing. Married to Rekha Gupta on 6th May, 1961, Prof. Gupta has two sons, Anil and Vikas and a daughter Meenakshi. He was elected as Lok Sabha member thrice from the Udhampur constituency and also remained Minister of State in the NDA government led by Atal Bihari Vajpayee and held different portfolios, including that of MoS, Defence. He was also elected to the State Assembly thrice from Jammu city.

Dhian Singh Kularia belonging to the Billawar area was quite popular amongst the people. He was a quiet and simple person and was elected to the State Assembly in the 1977 elections from

Billawar constituency and served the people of the area with great zeal.

In the Assembly, he was eager to raise the problem of the backward areas of Billawar and the people residing in remote areas.

□

Dedicated Activists of the Praja Parishad

There were at least eight activists by the name of Amar Nath in the Praja Parishad/Bharatiya Jana Sangh and they worked in various capacities. Four of them were Guptas. Amongst the Guptas, three were within a radius of only 200 metres in the Ghasmandi-Lakhdata Chowk of Jammu city.

Amar Nath Gupta, secretary of J&K Praja Parishad

Of them, Amar Nath Gupta, nicknamed Pahanda, held important positions including that of the city president and was elected Municipal Councillor and then Deputy Chairman of the MC. He took active part in all the party movements and was arrested.

His partner in business, Amar Nath Gupta was known as Amar Nath Gora. Another Amar Nath Gupta of the locality was nicknamed Comrade and Bounga. He was ever ready to take part in any agitation of the party and was arrested and jailed several times.

Yet another Amar Nath Gupta of Chand Nagar, Jammu was a humble worker. Being a gentle soul, he often took part in arrangement of meals at party functions and also arranged foodstuff for the refugees and migrants from PoJK/border areas.

Then there was another Amar Nath of Raghunathpura of Jammu city. During the agitation, he arranged food for underground and arrested workers. He was a dedicated activist of the RSS. He served in the OFD as an employee.

Amar Nath Gupta, Chand Nagar, Jammu 1929 to 13th April, 1984

Amar Nath Bhagat worked hard for upliftment of the downtrodden Scheduled Castes and others with dedication.

Another Amar Nath from the Sunderbani area worked in the office of Praja Parishad/Bharatiya Jana Sangh for a long time. He used to take special interest in looking into the problems of the border areas and was popularly known as Budhwar.

Lal Chand Aggarwal was a most gentle person, enjoying great respect amongst the trading community. He was associated with the RSS. He was also a respected activist of the Praja Parishad/Bharatiya Jana Sangh. His family members contributed a lot in activist movements for the sake of the society.

Lal Chand Aggarwal, Cashier, J&K Praja Parishad

Lal Chand held the office of the treasurer of the party in 1955-57.

Ram Nath Manhas was quite a prominent functionary of the Praja Parishad/Bharatiya Jana Sangh. He belonged to border area of Pargwal in the Akhnoor *tehsil* of Jammu district. He took part in various agitations of the party.

Manhas played an important role in organising the villagers to face the challenges posed by the Pak-designed attacks on the people, especially at nighttime, with the objective of forcing migration from the area. But Ram Nath and his colleagues made clear to the prominent villagers across the border that if this nuisance was not stopped immediately, it would lead to retaliatory actions. This warning had a salutary effect, so much so that even during the 1965 aggression of the Pakistani guerrillas supported by the Pakistan Army, they did not dare infiltrate the border villages.

Manhas was elected to the State Assembly in the 1977 elections and played his role in tackling the problems of the border villagers in general, more so those of the Chhamb sector. This area was part of his constituency. He took part in various agitations by the Praja Parishad/Bharatiya Jana Sangh and farced jail sentence.

Ram Nath Manhas
(died on 31st December, 2004)

Thakur Raghunath Singh Samyal, belonging to Samba in Jammu district, was a retired *tehsildar*, but was more of a poet than a politician. He was quite a jolly person and had developed the habit of using adjectives while calling and talking, making many smile over his way of narration. Samyal often used to accompany Panditji and narrate his verses and poems. The famous one was:

Raghunath Singh Samyal

"Dabiya dhol bajne jainya, te dogra des jangai jainya ho".

He was highly critical of the Sheikh and National Conference regime for which he had to face the wrath through stoppage of his pension and was jailed several times. He contested the Assembly elections but was defeated by foul means.

There were about half a dozen Praja Parishad/Bharatiya Jana Sangh activists who were named Banarsi Dass. One of them was Ranbir Singh Pura (RS Pura), who took active part in almost all the agitations and suffered jail terms. He held various positions in the *tehsil* unit of RS Pura.

Banarasi Dass Gupta
(Nai Basti)

Another Banarsi Dass Gupta was of Nai Basti, Jammu. He was elected as Municipal Councillor. He was arrested on various occasions, including the Emergency.

Banarsi Dass Gupta of Bishnah and another Banarsi Dass Gupta was a photographer of Ragunath Bazar.

Vaid Veshnu Dutt was born on 1st November, 1927 and did his matriculation in 1942 from Government High School, Udhampur. Thereafter, he joined the RSS. He was popularly known as Vaidji among the masses because of his profession, i.e., an Ayurvedic doctor.

Vaidji suffered jail in the 1952-53 agitation.

Vaid Veshnu Dutt acted as an active volunteer to help in the rehabilitation of refuges from PoJK/Punjab. He won the Municipal Committee election in the year 1956 and became Councillor of Jammu municipality.

He fought the Jammu municipality elections for a second time in 1972, won the elections and was elected as chairman of the JMC.

Vaid Veshnu Dutt with Jammu leaders

In 1975, during the Emergency, he led the underground movement successfully to oppose the oppressive and inhuman policies of the government. He later courted arrest.

In 1989, he was inducted into the BJP as a Central Working Committee member.

With the advent of jihadi militancy in Kashmir, he was appointed as chairman, J&K Sahitya Simiti and was instrumental in providing relief in cash and kind to the ousted Kashmiri Hindus to the tune of Rs. 6-7 crores in the early 1990's. In 1995, he became the president of BJP, J&K state and continued as president till 1997. He fought the election to the Lok Sabha in 1996 but lost to the Congress candidate. Again in 1996, he fought the Assembly election from the Jammu East constituency and won by a thumping majority.

In 1998, he fought the election to Lok Sabha from Jammu-Poonch constituency on BJP ticket and won by a margin of 1,27,000 votes.

In 1999, when the Vajpayee government fell by one vote, he was again nominated by the BJP to fight the election from the Jammu-Poonch constituency, which he won by a margin of 1,42,000 votes.

He passed away on 27th November, 2001 after a brief illness during his second tenure as Member of Parliament.

Shiv Lal was the district president of the Praja Parishad (rural) for many years and played an important role in organising the party units. Belonging to Rehial village of the Bishnah area of Jammu, he took part in every movement and suffered jail terms. He was a *hakim* by profession and quite popular amongst the people.

Shiv Lal Bishnah

Leading lights in Kathua—Being adjacent to Punjab, Kathua district was an important centre of Praja Parishad activities. At least two personalities from this area held the top posts in the party. They were Ruddar Mani Sangra and Thakur Baldev Singh. Moreover, Kathua was the centre of activities because several partymen in case of their warrants of arrest used to slip into Punjab, especially Pathankot, to breathe in the open.

In Kathua town, Chaggar Singh, Surinder Nath Ubbat, Vidya Parkash Padha, advocate, Om Wazir and some others were the

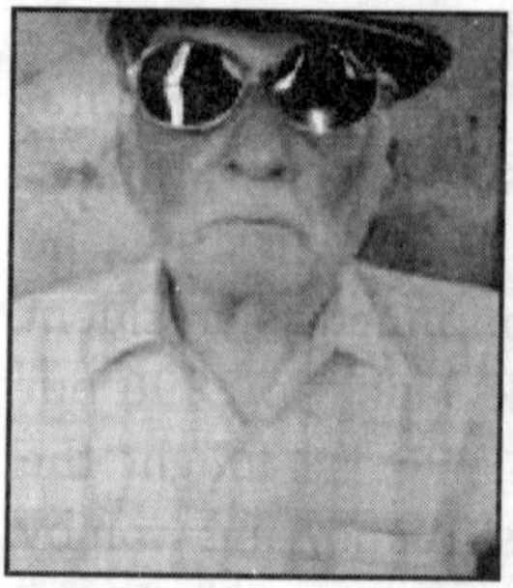

notable figures. They not only took active part themselves but also persuaded many others to take part in the *satyagraha* movement.

Several other noted activists of the district also included Radha Krishan Sharma, Om Parkash Sangra, Dawarka Nath of Basholi, Ishwar Dutt Shastri Maglooria, Jawala Parkash advocate, Gian Chand Sangra and Ranjeet Singh Zaildar. The latter was a leading figure who held important posts in the district and also in the state body.

Adv. Vidya Parkash Padha, Kathua, 1919-1985

Vidya Parkash Padha, belonging to the Kathua area, was well educated. He was a lawyer by profession and closely associated with the Praja Parishad and Jana Sangh.

He was a good orator and served the party in various capacities and took part in the movement for the removal of barriers between this state and rest of India. He was a popular figure and contributed to strengthen the Praja Parishad/Bharatiya Jana Sangh in the state. He was a founder figure of the Praja Parishad in Udhampur and also a member of the Praja Parishad executive. He courted arrest in the 1952 *satyagraha* and was shifted to Srinagar Jail along with Paras Ram and others. Along with some others, they too were lodged in Zenan Khana, a part of Srinagar Jail.

Deena Nath Gandotra, Udhampur

Dina Nath was also linked with some social organisations, including the Santan Dharma Sabha and was popularly known as Dinanath Mantri. Vaid Hari Ram of the RSS, in those days, was amongst the leading lights.

Mohammad Zubair Khattana was a leading personality amongst the Gujjar Bakarwal community. He was an admirer of Pt. Prem Nath Dogra. Along with his large number of followers, he used to participate in various functions of the Praja Parishad/ Bharatiya Jana Sangh.

Haji Mohammad Zubair, Khatana, 11th March, 1896 to 13th June, 1983

Bhikham Chand Magotra was one of the young revolutionaries in the 1953 agitation and lived in Udhampur. He played a leading role in Udhampur town in organising and leading the protest demonstrations and hence became a target of the then administration. He was arrested while leading one such demonstration in January 1953 and sentenced to four months, rigorous imprisonment with a fine. While they were being shifted to Srinagar Jail, it snowed heavily and they were stuck at the Banihal tunnel. As such, they had to spend three months of their jail term in the cold winter in Banihal, till the road for Srinagar reopened in the summer. The severe winter, poor living conditions and quality of food in the jail had an irreversible effect on his health.

Bhikham Chand Magotra

While a few sentenced people were released after they pleaded for pardon, Magotra was one of the few who chose to undergo the full jail term and not deposit the announced fine as a mark of protest. He was jailed for a further three months, which he spent in Srinagar's Hariparbat Jail.

Apart from health issues, Bhikham Chand Magotra sacrificed his established business of textiles and tea, since the stocks were seized by the administration and which got ruined during his seven months of imprisonment. Despite being the only son of his parents and sole bread-earner of the family, such was the undaunted conviction for the cause that he continued fighting for what he felt was the need of the hour. He was fully supported by his family and his wife Leela Rani was also arrested while protesting with other women against her husband's imprisonment.

Narsingh Dass Sharma, belonging to Jammu, was a humble worker and an RSS man. He did commendable work in organising strong Praja Parishad units in the Samba area with the cooperation of Mulkh Raj Pargal, Nank Chand, Swarn Singh, Atma Ram of Gurah Slathian and others.

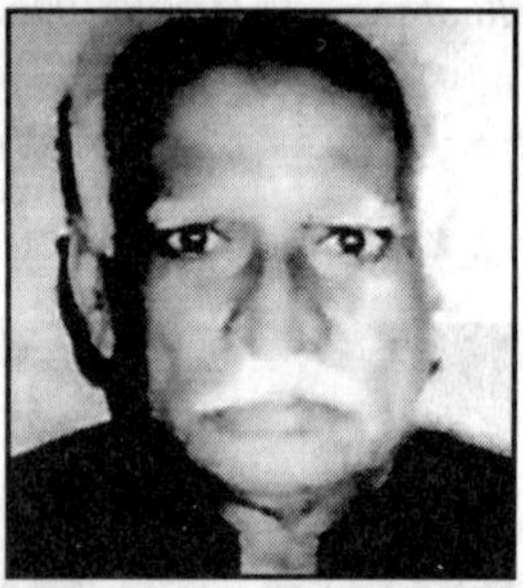

Narsingh Dass Sharma (22nd February, 1922 to 17th October, 1990)

Narsingh Dass was also the printer and publisher of the weekly party organ, *Deepak,* in the late sixties. He was killed in a road accident near Patni Top when he, along with Bhagwat Sarop, Budh Prakash Sethi and Ram Saroop, were coming after attending a party meet in Doda area. Two others were injured in this mishap.

Coming from village Nagri Padol of Kathua district, in Jammu, Sardari Lal was a well-educated person. Having remained with RSS activists during his education days, he was well versed with the outlook of nationalism and also had good knowledge of history. He could speak not only in Hindi and some other languages, but also deliver speeches in fluent English. Quite often he had some mental problems and used to deliver speeches at squares and even in various functions. The police had a tough time handling him.

Sardari Lal

In 1952, when the atmosphere was surcharged because of the separatist moves of Sheikh Abdullah, Dr. Karan Singh was elected as Sadar-i-Riyasat (president). The Praja Parishad was opposed to such moves. After his being elected as Sadar-i-Riyasat at Srinagar, the summer capital of the state, Dr. Karan Singh shifted to Jammu on November 18th. The ruling men of the National Conference and their cronies with the help of police arranged a big reception for the Sadar-i-Riyasat. A large number of reception gates were raised and the main bazaars were decorated with buntings, arches and welcome banners.

But minutes before the arrival of Dr. Karan Singh, Sardari Lal appeared in a busy lane and delivered a fiery speech against the raising of walls of separatism, detrimental to the unity of the country.

The people, who were already angry, led by Sardari Lal, smashed the reception arrangements in some areas of Ragunath Bazaar. Large crowds pulled down the gates, banners, etc. within minutes on the entire route to the palace. It was for the first time in Jammu that a member of the royal family had to face such a humiliating situation.

This incident gave a fillip to the preparations of the Praja Parishad for launching the *satyagraha* movement. As far as Sardari Lal was concerned, he passed much of his lifetime not only in Jammu jails and lockups, but also in several other places of the country for speeches delivered at places of his choice.

Sanji Ram Gupta was a leading activist of the Praja Parishad in the Bishnah-RS Pura area of Jammu district. He was arrested along with some other party functionaries during the early days of 1952-1953 Praja Parishad *satyagraha* movement. He had to be taken to Srinagar along with some others but before reaching Srinagar, the highway was closed because of heavy snowfall, due to which the arrested workers were held enroute near Banihal. In those days, there was no tunnel to reach the Valley due to which the road remained cut off on most winter days.

Sanji Ram Gupta

The buses carrying Sanji Ram and other arrested Praja Parishad workers were stuck near Banihal. The government authorities did not permit the return of the arrested activists despite the intense cold. There were no arrangements even for food, not to speak of lodging. These workers were kept in horrible conditions and after some days, they were lodged in sheds which were meant for keeping sheep and goat.

An account of this inhuman treatment meted out to Praja Parishad workers has been listed in the jail diary written by Sanji Ram. This has been published in the shape of a booklet titled as *Vishdhara-370*. This diary also details the painful and hell-like conditions that were created in Srinagar Jail.

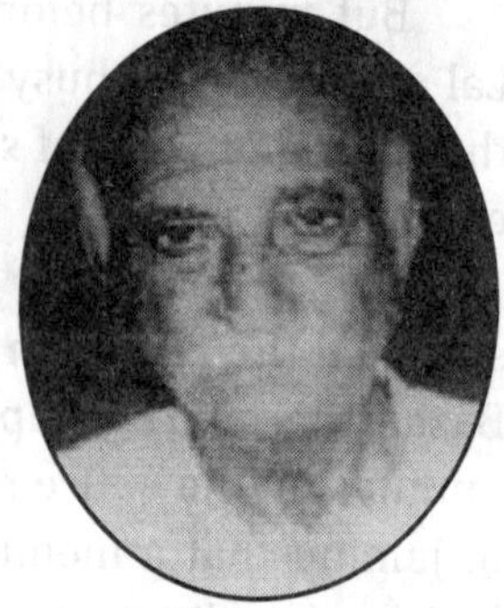

Atma Singh

Atma Singh, a pracharak of the RSS was a dedicated worker of the Praja Parishad. He was known for his organisational skills. He courted arrest and was kept in Reasi Jail.

Daya Kishan Gardish

Daya Kishan Gardish was a personality noted for his skill in writing in different languages, including English, Hindi, Persian, Dogri, but his mastery over Urdu was unmatched. Though he used to write for various opposing ideologies, Gardish was a nationalist from the core of his heart. He shifted to Jalandhar where he worked as an editor, spending most of his time in *Hind Samachar* and its group of newspapers.

Hirda Singh

His column, *'Saras ki Udaan'* used to be quite sarcastic and was popular among a large number of readers.

He was a great supporter of the Praja Parishad and more so of Pandit Prem Nath Dogra. During the election days, Gardish used to visit Jammu and extend his helping hand for writing posters in which he had great expertise.

He was a Dogri singer with an ever-smiling face. He courted arrest and was kept in Central Jail, Jammu.

Like many others, Sant Mehar Singh was enamoured by the leadership of Pt. Prem Nath Dogra and took part in the party functions, programmes and movements.

Sant Mehar Singh

Several young activists possessed the name Ram Saroop. Ram Saroop Gupta, who had underwent a hunger strike for several days during the 1952 students' agitation on the issue of flag, suffered confinement in jail.

He was killed near Patnitop in a road accident when he, along with Narsingh Dass Sharma, Tilak Raj Pandoh were coming after a party meeting at Doda. Sharma and Pandoh were killed while Budh Parkash Sethi was injured. Another Ram Saroop Gupta of Akhnoor held various posts and was arrested in all the agitations.

Ram Saroop Gupta

Two other youth named Ram Saroop, took part in the student agitation of 1952 and wen hunger strike for many days. One of them was known as Captain Dass Saroop of Raghunath Pura, Jammu and the other was Sharma.

In the Pargwal area of Akhnoor, another Ram Saroop Sharma was a leading activist along with Ram Nath Manhas, MLA.

Tilak Chander Singh

Tilak Chander Singh was a Swayamsevak from his childhood. He was a member of the SNA (Students National Association) which was merged with the ABVP. He was associated with the Vishwa Hindu Parishad and other social organisations. He was general secretary, Jammu Provincial Teachers' Association, senior vice-president, J&K and Ladakh Teachers' Federation.

Tilak Chander was commanded to discharge his duties as in-charge of publicity with headquarters at Samba. He left his college studies along with other colleagues to discharge his duties. The headquarters at Mangi Thalora (Samba) were raided by the police in the early winter of 1953, when the movement was at its peak. He was encircled in his hideout along with his companions.

Sulachan Singh

Lt. Sulachan Singh, president, Praja Parishad Gurha Slathia, led the first batch of Gurha Slathian, after a *havan yajna* performed by the village *pandit*, Tara Maniz, Bisheraji and Chaju Ramji. After a grand guard of honour ceremony presented by the ex-servicemen of the village the batch of *satyagrahis* left for Jammu to court arrest. Lt. Sulachan Singh shared a room with Pt. Prem Nath Dogra in Central Jail, Jammu.

Sansar Singh

A vocal Praja Parishad worker, Sansar Singh was in the prime of his youth when he courted arrest. He always led from the forefront. The government decided to shift some *satyagrahis* from Central Jail, Jammu to Srinagar. When the *satyagrahi* buses reached Banihal, all the *satyagrahis* alighted from their bus and vociferously protested against their being shifted to Srinagar.

Anchal Singh was a dedicated silent worker. D.D. Verma, in-charge of the movement, stayed in his house. The entire family looked after his security and other needs.

Anchal Singh, Mandi Rajgarh

Prabh Dayal Verma, Mandi Darbargarh

Khajur Singh, Mandi Garota

Inder Nath Khajuria, Mandi Darbargarh

Inder Singh, Mandigarh

Swaran Singh, Mandi Rajgarh

Master Jerman Singh, Mandi Andrar

He was a staunch party worker. His planning was meticulous. He was a trouble shooter of the party. His services were always required, whenever the situation was challenging. He was a loyal party worker.

Khajur Singh was an inspiring leader. He had a typical rural style of his own. He helped the poor and needy. He offered *satyagraha* at Jammu.

He was a dedicated and courageous leader and courted arrest at Jammu.

Inder Singh from Mandi Garh courted arrest at Jammu and was afterwards shifted to Srinagar Jail.

Lt. Diwan Chand

A firebrand leader popularly known as Bhagat Singh, Inder Singh rose to the position of general secretary of the state BJP. During the Praja Parishad struggle, he was in-charge of Kathua district.

He was a founder-member and first director of Ram Leela Club, Gurha Slathian. He was an artist of high calibre and an eminent social worker. He resigned from his government job and later went to Himachal to earn his livelihood. He was wedded to the RSS ideology.

Diwan Chand was a photographer by profession but took keen interest in various functions of the Praja Parishad/ Bharatiya Jana Sangh. He was arrested in the *satyagraha* movement.

He belonged to Panjtirthi area of the Jammu North Assembly constituency, which was represented by Pt. Prem Nath Dogra. He campaigned for Dogra in the 1957, 1962 and 1967 elections. He was one of the leading team workers who felt proud to work for the success of this great leader.

Lt. Devraj Gupta (Dabba Sahib)

Krishan Lal Gupta (1933-2015)

Lt. Durga Dass Gupta (15th May, 1923 to 25th June, 1996)

Revolutionary Poetry

As usual, in big movements as in the Praja Parishad struggle for removal of barriers between J&K and the rest of India, several persons used to recite their poems which attracted the audience a lot.

One such poem used to be recited by Sardar Kartar Singh Rahi in his melodious voice. This was, *'Raj meare ranjana da aapemuk jao ga.'*

Another such poet, who had earned popularity amongst the audience wwas Gajan Singh Gadgaj. In his thundering voice, he used to narrate: *'Gad gad gad aj, verian nun keh dey paij athu paij-gad gad gadgaj...'*

Durga Dass Gupta of Samba had been indirectly attacking the controversial utterances of the Sheikh by saying: *'Mean mean keare mera bilaa, mera dil jeali ao gya."*

Another such poet and Praja Parishad activist was Dev Raj Dabba. His poetry was popular because of being severely critical of the opportunists and would conclude with saying, *'Dabba bajda heo, dil kamdaee.'*

Durga Dass Dogra of Panjtirthi, Jammu, Mangor Ram Viffa and some others had been writing such poems, hitting at the National Conference leaders and causing uneasiness for them.

Such poems were quite often circulated through cyclostyled papers. Another noted local poet was Mohan Lal Sapolia who had written many poems, of which one was: *'Aes Bharat dae, tae Bharat sadda.'*

Another of his poems was: *'Mera des meri akhian de bahar sajna.'* Similarly, Raghunath Singh Simial had written poems attacking the controversial utterances of Sheikh Abdullah.

Some such poets from adjoining Punjab also used to visit and recite their poems at the Praja Parishad meetings. They included Sardar Gurcharan Singh Deepak, Tilak Raj Tilak, Suman Amritsari and others.

All such poems became quite popular as to become *lokgeet* (folk songs) in villages.

श्री तिलक राज शर्मा

Tilak Raj Sharma

Kuldeep Raj Gupta, Rajouri

Prominent BJP leader Kuldeep Raj Gupta joined the Praja Parishad 'accidentally'. According to him, "It was 1953, when Gupta was 17 years old and was at Sunderbani for some time with his relatives. At Sunderbani, the Praja Parishad was protesting against the permit system and dual system of governance. The protestors tried to unfurl the tricolour on certain buildings. The situation suddenly took an ugly turn and the police opened fire on the protestors, in which three persons were killed. Those who were martyred in this incident were Ram Lal, Krishan Lal and Beli Ram. This incident shocked Kuldeep Raj Gupta and he became a part of the agitation. He was supplied with some posters to paste at Rajouri which he did during the evening. The consequence of this was that at dawn, he was officially introduced into the Jana Sangh and was appointed as the president of Rajouri-Poonch district and later as state secretary.

Hans Raj Dogra, Jammu

Hans Raj Dogra took an active part in almost all the movements of the Praja Parishad/Bharatiya Jana Sangh and that of the BJP and suffered jail as well. He held various positions, including that of the treasurer of the party. He took active part in different social organisations, including those of the backward classes. He was elected to the State Assembly from Jammu West and served the people from 1996-2002.

Kushak Bakula
21st May, 1917 to
4th November, 2003

Ladakh Unhappy

While Jammu was struggling against the ill-conceived moves of the pseudo-

Sham Sunder Bhatia, Pracharak, RSS (22nd September, 1925 to 28th October, 2012)

secularists of the National Conference/Congress, the peace-loving Ladakhis were also not happy with the Sheikh.

Kushak Bakula, the great Buddhist leader, who was a Minister of the state, voiced his displeasure several times. The Praja Parishad/Bharatiya Jana Sangh managed to establish its units in both Ladakh and Kargil areas. Fed up with the discriminatory approach of the National Conference/Congress leadership, Ladakhis had been voicing their demand for Union Territory status for their region.

Sham Sunder Bhatia was a dedicated worker of the Praja Parishad. He was known for his organisational skills, and also received the *Simriti Chihn* from the RSS in 2002.

Tilak Raj Kaila, Gali Devi Dawara, Jammu (2nd November, 1930 to 26th February, 2002)

Tilak Raj Kalia lost his job at the Drug Research Laboratory, Jammu for being an activist of the RSS, but escaped arrest in the 1952-53 agitation in Jammu and left for Dehradun and got a job there.

Hailing from Udrana, an important locality of the charming valley of Bhaderwah in the erstwhile district of Doda in Jammu region, Daya Krishan Kotwal worked for the Praja Parishad and Bharatiya Jana Sangh by holding different positions in difficult circumstances.

Lt. Daya Krishan Kotwal, Tiger of Bhaderwah (29th April, 1927 to 9th April, 2013)

When the Muslim-majority district of Doda was erected in 1950 with a design, the young leader, Daya Krishan played an important role in frustrating the communal designs of the ruling *junta*. For his daring moves, Daya Krishan was known as the 'Tiger of Bhaderwah'.

For his organising skill, he held various positions in the Praja Parishad and *pradesh* Bharatiya Jana Sangh. In the difficult days of the nineties, Daya Krishan was elected as *pradesh* president of the BJP. He was also an elected member of the Legislative Council of the state.

Abdul Rehman was very young when he came in contact with some passionate social activists of Bhaderwah. They encouraged him in the Praja Parishad and managed his stay in Jammu where he was nurtured as a political leader in the Praja Parishad/ Bharatiya Jana Sangh.

Sheikh Abdul Rahman

He pleaded with the Praja Parishad/ Bharatiya Jana Sangh to adopt the outlook to put this state at par with other parts of India. He was inducted also in the All-India Working Committee of the Bharatiya Jana Sangh and was given the party mandate from the Jammu North Assembly constituency, which was represented by Pt. Prem Nath Dogra.

After the death of Panditji in 1972, due to some differences, Sheikh went astray along with several others. Later on, he frequently changed parties, but remained active throughout his life.

Hans Raj (Ramnagar) Secretary (Org.), Teh. Ram Nagar Praja Parishad

In the Ramnagar *tehsil* of Udhampur, Hans Raj Gupta was a law graduate and an advocate by profession, but he was an important functionary of the Praja Parishad and the Bharatiya Jana Sangh too.

He took part in all the *satyagraha* movements and organised the people of the area to court arrest and take part in the party activities.

His younger brother Om Prakash

had taken part in the 1952 agitation against the hoisting of the National Conference's *halwala* flag in the Government College, Jammu. He was amongst those students who underwent a 32-day hunger strike and faced imprisonment too.

Om Prakash was dedicated to patriotic feelings and played his role in strengthening the nationalic outlook, like a true Swayamsevak.

Kotwal Kripa Ram

The president of the Bhaderwah Praja Parishad named Kotwal Kripa Ram, businessman by profession, devoted much of his time to build a strong unit of Praja Parishad/Bharatiya Jana Sangh in Doda areas, facing all the difficult situations created by the secessionists and pseudo-secularists.

He was the *tehsil* president of Bhaderwah and was a popular figure of the district. He nurtured some small children in a passionate manner with the desire to make them useful activists with a national outlook.

Onkar Singh,
president, Praja Parishad
tehsil *Reasi*

Onkar Singh was a notable activist of the Praja Parishad/Bharatiya Jana Sangh. He took a leading part in the party movements in Reasi area and faced arrest and jail.

He was loved more in the party circles and by the people in general but also for being the grandson of the great General Zarawar Singh, who had extended the frontiers of Jammu & Kashmir state to Ladakh and partially of Tibet, braving many odds. He resided at Vijaypur Reasi.

A senior party activist, Subedar Hari Singh was an ex-serviceman belonging to Samwan village in the border area of Planwalla, then *tehsil* Akhnoor of Jammu district. He was a member of the Praja Parishad/*pradesh* Bharatiya Jana Sangh executive and took active part in various movements.

The Subedar played an important role in organising the villagers to face the attacks of Pak-sponsored intruders who used to chop off heads and limbs to terrorise people and force them to migrate from the border areas.

Subedar Major Th. Hari Singh

Vice president of J&K Praja Parishad and belonging to Nagri Padole in Kathua district, Ranjit Singh was a noted personality and took part in various agitations despite being aged. Not only did he himself take part but also prepared many others to face the regime's wrath with determination.

Thakur Ranjit Singh

Ranjit Singh held important positions in the Praja Parishad/Bharatiya Jana Sangh and remained vice-president of the party for many years.

As president, *tehsil* Jammu Praja Parishad, Thakur Basant Singh belonged to a village of Jammu district. He was an ex-serviceman and a migrant from PoJK and had opted to wear only one *khadi dhoti* to protest against the atrocities on the *satyagrahis* and took part in the Praja Parishad struggle for placing J&K state at par with other parts of the country.

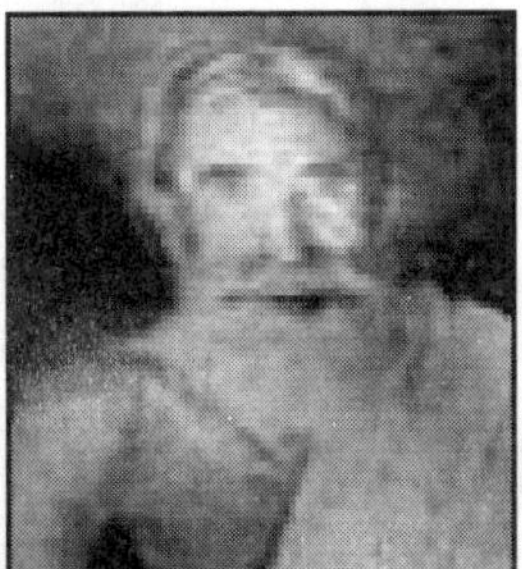

Thakur Basant Singh 'Tyagi'

Basant Singh the created a complex problem for police by offering *satyagraha* along with not only the members of his family, but also his goat and some cattle in the 1952-53 agitation. He remained in jail in the severe winter in just one *dhoti* for several months.

Nand Lal Bhagat

Nand Lal Bhagat was a dedicated Harijan activist of the Praja Parishad and Bharatiya Jana Sangh. Belonging to the Miran Sahib area of RS Pura *tehsil*, district Jammu, he was a great admirer of Pt. Prem Nath Dogra and took part in all the movements and courted arrest to suffer in jail.

Manmohan Gupta, Kishtwar, senior leader of Praja Parishad

Nand Lal also contested the Assembly elections even when the other Harijans were terrorized in order to prevent them from contesting against the National Conference candidates to ensure 'unopposed' success.

Despite being economically poor, Nand Lal was rich enough to face the onslaught of the money power of the ruling party.

There were some prominent activists who played their important role in establishing the Praja Parishad/Bharatiya Jana Sangh units at far-off places in the erstwhile district of Doda.

Among them, Manmohan Gupta and his colleagues from Kishtwar visited far-off places, facing heavy odds to mobilise the people against the designs of separatists.

In Kishtwar, Sant Ram of Matta and others were ever ready to come to the rescue of townsmen who were often harassed by the National Conference and other communal elements.

Manmohan Gupta and others also established strong units of the party in remote areas of Padder with the help of Janki Nath and some others.

Sant Ram, secretary, tehsil *Kishtwar, Sham Lalji, Parkash Ram, activist Praja Parishad, Ramban*

In this highly sensitive Doda district, Natha Singh, Labhu Ram, Kasturi Lal, Sardar Mehar Singh and others played a commendable role in building a strong party unit. Labhu Ram also contested the Assembly polls but was defeated by a narrow margin.

Dr. Ved Parkash Gupta, Nowshera

Dr. Ved Parkash was basically a chemist but because of his background, he established a small hospital-like institution in the border town of Nowshera and became popular.

During the Praja Parishad struggle, especially in the 1952-53 agitation, he played his role like a dedicated activist. He was in-charge of the Hindi section for preparing publicity material and handling a difficult task of underground operations of one of the cyclostyle machines, which were on the special radar of the police.

Jodh Ram Sharma (1906-1989)

Jodh Ram Sharma was the eldest brother of Niwas (father of Chander Prakash Ganga) and activist of the Praja Parishad. He was jailed for 10 months during the 1953 Praja Parishad agitation.

He was a great activist from Hiranagar during the 1953 Praja Parishad agitation. He was an activist from Jammu and was jailed during the agitation.

Adv. Jawala Parkash Gupta (10th August, 1916 to 26th September, 1996)

By profession, Chatru Ram Dogra was a photographer, whose number was few in the capital city of Jammu in those days and hence was a well-known figure. But more than as a photographer, Chatru was known for his agitational role. In the 1942-43 food agitation, he and his family members including his wife played quite a leading role.

Radha Krishan Sharma (22nd November, 1927 to 14th February, 1993)

In the early fifties, Chatru was actively associated with the Praja Parishad and got arrested at different times. He was also a member of the Working Committee of the Praja Parishad when Pt. Prem Nath Dogra was the president.

Chatru Ram Dogra

During the Praja Parishad/ Bharatiya Jana Sangh agitations, Dogra's wife and daughter Bimla Dogra played important roles in organising women activists.

Satpal Sharma of Nowshera was a dedicated worker and played a role in organising nationalists of the border areas. He always extended his helping hand to the victims of firing and attacks of Pakistani invaders.

Lt. Satya Paul Sharma (1939-2000)

By profession he was a doctor and enjoyed the goodwill of the people. He contested the elections too.

Several Sikh leaders, mostly linked

with the Akali Dal, not only supported the Praja Parishad/Bharatiya Jana Sangh movement but also took an active part and courted arrest. They included Giani Isher Singh and others.

Giyani Isher Singh, Sikh leader

Led by Sardar Basant Singh Sabar, many Sikh activists used to participate in the party functions.

Bachan Singh Panchi was also inducted as a member of the *pradesh* executive of the Bharatiya Jana Sangh and presented the problems of the migrants from the Pak-held areas at various fora.

Hem Raj Pujari, Katra (1st February, 1934 to 11th January, 1986)

Hem Raj Pujari was an important activist of the Praja Parishad/Bharatiya Jana Sangh at Katra Vaishno Devi. Along with Khem Raj, Faqir Chand Gupta and others, there was a big team of party activists who took active part in various movements and suffered imprisonment.

Bansi Lal Dogra

From Gurhaerahimna Akhnoor, Bansi Lal Dogra was an activist of the Praja Parishad and served jail sentences many times during this period.

□

Women's Wing of the Praja Parishad

WOMEN'S WING

Women played an important role during all the Praja Parishad/Bharatiya Jana Sangh movements. They not only organised processions defying prohibitory orders and faced *lathi*-charge and arrests, but also organised drives for collection of funds to help the families of jailed workers. Some women even contributed their ornaments to this end.

The most important part was played by Prof. Shakti Sharma (popularly known as Behenji), Susheela Mengi, Mata Parvarti, Parkasho Devi, Chatru Ram Dogra, Bimla Dogra, Susheela Devi (known as Reasiwali Mata), Taro Devi Chouhan and many others.

Shakti Sharma

Their significant role was in organising teams to reach Delhi and other important places to apprise the national leaders of the kind of atrocities and excesses being committed by the police and other forces on the arrested and jailed *satyagrahis*.

In addition to Jammu city, the women units were well organised at important places, including towns and even villages.

Susheela Mengi

Shakti Sharma, wife of Sham Lal Sharma was amongst the leading women leaders who played an important role during the Praja Parishad movement.

Susheela Mengi was amongst the leading activists of the Praja Parishad and Bharatiya Jana Sangh.

Susheela Devi (populary known as Mata Reasiwali)

Sheela Chauhan held important positions in the women's wing of the Praja Parishad and Bharatiya Jana Sangh

Parkasho Devi of Pratap Garh, Jammu, held party positions in the women's wing

Darshna Devi, wife of Dev Raj (Dabba) was an important functionary of the Praja Parishad and Bharatiya Jana Sangh in Jammu

Lt. Vinod Kumari Sharma

Brinda Devi, grandmother of Ashok Khajuria

Sukantla Devi

Sukantla Devi was arrested in 1953 and was tortured in police lockup for more than a month. She was kept under illegal confinement. She was arrested along with six other women in Jammu. She was the sister of party activist Kesho Ram.

Bimla Devi (Paggad) Sunderbani

Chanchla Devi, Akhnoor

Mahila leader, Soama Devi, Jammu

Taro Devi Abrol of Mohalla Gujaran, Jammu

Darshna Deviji w/o Sobha Ram Sharmaji r/o Gurah Jattan Ghagwal, D.O.B 1931-1973

Vimla Dogra (Paggad), daughter of Chattru Ram Dogra

As an activist during the Praja Parishad agitation, she actively participated during Dr. Syama Prasad Mookerjee's movement.

Sukantla Devi organised several public meetings and motivated people towards J&K's accession to Union of India, especially among women. She also organised movements against the dowry system and was a big supporter of joint families.

□

Frontline Workers

There was a huge team of Praja Parishad/Bharatiya Jana Sangh activists in Jammu and elsewhere who used to organise youths to take part in protest demonstrations and various agitations. They faced *lathi*-blows as also caught hold of tear gas shells and threw them back on the police personnel.

As the state police failed to suppress the agitators, at the instance of Prime Minister Nehru, the Punjab police was also summoned for their help and deployed at a number of places. These policemen carried long iron-capped *lathis*.

In the city, daredevil activists of the Praja Parishad/Bharatiya Jana Sangh faced the wrath of the police. They included Tilak Raj Pandoh, Bhagwan Dass Pahada, Dev Raj Dhabba, his brother Babu Ram, Om Parkash, Amar Nath Bounga, Tilak Raj Talwar, Mahashay Yashpaul, Mohan Lal Gupta, Mulkh Raj, Ishar Dutt Raina, Haider Noorani, Khushi Ram Padha, Shiv Kumar Sharma, Om Wazir, Aatma Ram Sharma, Sham Lal Sharma, Kulbir Gupta, Paras Ram, Shiv Lal, Ved Parkash, Papa Dina Nath and many others.

Lt. Tilak Raj Pandoh

Shiv Kumar Sharma, Pracharak

Mahashay Yashpaul, secretary, Jammu Praja Parishad and member of Pradesh *Committee*

Om Wazir of Kathua took part in various agitations and suffered jail terms

Baldev Raj of Gajansoo district, Jammu was an active figure of the area

Paras Ram Pachialo, Udhampur, senior activist of the Praja Parishad, suffered jail for several months

Mulkh Raj Peer Mitha, Jammu

Mohan Lal Gupta, Bishnah

Late Kesho Ram Arora

Ishar Dutt Raina, senior leader, Praja Parishad Kaniyala Dansal (1910 to 1980)

Vaid Chajju Ram Sharma, Gharota activist of Praja Parishad, passed away in the year 2006

Khushi Ram Padha, senior leader, Praja Parishad (1922-1978)

Kulbir Gupta, Udhampur

Shiv Lal, Udhampur

Papa Dina Nath, Udhampur

Chhajju Ram Shastri, founder member of Praja Parishad (D.O.B 19th April, 1923) Village Chirayi, Teh. *& Distt. Udhampur. He also served as district president of the BJP four times from Udhampur Reasi*

Mahant Baba Durga Dass (21st July, 1920 to 24th June, 2000), activist of the Praja Parishad

Ved Parkash Chouhan, student leader

Pt. Rohlu Ram Akhnoor (1910-1985) joined the Praja Parishad movement during the year 1950-54 and was jailed several times

Yash Puri observed hunger strike for several days during the 1952 students' agitation

Puri Ram Manwal

Suraj Kapoor, prominent activist of the Praja Parishad

Ved Mittar, leader of the student wing, underwent 31 days' hunger strike in 1952

Pt. Vaid Prakash Raina (Kaniyala), Dansal Balraj Madok (Delhi), and Tilak Raj Sharma (Jammu) Praja Parishad leaders

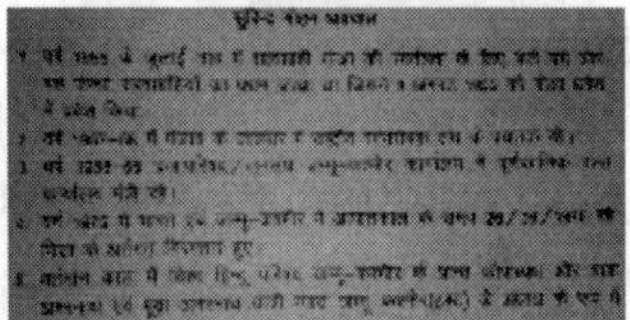

Role of Activists from the Valley

Several prominent activists from the Valley of Kashmir played their role in the Praja Parishad/Bharatiya Jana Sangh movement. They included Tika Lal Taploo, Makhan Lal Aima, Janki Nath, Som Nath Ugrah, Hyder Noorani, Prem Nath Butt, Piare Lal Goja and others.

Tika Lal Taploo

Amar Nath Vaishnavi served in various capacities in strengthening the spirit of nationalism. He was popular amongst various sections of the society for his dedication to serving the society.

It was broad daylight when the sky came under dark clouds upon the assassination of Pt. Tika Lal Taploo, who was the voice of Kashmiri Pandits in the Valley of Kashmir. The terrorists silenced this voice on 13 September, 1989 with their bullets threatening Kashmiri Pandits to remain silent or face the same consequences. This considered the start of terrorism in Kashmir.

This noble soul was born in 1930. He did his matriculation in 1945 from the Punjab University and M.A., LLB from the Aligarh Muslim University. He joined the Kashmir Bar in 1957 and played a leading role in the promotion of justice. He was enrolled as an advocate of the High Court on April, 1971. He was an RSS activist and was arrested many times while fighting for the cause of the people in Kashmir. He would not charge anything from his poor clients and would plead their cases in court, irrespective of their religion.

In 1975, when the notorious Emergency was declared, on the call of the Lok Sangh Samiti formed by various national parties under the leadership of Loknayak Jayaprakash Narayan, Tika Lal Taploo courted arrest at the historic Lal Chowk in Srinagar with some of his friends.

He was an active politican and rose to the high office of vice-president of the *pradesh* Bharatiya Janata Party. He was a fearless, transparent, honest and upright politician.

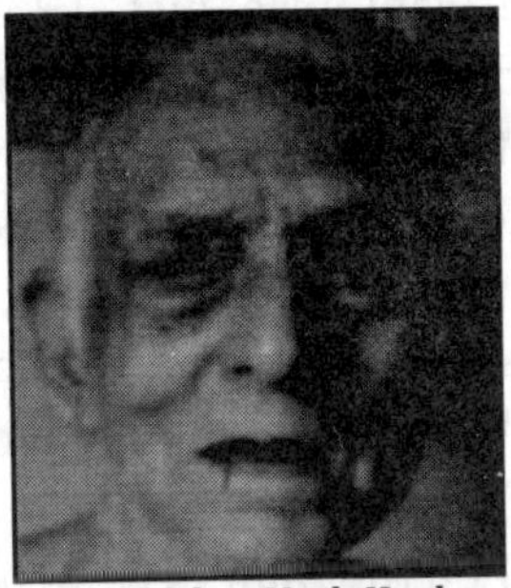

Pt. Omkar Nath Kaak

Amar Nath Vaishanavi

Prem Nath Bhatt, member executive, Praja Parishad

Haider Noorani, MP candidate, BJP in 1999; attacked and killed by terrorists

Every year, on its Infantry Day, the Indian Army commemorates the saviour of Kashmir, Mohammad Maqbool Sherwani. It has also constructed a Memorial Hall in his name in Baramulla town, but that is not all. None else observes a day for

Maqbool Sherwani

this saviour whom the invading Pakistani tribesmen captured on 7th November, 1947 and virtually crucified.

Highlighting Maqbool's daring deed, his first cousin Ghulam Mohammad Sherwani, general secretary, District Congress Committee, Baramulla, says, "Way back in 1947, the young Mohammad Maqbool Sherwani was just 19 but he single-handedly frustrated the advance of thousands of raiders (*kabailis*) from Baramulla, thus giving valuable time to the Indian Army to land in Srinagar and push back the raiders. The raiders put him on a wooden cross, nailed him and fired upon him 10-15 times. He remained in that state for two to three days. His body was brought down only when the army reached the place."

Ghulam Mohammad says that when the raiders were heading for Srinagar, Maqbool Sherwani misguided the infiltrators on to the wrong routes and made them lose four precious days so that the Indian Army could reach Srinagar for its defence. When Maqbool was captured by the raiders, the Amir of raiders softly said to him, "You are a promising young man. We will forgive you if you yourself join us. As positive proof of your change of heart, you must tell us the secret position of the militia (state force) and Indian troops in Shalteng and also show us the shortest route to the Srinagar aerodrome."

"No, that shall never be," was the firm reply of the saviour Sherwani. The Amir wrote "Sherwani is the traitor; his punishment is death" on a piece of paper in Urdu and pasted it on his forehead. The Amir ordered his men, "Tie his ears and his drooping head and arms straight to the posts so that every passerby can see him...Fire..."

On 8th of November, 1947, the Pakistani raiders were driven out of Baramulla. One of the first acts of the freed people was to reclaim the dead body of Sherwani and bury it in the graveyard of the Juma Masjid of the town with full military honours.

The Memorial Hall in the name of Maqbool Sherwani was constructed by the Indian Army. Since his childhood, Maqbool was a dedicated activist of Sheikh Abdullah. He was martyred before he could marry Zeba, to whom he was engaged. When Mohammad Ali Jinnah visited Kashmir and spoke at Baramulla propagating his Two-Nation Theory, Sherwani forced him to climb down from the platform and thus cut short his speech. Ever since the founding of the All Jammu & Kashmir National Conference in 1939 by Sheikh Abdullah, Maqbool Sherwani had been a staunch supporter of the national cause of the 40 lakh Kashmiris who demanded freedom from the Dogra monarchy. "But today the Sherwanis are being looked upon as 'traitors' and branded as 'Indian agents'. The successive governments have ignored them," says Ghulam Mohammad.

About Sheikh Abdullah, Ghulam says that he was a self-centered person who never cared for his loyalist workers after acquiring power. That 'tradition' still continues in the National Conference. "When my brother was assassinated, Maqbool's father Mohammad Abdullah Sherwani met Sheikh Abdullah and asked for a livelihood for his other son. Sheikh Abdullah did not care," he says.

Ghulam Mohammad is the only person from Maqbool Sherwani's family who joined politics in 1958 when he was serving in the Education Department. Later, he became an active member of the Indian National Congress in 1975. Asked about the Kashmir problem, he said there would be no end to the ongoing dialogue process being held between India and Pakistan and Kashmir would remain depressed.

He said, "Those who have visited Pakistan or PoK in private discussions have told me that they have no love for Pakistan." Commenting upon the political scenario of the state, he said, "Coalition governments in J&K state have never worked. When Mir Qasim was Congress Chief Minister, the party was being considered a pro-people's party and it flourished but after his removal, the party slipped into lobbyism. The Central leadership of the Congress is responsible for encouraging lobbyism between

Ghulam Nabi Azad (former) Union Health Minister and Prof. Saifuddin Soz (former state president of the Congress)."

Ghulam Mohammad said that he met Congress president Sonia Gandhi in 2009 with a memorandum on the grievances of the workers and requested her to set the state committee in order, but "till now nothing has happened". About the Congress-National Conference alliance, he said, "Both are cutting each other's roots. The coalition between the two has never ever percolated down to the grassroots."

□

Role of the Aged and Incapacitated

To what extent the masses were involved in ensuring the success of the Praja Parishad movement can be gauged from the fact that even dumb, incapacitated and aged did not lag behind.

Amongst such persons were the notable Jhalla brothers of Jain Bazar. They were Ram Lal and Des Raj. Ram Lal, who could not speak, played his part in pasting handwritten wall posters and had been contributing a part of their income to Pandit Prem Nath Dogra for the cause of the Praja Parishad/Bharatiya Jana Sangh.

The Jhalla brothers had a shop in Jain Bazar, Jammu. They were famous for preparing *pheniyan* and *kutlamas* (a particular type of preparation for special occasions by using *desi ghee* and *maida*).

Though the Jhalla brothers passed away several years ago, the shop is still known by their name.

SENIOR CITIZENS IN THE PRAJA PARISHAD

Though the Praja Parishad/Bharatiya Jana Sangh was known as a party of young men, some quite elderly persons also held party posts.

In Jammu city, Dewan Bishan Dass, Sham Lal alias Shamu Shah and others held important positions in the city committee of the Praja Parishad.

Ram Lal Arora

Sant Ram Arora

Bishan Dass Sharma

Pt. Gyan Chand Raina Dansal, Praja Parishad

Atma Ram Sharma, Akhnooor

Lal Chand Verma, Udhampur

Sham Lalji (Shamo Shah)

Bishamber Dass Sharma

Bhagwan Dass Padha of Tangewali Gali, Jammu; leading activist of the Praja Parishad/ Bharatiya Jana Sangh

Dina Nath Sharma, Deputy Chairman of the Jammu M.C. and leading activist of the BJS

Ch. Waryam Singh, Smailpur and his brother Ch. Nasib Singh of Bisjhnah area of Jammu; leading activists of the Praja Parishad/ Bharatiya Jana Sangh

Sat Pal Khajuria, secretary of the Praja Parishad from Samba, 1953

Sohan Lal, dedicated leader of the Praja Parishad (26th April, 1939 to 18th March, 2006)

Sat Paul Gupta

Satish Mahajan, Praja Parishad activist and ex-Councilor, Bakshi Nagar (23rd July, 1938 to 21st June, 2014)

Subedar Dharam Singh, senior activist, Teh-Akhnoor, Praja Parishad

Bal Krishan, Jammu Praja Parishad/ Bharatiya Jana Sangh/ Bharatiya Janata Party, senior activist of Panjtirthi, Jammu

Brij Lal Sharma, Katra Vaishnooo Devi (6th January, 1928 to 3rd February, 1995)

Swami Raj Katal of the Praja Parishad/ Bharatiya Jana Sangh, leading activist of Bhaderwah, Doda; shot dead by terrorists

Lt. Satish Kumar Bhandari from Doda

Ruchir Kumar, the hero of Doda, martyred on 7th June, 1994

Thakur Santosh, the hero of the Doda war

Poem written by Thakur Surjit Singh, senior activist of the Praja Parishad.

'लावारिस जागीर नहीं'

धुन : आओ बच्चो तुम्हें दिखाएँ···

उन्हें कयामत तक मिलने का, जम्मू व कश्मीर नहीं,
अंग अटूट है भारत का, यह लावारिस जागीर नहीं।

Thakur Surjeet Singh

1. जिसकी खातिर लाखों वीरों ने दी हँसकर कुरबानी, लहू शहीदों का बहता बन, जिसकी नदियों का पानी, हम दुश्मन की चलने देंगे, यहाँ कोई तदबीर नहीं, अंग अटूट है भारत का···
2. देखो हरे-भरे खेतों में, क्या सुंदर है हरियाली, मन मोहित करने वाली है, हँस के फूलों की लाली, बंदर के हाथों दी जाए, यह ऐसी तसवीर नहीं, अंग अटूट है, भारत का···
3. जिस धरती पर केसर फूल, हरे खेत हैं लहराते, सदियों से कश्मीर निवासी, भारतवासी कहलाते, कौन कहे यह भारत रूपी राँझा की प्रिय हीर नहीं, अंग अटूट है भारत का···
4. पूजा-पाठ, नमाज का झगड़ा, यहाँ नहीं तकरार है, रगों में सबकी एक लहू है, भाइयों जैसा प्यार है, जिसकी कड़ियाँ अलग-अलग हो, यह ऐसी जंजीर नहीं, अंग अटूट है भारत का···
5. कदम-कदम पर जो धमकाते थे, हमको तकरीरों में, देख लिये वह कितना दम है, भारत के रणवीरों में, अब तो गाजी भूल सकेंगे, भारत की शमशीर नहीं, अंग अटूट है भारत का···
6. हमें रोज जो अमरीका के टैंकों का डर दिखलाते, स्यालकोट, लाहौर गँवाकर, सिर धुनते थे पछताते, क्या रण-गाथा अपनी गाता, दर्रा हाजी-पीर नहीं, अंग अटूट है भारत का···
7. इस पर कब्जा के मनसूबे, बुरी तरह नाकाम हुए, हार-मार खा पाकिस्तानी, दुनिया में बदनाम हुए, सैर करें बागे जन्नत की, यह उनकी तकदीर नहीं, अंग अटूट है भारत का, यह लावारिस जागीर नहीं।
8. इस धरती को लहू से सींचा, लाखों वीर जवानों ने, भारत रूपी शमाँ पर, जलने वाले परवानों ने, क्या (निर्भीक) की कविता में, वह बिजली की तासीर नहीं, अंग अटूट है भारत का, यह लावारिस जागीर नहीं।

THE DODA AGITATION

The Muslim-majority district of Doda in Jammu region was created under a design by the interim regime of Sheikh Mohammad Abdullah in 1950, despite opposition by the Praja Parishad and some nationalists, but the opponents were dubbed as communalists. There was not much difference in the population. The ratio of Muslims and that of Hindus was about 55:45.

Adjoining Kashmir Valley, this district became a major centre of activities of the Kashmir Plebiscite Front, which was formed in 1954 after the Sheikh had gone astray and was jailed by his own colleagues in August, 1953. The Praja Parishad/BJS had strong units in some parts of this belt but the activists had to face tough times, both from the administration and the secessionists.

In 1990, when armed militancy assumed alarming proportions and the minorities were forced out from the Vale of Kashmir, Doda district became the next target of the ultras. Some local youths led by an ex-serviceman, Subedar Surjit Singh, formed Village Defence Committees, but these were not enough to meet the challenge.

In 1994, the BJP launched a movement at the national level: 'Save Doda district'. Thousands of BJP activists including the party's top leadership reached Jammu to court arrest. They included Atal Bihari Vajpayee, L.K. Advani, Dr. Murli Manohar Joshi and others. In the wake of this movement, a number of security arrangements were made. These also included a large number of VDCS and deployment of forces.

The extent of threat by the enemy could be well gauged that between 1991-2002, there were as many as about 60 incidents of massacres to terrorise and force migration, out of which about 40 were recorded in this district of Doda alone.

Since 2009, this vast belt of Doda has been divided into three administrative districts, viz. Doda, Kishtwar and Ramban.

There has been considerable change in law and order problems as also the political activities, but the BJP has made enormous sacrifices. Several of its activists have sacrificed their lives at the hands of terrorists.

Those who became victims of enemy bullets include:

i. Santosh Thakur
ii. Swami Raj Kattal of Bhaderwah
iii. Ruchar Kumar
iv. Satish Bhandari

□

Rare Pictures

Panditji with Durga Dass Verma, Shiv Charan Gupta, Sham Lal Sharma and other activists of the Praja Parishad

Atal Bihari Vajpayee and Rishi Kumar Koshal with other leaders at Jammu in 1952

Leaders of the Praja Parishad gathered for satyagraha *in 1953*

People waiting for message from Pt. Prem Nath Dogra under the national flag for satyagraha *in 1953*

Youth activists of the Praja Parishad on satyagraha *at Udhampur*

Photograph of the Praja Parishad satyagraha

Activists of the Akhnoor satyagraha—*Lala Ram Saroop Gupta, Pt. Bachitru Ram, Bava Durga Dass, etc.*

Women supporters of the Praja Parishad sitting on satyagraha

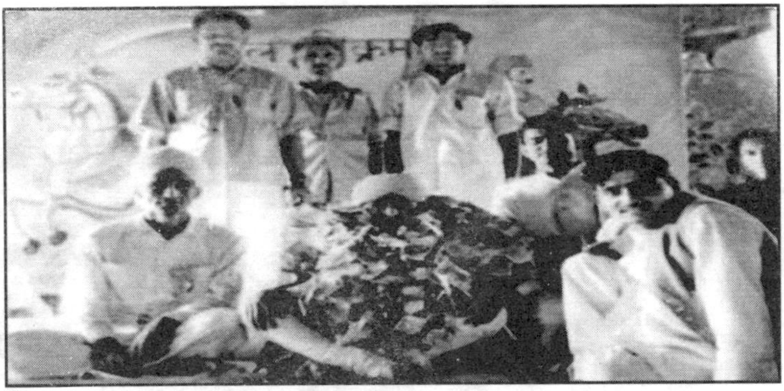

Warm welcome to Pt. Prem Nath Dogra at Hiranagar

Jammu & Kashmir currency in Samvat *1934*

Guruji and Maharaja Hari Singh at Srinagar in 1947 before accession

Atalji with Sheikh Abdullah

Rajju Bhaiya at Jammu

Atalji with Praja Parishad activists at Jammu after the death of Dr. Syama Prasad Mookerjee

Balraj Madhok, Atalji, Rajmata Vijaya Raje Scindia

Dr. Syama Prasad Mookerjee with Nehru and other national leaders

Leaders of the Praja Parishad and Jana Sangh after meeting

Balraj Madhok with Atalji

All India Jana Sangh president, Panditji sitting with Dev Prasad Ghoshe and Rama Rau (All India president of Jana Sangh) and Deendayal Upadhyay a (general secretory) in 1954 at Jammu

Dr. Mookerjee with other leaders before entering Jammu & Kashmir

Mother and father of Guruji with Pt. Prem Nath Dogra, Bhagwat Saroop, Sham Lal Sharma, Narsingh Dass, Sudesh Gupta and other Swayamsevaks on their visit to Mata Vaishno Devi in the late forties

Dr. Syama Prasad with Sheikh Abdullah and Bakshi Ghulam Mohammad in Srinagar on 10th May, 1952.
At present, one of the party leaders of the BJP resides in the same house where Dr. Syama Prasad Mookerjee is seen interacting with Sheikh Abdullah and Bakshi Ghulam Mohammad

Rare photo of senior leaders, including Atalji

जनसंघ के पूर्व अध्यक्षगण डी.पी. घोष, प्रेमनाथ डोगरा, पीतांबर दास, बलराज मधोक एवं दीनदयाल उपाध्याय सहित आए प्रचारकगण कुशाबाऊ ठाकरे, केदारनाथ साहनी, के.आर. मलकानी, नानाजी देशमुख, सुंदर सिंह भंडारी, जगन्नाथराव जोशी, दत्तोपंत ठेंगड़ी एवं जगदीश माथुर

L.K. Advaniji, Dhan Raj Balgotra, Krishan Lal Sharma, Amar Nath Bhanda along with local leaders at Jammu

Senior BJP leader, Shiv Charan Gupta discussing a point with Venkaiah Naidu at a BJP rally at Zenana Park, Jammu

Pandit Prem Nath Dogra welcomes Guruji

Pramod Mahajan addressing a gathering at Jammu

Dattopant Thengadi at Jammu

Atalji with Pt. Deendayal Upadhyay at Jammu

Statue of Dr. Mookerjee at Lakhanpur where L.K. Advani, Mohan Bhagwat, Nitin Gadkari along with other national leaders are seen

Panditji with Megh Raj Bali and Muslim leaders at Rajouri

Kusha Bhau Thakre at the Jammu Press Conference with local leaders

Atalji, L.K. Advani with Jammu leaders at lunch

Mata Vijaya Raje Scindia delivering her address at a mega rally of the Hindu Sammelan in Jammu

Pandit Prem Nath Dogra at a public meeting at Akhnoor

Panditji touring a village area in 1952

Madhukar Dattatreya Deorasji (third RSS chief)
at the residence of Sham Sunder Bhatia in Jammu

Pt. Prem Nath Dogra, Pt. Deendayal Upadhyay and Rishi Kumar Koushal at a Press Conference in Jammu

L.K. Advani with Atalji at his residence

Atalji with Rajnath Singh

जमीन पर बैठकर नेताओं के भाषण ध्यान से सुननेवाला ये महान् व्यक्ति आज इस महान् देश का प्रधानमंत्री है

Murli Manohar Joshi, Narendra Modi and Chaman Lal hositing flag at Lal Chowk, Srinagar on 26th January, 1992

L.K. Advani inaugurating Sindhu Darshan at Leh, 2003

Atal Bihari Vajpayee in Jammu

L.K. Advani, Kedar Nath Sahani, Vashnavi, Bhagwat Swaroop along with local leaders

Sikander Bakht with Prof. Chaman Lal Gupta

Narendra Modi with Sunder Singh Bhandari

Dr. Syama Prasad Mookerjee's last picture in Jammu, saying, 'Bharat Mata ki jai'

Dr. Mookerjee and his two companions imprisoned in a small cottage near Nishat Garden and which is designated as sub-jail. The sub-jail is not equipped with any facilities, not even a telephone

Speeches of Nationalist Leaders on the Praja Parishad Agitation

SPEECH OF N.C. CHATTERJEE, M.P.

In the House of the People on Kashmir issue on 26th June, 1952:

Mr. Speaker,

Sir, until now India had placed herself under a self-denying ordinance with regard to Kashmir. There was a general feeling of reluctance to say anything which might help Pakistan in its anti-Indian propaganda. But, sir, unfortunately, some of the recent speeches of Sheikh Abdullah as the Chief Minister of the state of Jammu & Kashmir compel us to speak out our mind; especially the resolutions passed by the Kashmir Constituent Assembly compel us to review the constitutional position and both the Government of India and the House of the People should address themselves seriously to the situation which is now facing us.

BIGGEST BUNGLING

Mr. Alam Campbell Johnson has said in his book, *Mission with Mountbatten*, that when Sheikh Abdullah was nominated to represent India at Lake Success, there was uneasiness in high quarters because he was known as a 'flamboyant personality' and when a flamboyant personality makes flamboyant speeches, difficulty comes into being. Sir, we maintain that our government has bungled badly over the Kashmir issue. *The biggest bungling was to refer the Kashmir problem to the UNO.* The big leaders were afraid and succumbed to the machinations of the imperialists, who were supposed to be friends of India. The sooner we get out of the UNO and withdraw this problem, the better for India and for Kashmir. *The second bungling, sir, was the 'ceasefire' order*. While the valiant army had reached Kashmir and was chasing the marauders and aggressors who were helped by Pakistan and the whole territory was going to be cleared by our valiant soldiers, this unfortunate 'ceasefire' order went. The result is that Kashmir territory, which is under the law, under the constitution and by all cannons of morality and justice, Indian territory, one-third of it—more than that—is today occupied by these illegal tresspassers, who are still sticking to it and we are passive spectators and cannot do anything.

The third bungling, sir, to my mind, the most tragic thing which happened in Indian history, *was this offer of a plebiscite*, which should never have been given. I maintain and I say with all earnestness that under the law, under the constitution, accession to the Dominion of India under Section 6 of the Government of India Act, as amended after the Indian Independence Act, was final and irrevocable, and there ought not to have been any question of plebiscite. *This tragic offer of plebiscite led to all this result and we are faced today with a serious situation*. Indian blood had been shed on the Valley of Kashmir, 150 crores of rupees of the Indian taxpayer's money has been spent there and more will have to be spent there and yet we are not out of the woods. Not only that, sir, this is responsible for the uncertain situation and for the pandering of communalism which the government of Kashmir is today doing. Look at it. Sheikh Abdullah says: 'How can I face the Kashmiri Muslim?' That is an astonishing statement! What about the poor Hindus of J&K? What about the people of Jammu?

Ghulam Qader (Jammu & Kashmir): *"Kashmir me* communalism *hai, uska aap ke pass kya sabut hai?"*

ACCESSION FINAL; IRREVOCABLE

N.C. Chatterjee: Sir, I hope I will go on uninterrupted. My hon'ble friend will have his turn. Sir, we expected a different stand from Sheikh Abdullah. He has gone to talk like this because of this offer of plebiscite, which ought not to have been given. *I maintain that the accession is final and irrevocable.* Under our constitution too, Kashmir is an integral part of India. Under Article 1, the Union consists of a federation of states and it is a Part 'B' state. There cannot be any going back on that. But the unfortunate thing is that the Constituent Assembly is doing something there which is against the spirit of our constitution. I know my hon'ble and learned friend, Dr. Katju, will point to me Article 370 of the constitution. Article 370 itself says, sir, that "for the purposes of this Article, the government of the state means the person for the time being recognised by the President as the Maharaja of Jammu & Kashmir acting on the advice of the Council of Ministers for the time being in office under the Maharaja's proclamation, sir, before me. It was read out to the Constituent Assembly of India by the Hon'ble Mr. Gopalaswami Ayyangar on the 17th October, 1949. That proclamation signed by the Maharaja said as follows:

I hereby ordain as follows:

'My Council of Ministers shall consist of the Prime Minister and such other ministers as may be appointed on the advice of the Prime Minister. I have by royal warrant appointed Sheikh Mohammad Abdullah as the Prime Minister with effect from the 1st day of March, 1948.'

Then, Mr. Gopalaswami Ayyangar pointed out that the proclamation set out another sentence as follows: 'The Prime Minister and other ministers would function as a Cabinet and act on the principle of joint responsibility.'

A TRAVESTY OF FACTS

'Sir, I maintain it is absolutely a travesty of facts to say that they have achieved a wonderful thing—this wonderful Constituent Assembly of Kashmir—by abolishing despotism, or tyranny or any unconstitutional rule of a tyrant who was sitting on the throne as the Maharaja. Immediately, this proclamation was promulgated by the Maharaja and Article 370 of the constitution came into operation. The Maharaja of Kashmir was nothing but a constitutional ruler just as the other *Rajpramukhs* are, and *it is absolutely wrong to say that they are going to remove or liquidate the Maharaja and a triumphant progress in democracy is being achieved in that wonderful state of Jammu & Kashmir*. But, sir what about Article 366? I would request my learned friend, Dr. Katju to remember Article 366. It is not in Part XXI, not in the chapter dealing with temporary and transitional provisions. In clause (21) of Article 366, there is a definition of *'Rajpramukh'*; it says as follows:

'Rajpramukh' means:

a. In relation to the state of Hyderabad the person who for the time being is recognised by the President as the Nizam of Hyderabad.
b. In relation to the state of Jammu & Kashmir or the state of Mysore, the person, who for the time being is recognised by the President as the Maharaja of that state.'

SOVEREIGNTY OF PARLIAMENT

Now this is our Constitution. I am not for any particular Raja or Maharaja. I am not one of those who would support any vestige of feudalism in the Republic of India. But this is our constitution and the Constituent Assembly of J&K must recognise the sovereignty of the Indian Parliament, the sovereignty of the Indian Republic and that this constitution is the paramount and organic law which it cannot transgress. Here, you place the Nizam of Hyderabad on the same footing as the Maharaja of Kashmir and the Maharaja of Mysore. You have made all of them constitutional rulers, constitutional Heads of States. What right has this Constituent Assembly to drive this kind of wedge in the constitution and declare by its unilateral action that it will liquidate the rule of the Maharaja? This cannot be. I say with respect, dealt with by Sheikh Abdullah or by Pandit Jawaharlal Nehru, this must be done by bilateral action, if at all, by amendment of the Constitution. Therefore, this must be done by this Parliament functioning as the supreme sovereign authority.

First of all, I maintain that they must recognise the sovereignty of the Indian Parliament. They must recognise that the constitution is the paramount law which the Constituent Assembly of Kashmir cannot transgress. They cannot infringe its letter and they cannot infringe its spirit; they must act within the framework of the constitution. If Sheikh Abdullah cannot be brought to his senses, if he stands for a republic, have you heard of a republic within a republic? If we allow this to be done, tomorrow the Constituent Assembly of Kashmir may say, "We shall cease to be Part 'B' state." They cannot do that, I maintain under this constitution. Day after tomorrow they will come and say: 'We shall not accede to India even in three matters—defence, communications and external affairs.' I maintain that cannot be done as that would be an outage on our Constitution.

A DANGEROUS PRECEDENT

Once you allow this constitution to be tampered with in that manner, you will be setting a dangerous precedent. It will have serious repercussions on the other states and their constitutional position would be affected. We have got to reflect on this. If this Parliament or the Prime Minister of India, or the Government of India cannot induce the Constituent Assembly or Sheikh Abdullah to come to their senses, if they are determined to say, "We shall have a separate flag of our own; we shall have an elected head as president; we are not going to recognise Article 366 or the other provisions of the Constitution", it would mean an abridgement of the powers of this Parliament. Sir, by this constitution—I have not got the time, otherwise I could read it out to you—there is a definite legislative abridgement of the power of this Parliament to liquidate the rulers. There is a provision that even this Parliament, in exercise of its legislative powers, cannot legislate to liquidate the rulers, nor can any legislature of a state exercise this power to the detriment of the guarantees given by the government in Instrument of Accession. By certain solemn documents, guarantees and assurances have been given to the rulers of Indian states, and we will have to implement those pledges. Will you, as Members of this Parliament, allow this government, with whose support Sheikh Abdullah and his ministry are operating, to do anything to infringe the spirit of this constitution, to do something against this constitution? They cannot do it. But if they cannot induce the Constituent Assembly to give up its stand of having a republic within a republic of having a separate flag of its own, and if the Constituent Assembly is determined to say, "We shall not fully accede to India, and we will not allow the people of Jammu to have their legitimate expression of self-determination and complete accession to India", then sir, I submit that the representatives of Jammu & Kashmir should not be allowed to participate in any discussion or in any voting in this House, excepting in respect of these three subjects of defence, communications and external affairs. What right have they to participate in our internal affairs?

THE INCONGRUITY

Sir, I remember in the Irish debates in the British House of Commons, when Ireland was acceding under the Home Rule Bill of Gladstone, only in respect of certain subjects like defence and external affairs, it was made clear that no Irish members could sit in the House and vote on other subjects. Sir, there is an incongruity that should be faced. I am reading to you a very thoughtful address by Mr. Kodanda Rao, a distinguished member of the Servants of India Society. He has written: "If the Maharaja's Dogra administration had its black spots, the Nizam's Razakar government had blacker spots. India had to fight to save Kashmir from outside hostiles, the raiders and Pakistan. India had to fight Hyderabad to save it from internal hostiles, the Nizam and his Razakars. Indeed, if the Maharaja deserved to be deposed, the Nizam deserved it infinitely more. And yet the Maharaja has been deposed while the Nizam has been made the *Rajpramukh*. While the Government of India has been chivalrous towards the hostile Nizam who defied them, they have been mean towards the friendly Maharaja who sought their protection."

Sir, he is a man who weighs his words. The language is strong, but I maintain it is a fair description of the position. How will you face the country and say that you will keep the Nizam in office as *Rajpramukh* under the Article 366, clause (21), and tolerate this unilateral action of Sheikh Abdullah and his Constituent Assembly to liquidate the hereditary ruler of Kashmir? You cannot do it under the constitution and it should not be left to any powerful personality here. It ought to be thrashed out. But if they do it, I maintain that their representatives should not be allowed to function here in this Parliament, discussing and participating in all votes for grants on every possible and impossible matter relating to the internal administration of India. That would be most improper, and that should not be tolerated.

DON'T TAMPER WITH THE CONSTITUTION

Lastly, sir, I would say that this flag question cannot be brushed aside. I know Sheikh Abdullah has been delivering speeches in diverse degrees of warmth and eloquence to suit different occasions. The latest Eid broadcast has toned down his previous somewhat indiscreet utterances. We are thankful for it.

But, sir, are you going to allow any state to have a separate flag of its own? Is it not an expression of hostility towards the Union, towards our flag, towards our sacred flag which is the emblem of India's sovereignty? Are you going to tolerate that? And would you allow all other states to have separate flags of their own? The Constitution of India says that there shall be one elected President and none else who will be the Head of the State. The other constituent federating units will have nominated heads, either as *Rajpramukh* or as Governor. Nobody else will be the elected head of India or her constituent units. Will you allow Kashmir to go its own way in defiance of the letter of the constitution, in defiance of the fundamental scheme of our constitution? I hope that will not be allowed to be done. Sir, this thing should be made clear, that it is not a question of the liquidation of a despotic monarchy. It had already been liquidated, finally liquidated. There is no question that a Tudor tyranny or Stuart despotism is being wiped out by the sagacious wisdom of somebody in Kashmir. It has already been done. It is a closed chapter. Sir, my appeal to the Prime Minister and to Dr. Katju is: do not allow this constitution to be tampered with or whittled down. Do not allow these disruptive forces to operate by saying they will have a separate flag or that they will not have parity with other Part 'B' states or that they will have their own elected President. It is a dangerous innovation. You should not tolerate that. That would not be showing true allegiance to India. What is our predicament? India has spent Rs. 150 crores and more and Indian blood has been shed in the Valley of Kashmir. That has been done, but we do not want this kind of treatment in return. Then, we shall have to say: "*Ingratitude, thy name is Kashmir*." That should not be tolerated. That should be put a stop to. Our Prime Minister and our Minister of States should be firm in dealing with this kind of encroachment, which is an outrage on our constitution, which is an outrage on the cherished document, which is the supreme organic law of the country.

DR. SYAMA PRASAD MOOKERJEE, LOK SABHA DEBATE, 7TH AUGUST, 1952

THE KASHMIR ISSUE

I agree with the Prime Minister that the matter of Kashmir is a highly complicated one and each one of us, whatever may be our point of view, must approach this problem from a constructive stand-point. I cannot share the view that we are creating a new heaven and a new earth by accepting the scheme which has been placed before the House on the motion of the Prime Minister. The question can be divided into two parts—one relates to the international complications arising out of Kashmir and the other relates to the arrangements that have to be made between Kashmir and ourselves regarding the future constitution of Kashmir.

It has been said that I was a party when the decision was taken to refer the Kashmir issue to the UNO. That is an obvious fact. I have no right and I do not wish to disclose the extraordinary circumstances under which that decision was taken and the great expectations which the Government of India had on that occasion, but it is a matter of common knowledge that we have not got fair treatment from the United Nations as we had expected. We did not go to the UNO with regard to the question of accession, because accession then was an established fact. We went there for the purpose of getting a quick decision from the UNO regarding the raids which were then taking place by persons behind whom there was the Pakistan government. The raiders merely acted on behalf of somebody else. So now, we should withdraw ourselves, so far as consideration of the Kashmir case is concerned, from the UNO. We can tell them respectfully that we have had enough of the UNO and let us now consider and try to settle the matter through our own efforts. I am not suggesting that India should withdraw from the UNO. The only matter regarding which the dispute still persists is the occupation by the enemy. The Prime Minister said today that that portion is there. It is a matter for national humiliation. We say that Kashmir is a part of India. It is so. So, a part of India is today in the occupation of the enemy and we are helpless. We are peace-lovers, no doubt, but are peace-lovers to be occupied by the enemy? Of course the Prime Minister said: thus far and no further. If the raiders enter into any part of Kashmir, there will be war on a bigger scale between India and Pakistan.

Is there any possibility of our getting back this territory? We shall not get it through the efforts of the United Nations; we shall not get it through peaceful methods; by negotiations with Pakistan. That means we lose it, unless we use force and the Prime Minister is unwilling to do so. Let us face facts: are we prepared to lose it?

It has been said that there is some provision in the constitution that we are bound by the pledges which have been given. Pledges? Undoubtedly, so many pledges we have given. We gave a pledge to Hyderabad. Did we not say that there would be a Constituent Assembly for Hyderabad? It was to be decided by the Legislative Assembly of Hyderabad. But is not Hyderabad already a part of the Indian Union? We gave pledges also to those princes whom we are liquidating in different forums today. If we talk of pledges, we have given one to minorities in East Bengal. That was given after the attainment of Independence. The Prime Minister said the other day that even if Kashmir had not acceded in India, when Kashmir was attacked by the raiders on humanitarian grounds, the Indian Army could have marched to Kashmir and protected the distressed and oppressed. I felt proud. But if I make a similar statement, or even a similar suggestion for the purpose of brethren and sisters, through whose sacrifices, to some extent at least, freedom has been achieved, I am a communalist, I am a reactionary, I am a war-monger! Pledges? Undoubtedly pledges have been given. I am also anxious that pledges should be respected and honoured. What was the nature of the pledges? We did not give any new pledge to Kashmir. Let us be clear about it.

What was the set-up we accepted when the British withdrew from India? There was the Indian India divided into India and Pakistan and there was, if I may call it, the princely India. Every one of those 500 rulers got theoretical independence and they need have acceded to India only with relation to three subjects. So far as the rest were concerned, it was purely voluntary. That was the pattern which we accepted from the British Government. So far as the 498 states were concerned, they came to India, acceded to India on 14th August, 1947 in relation to three subjects only, but still it was accession, full accession. Later on, they all came in relation to all these subjects and were gradually absorbed in the Constitution of India that we have passed. Supposing some sort of fulfilment of the pledge that we are thinking of so literally in relation to Kashmir, was demanded by these states, would we have agreed to give that? We would not have, because that would have destroyed India. But there was a different approach to the solution of those problems. They were made to feel that in the interest of India, in their interest, in the interest of mutual progress, they will have to accept this constitution. We made elaborate provisions for nationally absorbing them into its fabric. No coercion; no compulsion. They were made to feel that they could get what they wanted from this constitution.

May I ask: Was not Sheikh Abdullah a party to this constitution? He was a member of the Constituent Assembly, but he is asking for special treatment. Did he not agree to accept this constitution in relation to the rest of India, including 497 states. If it is good enough for all of them, why should it not be good enough for him in Kashmir?

We are referred to the provision in the constitution. The member from Bihar said there was going to be compulsion; that we are going to hold a pistol at the head of Jammu & Kashmir saying that they must accept our terms. I have said nothing of the kind. How can we say that? What is the provision we have made in the constitution? Article 373: read it and read the speech of Gopalaswami Ayyangar when he moved the adoption of that extraordinary provision. What was the position then? All the other states had come into the picture. Kashmir could not because of special reasons. They were: first the matter was in the hands of the Security Council; secondly, there was war; thirdly, a portion of Kashmir territory was in the hands of the enemy and lastly, an assurance had allowed the state to be formed and the wishes of the people of Kashmir ascertained through a plebiscite. Those were the factors that had yet to be fulfilled and that was why a permanent decision could not be taken. It was a temporary provision.

He said categorically that he and also the Kashmir government hoped that Jammu & Kashmir would accede to India just as any other state has done and accept the provision of the constitution. It is not a question of compulsion on our part. The Constitution of India does not say that whatever the Constitution Assembly of Jammu & Kashmir would ask for India would give. That is not the provision. The provision is: agreement, consent.

Certain proposals have been made today. Some of us do not like them. What are we to do? If we talk, we are reactionaries, we are communalists, we are enemies. If we keep quiet and if a catastrophe comes after a year, then, you were a party to it, you kept quiet; therefore, you are stopped from saying anything.

I am most anxious, as anxious as anybody else that we should have an honourable, peaceful settlement with Kashmir.

I realise the great experiment which is being made on the soil of Kashmir. Partition did not help anybody. I come from an area where sufferings are continuous; they are going on. We feel every day, every hour, the tragic efforts of Partition, the tragic possibilities of approaching this national problem from a narrow, communal and sectarian point of view. Why did we not utter a single word against the policy of Sheikh Abdullah so long? I could have spoken. I came out of this government two-and-a half years ago. On the other hand, I supported, whatever I spoke publicly, the policy of the Kashmir government. I said that this was a great experiment which was going on and we have to keep quiet and see that the experiment is made a success. We must be able to show that India is not only in theory, but also in fact, a country where Hindus, Muslims, Christians and everyone will be able to live without fear and with equality of rights. That is the constitution that we have framed and which we propose to apply rigorously and scrupulously. There may be some demands to the contrary here and there, but do not regard that. Whenever an attack is made on certain matters of policy, some narrow, sectarian, communal motive is promoting us. Rather, it is the fear that history may repeat itself. It is the fear that what you are going to do may lead to the 'Balkanisation' of India, may lead to the strengthening of the hands of those who do not want to see a strong and united India; may lead to the strengthening of those who do not believe that India is a nation but is a combination of separate nationalities. That is the danger.

Now, what is it that Sheikh Abdullah has asked for? He has asked for certain changes to be made in the Constitution. Let us proceed coolly, cautiously, without any heat or excitement. Let us examine each of them and ask him and ask ourselves: if we make an allowance in respect of these matters, do we hurt India, do we strengthen Kashmir? That will be my approach. I shall not say anything blindly because it transgresses some provisions of this book, the *Constitution of India*. I would not do so. I would have liked the Prime Minister to have sent for some of us in the Opposition when Sheikh Abdullah was here. He faces us today with his decisions. I do not like these public discussions because I know their repercussions may not be desirable in some quarters. He might not have accepted our suggestions, but I would have liked to have met him–those of us who differ from the Prime Minister's attitude on this question. I met him at a private meeting and we had a full and frank discussion. But we would have liked to have met Sheikh Abdullah and others in a friendly way and explained our point of view to them. We want to come to an agreement: an agreement which will make it possible for India to retain her unity and Kashmir to retain her separate existence from Pakistan and be merged with India.

Since when did the trouble start? Let us look at it dispassionately. Since Sheikh Abdullah's return from Paris some time ago, statements started to be made by him which disturbed us. Even then we did not speak out. His first statement that he made in an interview which he gave when he was abroad about his vision of an independent Kashmir, and then when he came, he amplified it. Then the speeches which he has made during the last few months were of a disturbing character. If he feels that his safety lies in remaining out of India, well, let him say so. We will be sorry for it, but it may become inevitable. But if he feels honestly otherwise, as I have always hoped and wished, then certainly it is for him also to explain why he wants these alterations to be made.

...Sheikh Abdullah spoke in the Constituent Assembly of Kashmir about three or four months ago–words which have not been withdrawn, but words which created a good deal of affiliations. I do not know whether the Prime Minister saw this: "We are a hundred per cent sovereign body. No country can put spokes in the wheel of our progress. Neither the Indian Parliament nor any other Parliament outside the state has any jurisdiction over our state."

It is an ominous statement. I shall make an offer to the Prime Minister and to Sheikh Abdullah. I shall give my full, whole-hearted support to the scheme as an interim measure... The Prime Minister said today that nothing is final. It cannot be final because things have to be discussed in their various details. But even then, I am prepared to give my support. Let two conditions be fulfilled.

Let Sheikh Abdullah declare that he accepts the sovereignty of this Parliament. There cannot be two sovereign Parliaments in

India. You talk of Kashmir being a part of India, and Sheikh Abdullah talks of a sovereign Parliament for Kashmir. It is inconsistent. It is contradictory. This Parliament does not mean a few of us here who are opposing this. This Parliament includes a majority of people who will not be swayed by any small considerations. And why should he be afraid of accepting the sovereignty of this Parliament of free India?

Secondly, it is not a matter of changing the provisions of the constitution by the President's order. Let us look at some of the changes which are being sought for. We are supporters of the Maharaja! That is what is said against us. I have never met the Maharaja. I do not know him personally. We are not supporters of this Maharaja, or of any Maharaja as such. But the Maharaja is there not by his own free will. The Parliament of India, the constitution has made him what he is, namely the constitutional head of Jammu & Kashmir. And what is the irony? At present Sheikh Abdullah's government is responsible to one who is being described as a wretched fellow, who has to be turned out lock, stock and barrel. The Maharaja is there as a constitutional head. If you feel that this should be taken out, change your constitution. Say that there will be no hereditary *Rajpramukhs*. It is a matter worthy of consideration. Let us consider it. But see the way in which it has been put: a Hindu Maharaja is being removed. That is one of the war cries in Pakistan. But who finished the royal powers of Hindu Maharajas? Not Sheikh Abdullah, but the constitution of free India. We did it. We said that no ruler would have any extraordinary powers, that he will be just head of the government which may be technically responsible to him but later on, responsible to an elected legislature. But now great credit is being taken that a unique performance is being done in Kashmir. In every speech of his he gave: the Maharaja, the Dogra *raj* is being finished. Is that propaganda? Is that necessary? You are flogging a dead horse. It is finished. What is the use of saying it?

What about the elected Governor? I have got here the proceedings of the Constituent Assembly. The Prime Minister will remember that in our own constitution we at first made a provision for an elected Governor, and then later on Sardar Patel and the Prime Minister and others felt that in the democratic set-up that we contemplated, an elected Governor had no place. Read the speech. It was stated that the Governor will be there to act as the representative of the President and if the Governor is elected by the people or the legislature and the Chief Minister also will be elected: as such, there is every likelihood of a clash; then again, the Governor will be a petty man. And the Prime Minister pointed out all these considerations and claimed that there was a very special reason why, in order to retain the unity of India and contact between the Centre and all the states, the Governor should be nominated by the President. You just ignore these basic points because Sheikh Abdullah says, "I want an elected head now." Why can you not tell him and others what you have done in the constitution—that organisationally we provided for an elected Governor but after a good deal of thought we did away with that? Even then, I say that today in your wisdom you feel that an elected head is a necessity and it will help you consider it. Bring it up as a specific proposal. Let us discuss the pros and cons of it but suddenly my friend Mr. Hiren Mukerjee says, "People are calling for an elected head." People are clamouring for an elected head everywhere. Are you going to have elected heads everywhere? In fact, as things are happening we may abolish Governors altogether. Governorships are often reserved for various classes of persons—disappointed, defeated, rejected, wanted to be ministers and so forth. We need not have this class at all. Or, if you want to have them, have them; I am not particularly interested, but this is a change for which no justification is given.

And then the flag. The flag has a significance; it will not do for the Prime Minister to say that it is a matter of sentiment. It was announced in the papers three days ago that the Indian flag will fly only on two ceremonial occasions and otherwise the state flag alone will fly there. If you feel that the unity and integrity of India are not affected and it will not lead to fissiparous tendencies being generated, accept it and do it for all. But why do it as a matter of surrender to Sheikh Abdullah's demand?

He wanted to call himself the Prime Minister. That is how he first started. Some of us did not like it. We know one Prime Minister of India, including Kashmir, and that is the Prime Minister who is sitting here. How can you have two Prime Ministers, one Prime Minister in Delhi and another Prime Minister in Srinagar, who will not call himself the Chief Minister, but a Prime Minister? At first I thought it was a small matter and we should not look at it but see how the process is developing: some sort of special treatment at every step and he must be treated in a very different way. Look at the citizenship rights and fundamental rights. What is it that we are doing? Has the House considered it? Has the House discussed the pros and cons of the recommendations which have been made? You are changing without giving much thought to the provisions of the constitution regarding citizenship. It was said that rich people are rushing to Kashmir and purchasing property. As the Prime Minister mentioned in his statement in Article 19(5) there is a provision. We discussed this Article threadbare when we framed the constitution. There were attempts made by various provinces and they wanted to have some special protection against unauthorised purchases of land on a large scale. What is it that we have said? We have said that any State Legislature may pass a law, imposing reasonable restrictions regarding acquisition of property or movement from one state to another in the public interest or in the interest of Scheduled Castes and Scheduled Tribes. If Sheikh Abdullah feels that in Kashmir some special restriction should be done, the clause is there. I would like to ask the Prime Minister categorically about this. He has not mentioned it. He has skipped over it. Is it intended that the restrictions which the Kashmir Assembly will impose will be in accordance with its exception or is it proposed to give it something more? There are four classes of citizens. I have got the details, but I have not the time to go through them. But those were done in the time of the much cursed Maharaja. Are they to be maintained or are they going to abolish the four different categories of citizenship? I am reminded of a story which was written by Lord Curzon in a book. A distinguished nobleman from England went to the court of Shah of Persia, 50 or 60 years ago, accompanied by his wife. Both of them were presented and the Shah was a bit inattentive and the secretary asked: "What should be the honour done to the lady?" There were three different categories of Order of Chastity and the award was made 'Order of Chastity—class three'. That is how the order came out and then it was realised that something had been done which was of a staggering character, and of course, amends were made after the damage was done. Four classes of citizenship in Jammu & Kashmir? What for? They should be abolished. There should be only one class of citizenship. Would Indians take all your property? It was not suggested that Indians should go and purchase property as they liked. Supposing some Indian comes and purchases some property, you may have legislative measures. We have accepted it. What is the fear? We have a Kashmiri Prime Minister of India We have a Kashmiri Home Minister of India. We are happy in India. We do not mind it. We welcome them. What is the fear? Is it feared that Indians will go and invade Kashmir and one of them will become the Chief Minister of Jammu & Kashmir? We are not going to raid Jammu & Kashmir. I have never visited this beautiful part. I would like to go and stay there for some time. I have not got the money to purchase a house. In any case, I would like to go there. This is what you have in regard to fundamental rights. You are having new changes there which are very difficult to justify. The Prime Minister mentioned two or three things–scholarships and services, etc. What is this, etc.? And why services? In services, do you want to make a difference between one citizen and another? Even there, as you know, in our constitution, Parliament and Parliament alone has the right to make special provision regarding entrance to services for those who have to be protected. Now there are similar demands made in the south. I have been going through their demands during the last few weeks. They also feel perturbed by the strict operation of some of these provisions. When you throw open the doors to them, they also will want similar protection.

There is another thing to which Prime Minister has not referred. I was really amazed to find how a special provision could be made. As you know, two lakhs of people have gone away to Pakistan. There is a provision that a special law will be incorporated to get these people back to Kashmir. War is still going on. On the one hand, fundamental rights regarding civil liberty are proposed to be made more strict and on the other, you are going to throw open the door and allow Pakistanis to go to Kashmir. For this, there is to be a special law and there is a special agreement. Why this anxiety on the part of Sheikh Abdullah to make a special provision for getting back those who ran away to Pakistan and who are not prepared to come? Is there any point in it? How will it affect security? Those who have been killed cannot go back. Those who are alive can come back tomorrow if they honestly believe in India and if they really want to live in Jammu, they must be tested. Let them come back. No special provision is needed for it. So far as Jammu is concerned, as you know, it was a most tragic state. It was done by both sides. There were Muslims who were bitter and there were Hindus who were bitter. That was a dark period when many parts of India were like that, but today, what is the position? You have allowed how many thousands, I forgot the number. They have come away from Jammu & Kashmir and are a burden on India. Why should not there be a special provision here in the agreement that promptly they will be taken back to Jammu & Kashmir?

There are several thousands of them who have come. Why are they not going back? I do not know how many *pandits* have come away from Kashmir. They also must go back to Kashmir. So far as the other portion is concerned, that also is a serious matter. In the one-third portion of Jammu & Kashmir which is now under Pakistani occupation, nearly one lakh Hindus and Sikhs have come and taken shelter, within the Kashmir territory. What will happen to them? They will have to be taken care of. You are thinking of those who have become Pakistanis for the time being. You will reconvert them and reconfirm on them the status of Kashmiri citizen but those unfortunate beings who today have taken shelter, how will they be given accommodation? Is there land enough for them? These are matters which had not received any attention.

As regards the emergency provision, it is an amazing stand.

If there is an emergency on account of internal disturbance, the President of India will not have the last say. Why this fear of the President of India? Can you contemplate a more gratuitous insult to the President of India? Here the Kashmir government must conform to the constitution. Why should they request if there is an internal disturbance which is the creation of their own misdeeds?

Why should they request you if, for instance, they are in league with others from the other side, China or Russia, through our other friends? Why should they come and request you for your interference? I would expect the Prime Minister to tell whether the other emergency provisions apply or not. As you know, there are two other very important emergency provisions in the constitution. Article 354 relates to application of provisions relating to distribution of revenues while a proclamation of emergency is in operation and the other Article is 356, relating to provisions in case of failure of constitutional machinery in states. Has Sheikh Abdullah accepted the application of Article 356 or has he accepted the more important provision contained in Article 360–provisions as to financial emergency? Has he accepted that provision? The Prime Minister does not make any reference to it. The Supreme Court's jurisdiction also has not yet been accepted.

I shall conclude by making this constructive suggestion. These comments which I made, naturally I had to make without commenting in detail on the reactions of Sheikh Abdullah. He wrote to me and said that he would like to meet me when he was in Delhi last time. I was not here on that day. So I could not meet him. I sent him a friendly reply. Perhaps I would meet him some time. It is not a question of his meeting me or I meeting him. I submit that we must proceed according to certain standards. First of all, there is no question of the President by virtue of his power to make orders altering the provisions of the constitution in material respect.

If the Prime Minister feels that a case has been made out for re-examination of certain important provisions, for instance, land, if you feel that and should be taken without payment of compensation, provide for it in the constitution. You consider all these items and make your provisions so elastic that you can apply them either to the whole of India or you can apply them to only such parts where this Parliament of India will feel that such special treatment is necessary. Proceed in accordance with a constitutional matter, do not just play with the constitution. It is a sacred document, and it is a document on which much labour and much thought were bestowed. If you feel some changes are necessary in order to take into consideration the new set-up that is slowly developing in India, whether in Kashmir or other parts of India, by all means let the people of the country have a chance to express their opinion.

Lastly, a charge was levelled that some of us have advocated separate consideration of Jammu and Ladakh. I would assure you and the House that I do not want that Jammu & Kashmir should be partitioned. I know the horrors of Partition. I know the results which may occur if Partition comes. But the responsibility for preventing Partition will rest on those who are today the masters of Jammu & Kashmir and are not prepared to adopt the Constitution of India. What is the crime if today the people of Jammu claim that they should be treated separately, in the sense that they should be allowed to join fully with India? Mark it, it is not a question of running away from India if they say that they would like to accept in toto the Constitution of free India. Is there any crime that they then commit? I am not suggesting that you partition Jammu & Kashmir I am not suggesting that you send Kashmir or Kashmir Valley out of India, and it is not for me or for us sitting in this House to decide this matter. As the Prime Minister pointed out very rightly that the people of that territory will have to decide. Now suppose the people of Jammu and Ladakh feel that either it should be full accession in relation to the whole of Jammu & Kashmir, or if that is not acceptable to Sheikh Abdullah, then, at least these two provinces, the two separate entitles could be justified historically or otherwise, that they should be allowed to join with India. Let Kashmir continue in any way that it pleases—even with more autonomy, with less possibility of interference by India. That is a possibility which we cannot rule out. I hope that this question will be considered in its full possible implications.

My friend from Kashmir, Maulana Masuodi, for whom I have very great regard—I tried to follow his speech this morning referred to Jammu, the last question which I would answer. Well, If the demand is made by Jammu. He said Jammu is a province which in 1941 had a Muslim-majority. He said that, but did not complete the story. Undoubtedly it was a Muslim-majority province in 1941, but had became a Muslim majority including those districts which have now fallen into the Pakistani-occupied area. So, if you exclude those areas—I am not saying surrender to them—I am very glad he has put the question. The Prime Minister says that the area will not be re-occupied, but it is a different question. You are not going to re-occupy it, and it is not possible. In any case those people have worked against Jammu & Kashmir. They became, as has been repeatedly said, more friendly to Pakistan than to India. If you take the 1951 Census figures—the figures have not been published, but it is on the basis of the territory that is under our occupation—75 per cent of the population of Jammu will be Hindus. But I am not proceeding on the basis of Hindus and Muslims. Let me make it clear, I am proceeding on the basis of the will of the people to come to India either in whole or in part. If these two provinces, Ladakh and Jammu, say that they will come to India with all these subjects, make it possible for them to do so.

The same right which you claim for Kashmir may also be demanded by the people of Jammu and Ladakh. Let us proceed in a friendly spirit. Sheikh Abdullah himself said about a month ago that he would have no objection if the people of Jammu and Ladakh really felt that they would go to India. I am not saying that you have it done immediately or that you proceed in that way, but let it be possible for the people residing in those areas to make up their minds as to which way it will be good to proceed, and it will also be consistent with the same principles of self-determination which constitute the basic claims of Sheikh Abdullah, supported by the Prime Minister.

□

Martyrs of the 1952-53 Praja Parishad Movement

'शहीदों की चिताओं पर लगेंगे हर बरस मेले, वतन पर मिटने वालों का यही आखरी निशान होगा'

1953 के ऐतिहासिक एक विधान-एक निशान-एक प्रधान आंदोलन के शहीदों को शत-शत नमन

1	Mela Ram	Chhamb
2	Nanak Chand	Dhonchak, Jourian
3	Basant Chand	Mattu, Jourian
4	Baldev Singh	Rati Dhanda
5	Sain Singh	Bhopur, Sunderbani
6	Waryam Singh	Bhopur
7	Trilok Singh	Pragwal
8	Baba Krishan Dass	Pukharni, Sunderbani
9	Baba Ramji Das	Sodra, Sunderbani
10	Beli Ram	Nandani Sunderbani
11	Bikham Singh	Hiranagar (Mandi)
12	Behari Lal	Hiranagar (Chann Moria)
13	Shivaji	Balot, Ramban
14	Devi Saran	Balot, Ramban
15	Bhagwan Dass	Kanthi, Ramban

जिएँ देश के लिए, देशहित तिल–तिलकर मर जाना सीखें।
असिधारा का व्रत अपना–अपना कर, बूँद–बूँद ढल जाना सीखें।

अडिग रहे जो जंजा में भी ऐसी ज्योति जगाना सीखें।
जननी के पावन चरणों में जीवन–पुष्प चढ़ाना सीखें।

□

List of Activists of the Jammu & Kashmir Praja Parishad

The Dogras of Jammu salute the great patriots for their supreme sacrifices and for facing atrocities for the honour of the national tricolour during the 1953 historic agitation of the Praja Parishad.

Jammu		
1	Pt. Prem Nath Dogra	
2	Vaid Veshnu Dutt	
3	Bhagwat Saroop	
4	Tilak Raj Sharma	Jammu
5	Mulkh Raj Pargal	
6	Dr. Om Parkash Mengi	
7	Prof. Chaman Lal	
8	Gopal Dass Sachar	
9	Sham Lal Sharma	
10	Amar Nath Gupta	
11	Om Prakash, Book-seller	
12	Dwarka Nath, Advocate	
13	Charan Dass	
14	Barkat Ram	
15	Shiv Kumar	Mirpurwala
16	Miyan Singh	

17	Punnu Ram	
18	Mehta Shiv Dass	
19	Ram Nath, Advocate	
20	Lal Chand Agarwal	
21	Rashpal Singh	
22	Chajju Ram	Smailpur
23	Shambu Singh	
24	Sita Ram	Seiwala
25	Shatrugan	
26	Basant Singh Tyagi	
27	Isher Dass	
28	Chuni Lal	
29	Teja Singh	
30	Sansar Chand	
31	Tilak Raj Pandoh	
32	Bhagwan Dass Padha	
33	Dev Raj Dhabba	
34	Babu Ram	
35	Om Parkash	
36	Amar Nath Bounga	
37	Tilak Raj Talwar	
38	Mahashay Yashpaul	
39	Mohan Lal Gupta	Bishnah
40	Mulkh Raj	Peer Mitha
41	Ishar Dutt Raina	
42	Ved Prakash Gupta	Kotliwale
43	Om Prakash	Kotliwale
44	Vishwa Mittar	Kotliwale
45	Kasturi Lal Gupta	Jammu
46	Sant Ram Arora	Jammu
47	Jagmohan Khanna	Jammu

48	Nagar Mal	Jammu
49	Diwan Singh	Jammu
50	Chatru Ram Dogra	Jammu
51	Giyani Isher Singh	Jammu
52	Banarsi Dass Gupta	Nai Basti, Jammu
53	Bodh Raj Gupta	Jammu
54	Sant Ram Tej	Jammu
55	Bhim Singh (Sewak)	Jammu
56	Mulk Raj Sharma	Jammu
57	Rattan Chand, Advocate	Bishnah
58	Dewan Bishan Dass	
59	Bhagwan Dass	
60	Durga Dass Verma	
61	Jagdish Chander Shastru	
62	Chhaju Ram	Grota
63	Sita Ram	Kangrel
64	Sita Ram Gupta	Doomi
65	Shiv Ram Gupta	Editor, *Amar*
66	Gian Chand	(Mirpur) Editor, *Sadakat*
67	Sodagar Mal	
68	Krishan Lal Gupta	
69	Shankar Das Bhagat	
70	Th. Durga Dass Charak	Jammu
71	Dev Raj (Dabba)	Jammu
72	Giani Kirtar Singh Rahi	Jammu
73	Babu Ram	Jammu
74	Sardari Lal	Jammu
75	Narsingh Dass Sharma	Jammu
76	Daya Krishan Gardish	Jammu
77	Haji Zuber	Bakarwal leader
78	Col. Peer Mohammad Khan	Jammu

79	Haider Noorani	
80	Ved Prakash Chauhan	Jammu

Kathua		
1	Thakur Ranjeet Singh	Nagri Prol
2	Krishna Chand	
3	Thakur Kharak Singh	
4	Ch. Dhayan Singh	
5	Kan. Prtithvi Paul Singh, B.A., L.L.B.	
6	Lala Tej Ram, Advocate	
7	Lala Harnam Dass	
8	Lala Beli Ram	
9	Rattan Chand	
10	Pt. Ram Rattan	
11	Ch. Parshotam Singh	
12	Om Prakash Wazir	
13	Surinder Nath Ubbat	
14	Ch. Chhagar Singh	
15	Vidhya Prakash Padha, M.A., L.L.B.	
16	Amar Singh	
17	Sardari Lal	Nagri Prol
18	Lala Puran Chand	
19	Lala Behari Mal Shah	
20	Lala Jagat Ram Shah	
21	Puran Singh	

Hiranagar		
1	Luder Mani Sangra	
2	Zaminar Kaka Singh	
3	Th. Baldev Singh, Advocate	
4	Capt. Thakur Dass	
5	Subedar Bhola Singh	

6	Pt. Gian Chand Sangra	
7	Vishwa Nath	
8	Tejey Singh	
9	Maj. Multan Singh	
10	Sardar Bhadur Subedar Chhattar Singh	
11	Girdhari Lal	
12	Rameshwar Chander Bali	
13	Jawalla Prakash, Advocate	
14	Bhagat Ram	Chhan Jourian
15	Des Raj	Chhan Jourian
16	Shankar Dass	Chhan Jourian
17	Radha Krishan	Manager, Govt. Press
18	Ishwar Dass Shastri	Hiranagar
19	Lt. Nand Lal Sangra	

Basholi/Billawar		
1	Jagdish Sharma Vaid	
2	Hari Chand Shah	Bhaddu
3	Hem Raj	Bani
4	Khushi Ram Padha	Basholi
5	Dhayan Singh	Billawar
6	Prem Gupta	Billawar
7	Hans Raj (Noor)	Billawar
8	Hari Krishan Zargar	
9	Pitamber Nath	
10	Ram Chand	
11	Isher Dutt Shastri	Parcharak
12	Ch. Diwan Chand Gupta	Billawar
13	Dina Nath Sapolia	

Akhnoor		
1	Thakur Seh Dev Singh	
2	Hari Singh	
3	Sat Dev	
4	Dev Raj	
5	Mela Ram	Chhamb
6	Rajinder Singh (MLA)	
7	Bansi Lal	Jourian
8	Ram Nath Manhas Pargwal	Chhamb
9	Amar Nath	
10	Subedar Waryam Singh	
11	Manhore Lal	Akhnoor
12	Suresh Chand	Akhnoor
13	Padam Dev	Akhnoor
14	Pt. Shanti Saroop	Jourian
15	Pt. Kunj Lal	Sohal
16	Dina Nath	Khadadra
17	Ram Rakha Mal (Koda Shah)	Saran
18	Bansi Lal	
19	Ram Saroop Gupta	
20	Gian Chand, Shopkeeper	
21	Lt. Baldev Raj	Gajanso, Marh
22	Lt. Bishamber Dass Sharma	Floura
23	Lt. Rashpal Singh	Gho-Manasa
24	Lt. Dr. Sansar Chand Sharma	Gho-Manasa
25	Lt. Meva Singh	Kukdiyan
26	Lt. Rala Ram	Rathua
27	Sansar Chand Sharma	Lambhardar Marh
28	Bansi Lal	Karlupwale
29	Sat Paul Saraf	Akhnoor
30	Lala Hans Raj Gupta	Sajwale (Pragwal)

31	Chaman Lal, Tailor	Akhnoor
32	Atma Ram Sharma	Akhnoor

Reasi/Sunderbani/Nowshera		
1	Jagdish Verma	
2	Th. Hari Singh	Mogla
3	Pt. Beli Ram	Sunderbani
4	Hakim Ram Saran Dass	Nowshera
5	Munish Lal	Nowshera
6	Gian Chand	Nowshera
7	Dr. Ved Prakash	Nowshera
8	Th. Tara Singh	
9	Hakim Kasturi Lal	
10	Ch. Birbal	Chhamb
11	Subedar Jagat Ram	
12	Inder Prakash	
13	Dr. Satya Paul Sharma	Nowshera
14	Krishan Chand	Taryath
15	Ram Saran Dass	Mogla
16	Capt. Onkar Singh Vijaypur	Reasi
17	Mehta Malik Ram	Nowshera
18	Pashori Lal	Nowshera
19	Bhola Ram	Mogla
20	Karan Chand	Mogla
21	Bimal Devi (Paggar)	Prore (Sunderbani)
22	Munish Ram Gupta (Pappu)	Sunderbani
23	S. Parabh Dayal Patrara	Sunderbani
24	Prema Pehlwan	Sunderbani
25	Numberdar Chet Ram (Deeng)	Nowshera
26	Amar Nath	Mogla
27	Pritam Dass	Sunderbani

28	Rishi Kumar Koshal	Reasi
29	Gouri Mal	Reasi
30	Mistri Gulam Mohammad	Reasi
31	Th. Gian Singh	Seyul Sui
32	Sat Pal Sharma	Nowshera
33	Shiv Nath Nanda	Reasi
34	Krishan Dutt Sharma	Reasi
35	Kasturi Lal	Sunderbani
36	Ram Prakash	Nargotra
37	Krishan Lal	Sunderbani
38	Madam Lal Nagi	Sunderbani
39	Kaka Ram Banpuri	Sunderbani
40	Rakhi Ram Shoor	Sunderbani
41	Zamindar Phoola Ram	Changi Kangrel (Sunderbani)
42	Kasturi Lal Gupta	Sunderbani
43	Ram Nath Nagotra	Sunderbani
44	Master Ram Dass Lakhanpal	Reasi
45	Madho Lal Nanda	Reasi
46	Pt. Bichetru Ram	Ghar
47	Pt. Brindaban	Ghar
48	Pt. Pers Ram	Ghar
49	Pt. Lachaman Dass	Dana

Samba		
1	Lala Shanti Saroop	
2	Jagdish Shastri	
3	Sohan Lala Spolia	
4	Master Dhyan Singh	
5	Th. Tarpat Singh	Gurha Salathia
6	Maj. Harbans Singh	Gurha Salathia
7	Maldar Karnel Singh	Gurha Salathia

8	Nanak Chand	Gurha Salathia
9	Kalwant Singh	Gurha Salathia
10	Govind Ram	Gurha Salathia
11	Durga Dass Gupta	Samba
12	Shiv Lal	Riahal/Kirial
13	Pt. Peras Ram	Bishnah
14	Sanji Ram Gupta	Bishnah
15	Atma Singh	Gurha Salathia
16	Hirda Singh	Gurha Salathia
17	Tilak Chander Singh	Gurha Salathia
18	Sulachan Singh	Gurha Salathia
19	Sansar Singh	Gurha Salathia
20	Anchal Singh	
21	Prabh Dayal Verma	Mandi Darkargarh Gurha, Salathia
22	Khajur Singh	Mandi Darkargarh Gurha, Salathia
23	Inder Nath Khajuria	Mandi Garh Gurha, Salathia
24	Inder Singh	Mandi Garh Gurha, Salathia
25	Sawaran Singh	Mandi Raj Garh Gurha, Salathia
26	Th. Dhyan Singh	Gurha Salathia
27	Master Jerman Singh	Mandi Andrar Gurha, Salathia
28	Sardari Lal	Nagri Padol
29	Ganpatiji Acharya	Bishnah
30	Nand Lal Bhagat	Miran Sahib
31	Raghunath Dass	Samba
32	Chet Ram Khajuria	Bohre camp
33	Laiq Singh	Bohre camp

34	Chajju Ram Khajuria	Samba
35	Krishan Lal	R.S. Pura
36	Sat Paul	Samba
37	Amar Nath Bawa	Ratian
38	Devikia Nandan	Samba
39	Nanak Chand Sharma	Samba
40	Niseeb Singh	Smailpur (Bishnah)
41	Waryam Singh	Smailpur (Bishnah)
42	Lala Amarnath	Khairi (Bishnah)
43	Lala Buta Ram	Sarore (Bishnah)
44	Jagdish Raj	Bishnah

Poonch		
1	Shiv Rattan Prui	
2	Lala Ram Saroop	
3	Mahesh Chander Sharma	
4	Pritam Lal Anand	
5	Dina Nath, Poonch	
6	Lala Jagan Nath	

Udhampur		
1	Shiv Charan Gupta	
2	Hari Ram Vaid	
3	Faqire Chand	Jaganoo
4	Bal Krishan	
5	Hans Raj, BA, BT	Ram Nagar
6	Mahashya Yash Pal	Mirpur, Jammu
7	Paras Ram Pachala	Udhampur
8	Gouri Ram Shah	Udhampur
9	Th. Bharat Singh	Ram Nagar

10	Papa Dina Nath	Udhampur
11	Shanti Lal Verma	Udhampur
12	Krishna Singh (Papa)	Udhampur
13	Bodh Raj (Prohil)	Udhampur
14	Suraj Prakash Gupta	Udhampur
15	Lal Chand Verma	Udhampur
16	Des Raj Jandial	Udhampur
17	Babu Ram Gupta	Udhampur
18	Shiv Lal Pakhetra	Udhampur
19	Krishan Lal Pandit	Udhampur
20	Dina Nath Gandotra	Udhampur
21	Shiv Lal Kailu	Udhampur
22	Krishna Anand Baria	Udhampur
23	Charan Dass (Pachaila)	Udhampur
24	Th. Anant Singh	Udhampur
25	Neel Kanth Shah	Basant Garh
26	Amrit Sagar	Udhampur
27	Om Prakash (Pachaila)	Udhampur
28	Kulbir Gupta	Udhampur
29	Des Raj Kailu	Udhampur
30	Ved Mittar	Udhampur
31	Suraj Kapoor	Udhampur
32	Dalit Parshotam	Udhampur
33	Puri Ram	Manwal Udhampur
34	Jia Lal	Udhampur
35	Amrit Sagar	Udhampur

Rajouri		
1	Paras Ram	
2	Megh Raj Bali	
3	Kuldeep Raj Gupta	

4	Nirmal Kumar Rishi	
5	Bakshi Vishwa Nath	
6	Bakshi Sandhya Dass	
7	Th. Sham Singh	
8	Th. Malook Singh	
9	Tej Ram	
10	Ram Lal	
11	Ata Ulla	
12	Shiv Ram	
13	Jagmohan Sharma	
14	Raghunandan Modi	
15	Krishan Lal	Chuga
16	Sr. Sat Pal	Rajouri

	Katra	
1	Hira Lal	
2	Bishan Dass	
3	Khem Chand Dubey	
4	Ram Lal	
5	Ram Saroop	
6	Tirth Ram Dogra	
7	Hem Raj Pujari	
8	Govind Ram	
9	Mohan Lal	
10	Krishan Kumar Padha	

	Doda District	
1	S. Bachan Singh	
2	Th. Dharam Singh	
3	Th. Shadi Ram	
4	Th. Madho Lal Gadhi	
5	Ram Saran	

6	Lal Chand Sharma	Manthala
7	Thakur Miyan Ram Lohar	
8	Th. Basant Singh, BA	(Bhagwah)
9	Hari Ram Sharma	
10	Dina Nath	Dessa
11	Kosri Singh	Kasti Garh
12	Jameet Singh	Assar
13	Lalman Singh	Ukhral
14	Ch. Anant Ram	Doda
15	S. Karan Singh	Samthi
16	Ravella Ram	Samthi
17	Guran Dittamal	Doda
18	Sadhu Ram	Doda
19	Nar Singh	Doda
20	Ram Chand	Marmat
21	Swami Raj Sharma	Doda
22	Faqire Chand Rajdhan	Doda
23	Om Prakash Kotwal	Doda
24	Tej Lal Padha	Doda
25	Surinder Kotwal	Doda
26	Faqire Chand	Adhwah
27	Harji Gadhi	Manthala
28	Salaq Ram	Manthala
29	Harji Gaddi	Manthala
30	Pt. Ishwer Lal Sharma	(Panwarra) Manthala
31	Lahru Ram	Chinta

Mahila Wing, Jammu		
1	Shakti Sharma	
2	Parkasho Devi	
3	Darshna Devi	

4	Suhag Rani	
5	Soma Devi	
6	Vinod Sharma	
7	Mata Parvati Devi	
8	Sushela Devi	
9	Raj Kumari	
10	Sita Devi	
11	Kailasho Gupta	
12	Taro Devi Abrol	
13	Brinda Devi	
14	Bimla Devi	
15	Susheela Mengi	
16	Vimla Dogra	
17	Sheela Chauhan	
18	Chatru Ram Dogra	
19	Sukantla Devi	
20	Chanchla Devi	

	Kishtwar	
1	Pt. Hari Lal	
2	Mehta Krishna Saroop	
3	Premnath Bhasin	
4	Sant Ram Parhiar	
5	Yash Prakash	
6	Lalal Amar Nath	
7	Prem Nath Goswami	
8	Wazir Shankar Nath	
9	Masat Ram	
10	Kirpal Singh	
11	Prem Lal	Atholi (Paddar)
12	Hem Raj	Thathri
13	Manmohan Gupta	Kishtwar

14	Janki Nath	Paddar
15	Charan Dass Gupta	Kishtwar

Ramban		
1	Labhu Ram	
2	Lalman Singh Pogal Parstan	
3	Hans Raj	
4	Kasturi Lal Gupta	
5	Th. Gaja Singh	
6	Padam Nath	
7	Th. Bhoop Singh	
8	Pt. Dina Nath	Batote
9	Bachan Singh Panchi	Batote (refugee leader)
10	Anant Ram	Batote
11	Kanshi Ram	Ramban
12	Thakur Dass	
13	Natha Singh (Parcharka)	Ramban
14	Jagat Ram Parhiar	Ramban
15	Sant Meher Singh	Batote

Bhadarwah		
1	Kirpa Ram Kotwal	
2	Madho Lal	
3	Daya Krishna Rathore	Bhallesa
4	Om Kishore	
5	Karan Chand	
6	Sheikh Abdul Rehman	Khallu
7	Amar Chand Kotwal	
8	Amar Nath	Doda
9	Amar Chand	Bhalla
10	Kotwal Swami Raj	

11	Hardyal Singh	
12	Daya Krishna Kotwal	
13	Swami Raj Katal	
14	Swami Raj, Advocate	

Kashmir		
1	Makhan Lal Aima	Parcharak
2	Omkar Nath Kak	Parcharak
3	Niranjan Nath Kaul	Parcharak
4	Tika Lal Taploo, Advocate	
5	Brig Nath Miya	Parcharak
6	Janki Nath Dhobi	Parcharak, USA, at present
7	Amar Nath Vaishnavi	Parcharak
8	D.P. Nakashi	Parcharak, Palampur/ Shimla (HP)
9	Som Nath	Hari Singh, High Street, Srinagar
10	Amar Nath	Nai Sarak, Srinagar
11	Prem Nath Bhat, Advocate	Anantnag
12	Hira Lal Chatta	
13	Prem Nath Miya	
14	Soom Nath Ogra	
15	Om Prakash Suri	

References

1. Verma, Durga Dass (1951), *Memorandum about Praja Parishad Stand*, New Delhi.
2. Gupta, Chaman Lal (2010), *Article 370–A Thorn*, Chaman Lal Gupta Foundation, Jammu, 182.
3. *Original Document of the Praja Parishad: Objectives over Separate Constitution.*

4. *Janta Ke Hridaye Samarat*, Jai Swadesh, Jammu, 13 September, 1955, Praja Parishad, Jammu.
5. *Original Documents.*
6. *J&K Legislative Assembly Debates,* 1958, 1960 & 1967.
7. Mahajan, Mehar Chand (1947), *Looking Back...*
8. India, Ministry of External Affairs: *Kashmir Issue.*
9. Sharma, G.D (2014), *Plight of Jammu & Kashmir : The Unknown Files*, Manas Publications, New Delhi, 552.
10. Gupta, Sanji Ram, *Jail Diary (1952-53).*
11. Agnohtri, Kuldeep Chand (2015), *Jammu Kashmir ki Unkahi Kahani*, Prabhat Prakashan, Delhi, 279.
12. *Meetings with Different Old Activists.*
13. Sharma, Sham Lal (1952), *Pandit Prem Nath Dogra: Ek Vyaktitva*, Vijay Printing Press, Jammu.
14. *Old Clippings of Various Papers.*
15. *Proceedings of Assembly Sessions, 1951 Onwards.*
16. *Teharike Kashmir Book.*
17. Gupta, Sanji Ram, *Vish Dhara 370.*

□

Letters and Paper Clippings for Reference

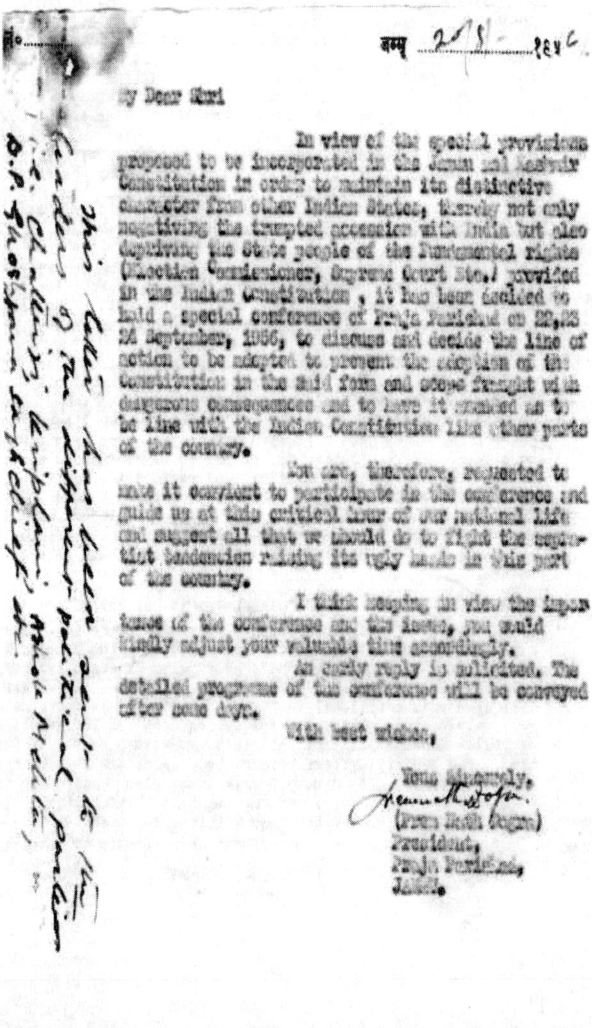

जम्मू 2/8/ १९५६

My Dear Shri

In view of the special provisions proposed to be incorporated in the Jammu and Kashmir Constitution in order to maintain its distinctive character from other Indian States, thereby not only negativing the accepted accession with India but also depriving the State people of the Fundamental rights (Election Commissioner, Supreme Court Etc.) provided in the Indian Constitution, it has been decided to hold a special conference of Praja Parishad on 22,23 24 September, 1956, to discuss and decide the line of action to be adopted to prevent the adoption of the Constitution in the said form and steps fraught with dangerous consequences and to have it amended as to be line with the Indian Constitution like other parts of the country.

You are, therefore, requested to make it convenient to participate in the conference and guide us at this critical hour of our national life and suggest all that we should do to fight the separatist tendencies raising its ugly heads in this part of the country.

I think keeping in view the importance of the conference and the issue, you would kindly adjust your valuable time accordingly.

An early reply is solicited. The detailed programme of the conference will be conveyed after some days.

With best wishes,

Yours sincerely,

(Prem Nath Dogra)
President,
Praja Parishad,
Jammu.

Jammu & Kashmir Praja Parishad

जम्मू-कश्मीर प्रजापरिषद

(Central Office Jammu)

Ref. No 94/2/P

Dated [illegible].7.1951.

Dear Sir,

This is in continuation of our previous letter No.91/2/P, 26.6.1951. It has been learnt from reliable sources that the Kashmir Government has come to harbour certain doubts and misgivings about the benefices of the Praja Parishad. Parishad has declared so many times in its statements as well as in public speeches that its aims and objects are to serve the people of Jammu and Kashmir State irrespective of religion, caste, creed or language and that it is national in out-look and considers every citizen of the State equal and that it is with the Government, as long as the Government is furthering those aims and objectives and where the Government departs from those aims and objectives, it would offer healthy opposition, but in no case it would disturb the peace of the State. So far and in future too the Praja Parishad will remain wedded to this policy inspite of provocation and incitement from some National Conference workers who are out to ~~create~~ produce wrong impressions ~~and~~ create bad blood and incite people to violence. They are acting on the policy of giving the dog a bad name and kill it. [illegible] National Conference workers are resorting to such tactics as will create disturbances in the State and thus strengthen the hands of Pakistan as will be clear from the facts detailed below:-

1. We have been charged with ~~giving~~ making provocative and offensive speeches, but the fact is that Mr. Motiram Baigra and his companions are openly preaching violence. He delivered a speech at Reasi saying that Praja Parishad people are murderers, dacoits and bad characters. They should be tied with ropes, seriously beaten, made to sit on donkeys and then driven out to be drowned in the river Chenab etc. He preached violence and excited the public, but the Praja Parishad people kept their heads cool and behaved nicely and saved the situation which otherwise would have become serious. [illegible] fact was brought to your notice at that very time and twice after that as well. But no notice has been taken of this inflammatory speech.

2. The incident of Sudhmahadev in Chaneni Illaqa, District Udhampur, has already been brought to your kind notice. The meeting organized by Praja Parishad was disturbed with the help of a Police Officer. A batch of fifty people armed with axes and lathies raised anti-slogans, terrorised the audience and abused the workers and fell upon them mercilessly. As a result thereof two persons were seriously beaten. The Sub Inspector on spot and the Superintendent of Police Udhampur did not entertain the written report of the victims. The Medical Officer refused to examine and issue a certificate of the injuries. The Deputy Commissioner also remained lukewarm and took no notice of these facts when brought to his notice. The victims had to be removed to Jammu Hospital for dressing etc.

On the other hand efforts are being made to involve our

Jammu & Kashmir Praja Parishad

जम्मू-कश्मीर प्रजापरिषद

(Central Office Jammu)

Ref. No .... -3- Dated........

and members who try to protect everybody and even shed their blood to defend them.

4. To condemn the unlawful action of the Goondas at Sudh Mahadev, the people of Udhampur observed complete hartal spontaneously to express their resentment at these inhuman and barbarious acts of the anti- national and anti-social elements. But the National Conference and the Kashmir Government took exception to it. They are against the people expressing their feelings and condemning such unjust, barbarous and inhuman acts, because the perpetrators belong to its group and that of Mr. Baigra. On the other hand, the people were victimized by cancelling the permits of some cloth dealers with a view to frighten, suppress and discourage the public. Similarly permits of four dealers of Samba have been cancelled as a result of hartal observed to protest against the arrest of Th. Raghunath Singh Samyal. These are clear instances of suppression and harassment.

5. The shopkeepers whose licences and permits have been cancelled approached the District Supply Officer, Udhampur, and requested him to tell the grounds upon which their permits were cancelled. He told them that he was helpless and that he had been verbally ordered by [illegible] Ali (Deputy Commissioner Udhampur) that licences and permits of all Praja Parishad dealers should be cancelled. When the dealers requested The District Supply Officer to furnish a copy of the orders in order that they might lodge an appeal, the District Supply Officer insulted and turned them out of his room.

6. Mr. Aga Nasir Ali, Deputy Commissioner, Udhampur, in a speech at village Jib in Udhampur District preached violence and exhorted the audience to receive the Praja Parishad people with lathies and ropes so that they might not dare again to enter their village.

7. On 8th Jeth 2008, Pandit Premnath Dogra, President, Praja Parishad, went on tour to Poni, where a public meeting was held at night. As a result of his visit to the place two Zaildars and two Nambardars have been suspended on the grounds that they took part in giving reception to Pandit Premnath Dogra. The ground is absolutely false because no such reception could be held at all at 9 in the night the time of his arrival in the town. It may be brought to your notice that this is not the first instance of this kind. This has becomes practice to harass and trouble the persons who take part in Pandit Jee's reception or attend our meetings. This is a travesty of democracy as in its practice here, the aggressor is encouraged the aggrieved is victimized exactly as the U.N.O. is doing in the Kashmir dispute.

9. On 12th Har 2008, S. Budh Singh, and Hon'ble Girdharilal Dogra went to Hiranagar for election propaganda. Failing to get a good audience, they arranged a Cinema Show at night through the State Publicity Department. During the show, Mr. Lalman, a Patwari at Hiranagar, stood up and began to deliver a speech which was full of malicious propaganda against Praja Parishad. Mr. Jawala

Jammu & Kashmir Praja Parishad

जम्मू–कश्मीर प्रजापरिषद

(Central Office Jammu)

Ref. No .... -4- Dated........

Prakash, a Vakil of Hiranagar, objected to this on the ground that he is an official and his position does not allow him to say anyth against or in favour of any political party. At this the said Pat wari raised a slogan " Sher-i-Duggar Murdabad". The public left th place. The Police Sub Inspector arrested Mr. Jwalaprakash along with Mr. Devkinandan our workder at Hiranagar. Next day both of t were produced before the court under section 151/107.

All these facts confirm the doubts and fears that the Government's efforts are directed against the Praja Parishad and that the Government will not allow fair and impartial elections. The Praja Parishad on the hand is endeavouring to maintain law and order in full appreciation of the critical situation and with a view to disillusion the Security Council that the elections in the State can be conducted fairly and impartially. I am afraid that if this process harassment and arrests are not put a stop to, the chances of healthy and peaceful atmosphere would be lessened and free and fair elections would not be possible.

Yours faithfully,

Durga Dass Varma
(Durga Dass Varma)
General Secretary,
All Jammu & Kashmir Government,
Srinagar.

Hon'ble Bakhshi Ghulam Mohammed,
Deputy Prime Minister,
Jammu & Kashmir Government,
Srinagar (Kashmir).

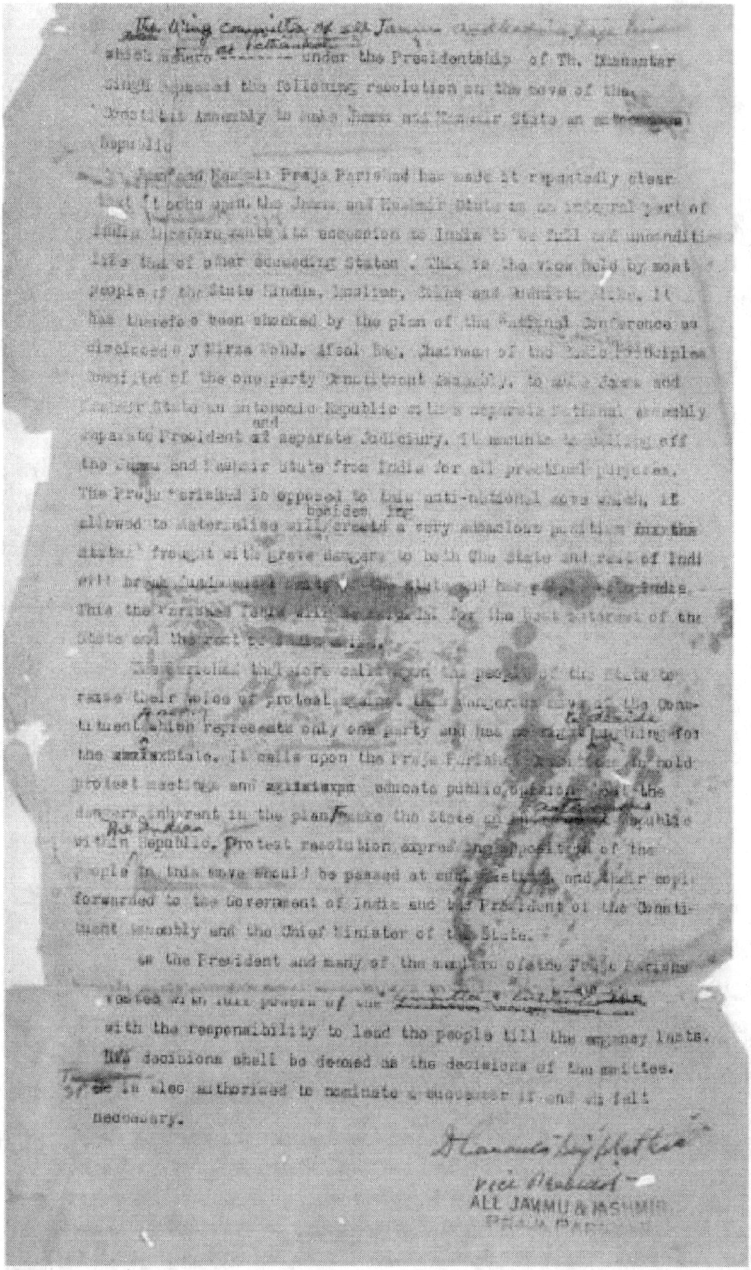

The Working Committee of All Jammu and Kashmir Praja Parishad at Pathankot which met [illegible] under the Presidentship of Th. [illegible] Singh passed the following resolution on the move of the Constituent Assembly to make Jammu and Kashmir State an autonomous Republic

Jammu and Kashmir Praja Parishad has made it repeatedly clear that it looks upon the Jammu and Kashmir State as an integral part of India. It therefore wants its accession to India to be full and unconditional like that of other acceding States. This is the view held by most people of the State Hindus, Muslims, Sikhs and Buddhists alike. It has therefore been shocked by the plan of the National Conference as disclosed by Mirza Mohd. Afzal Beg, Chairman of the Basic Principles Committee of the one party Constituent Assembly, to make Jammu and Kashmir State an autonomous Republic with a separate National Assembly separate President and separate Judiciary. It amounts to [illegible] off the Jammu and Kashmir State from India for all practical purposes. The Praja Parishad is opposed to this anti-national move which, if allowed to materialise will besides creating a very anomalous position [illegible] the State fraught with grave dangers to both the State and rest of India will [illegible] the State and her [illegible] India. This the Parishad [illegible] for the best interest of the State and the rest of India.

The Parishad therefore calls upon the people of the State to raise their voice of protest against this dangerous move of the Constituent Assembly which represents only one party and has no [illegible] for the State. It calls upon the Praja Parishad [illegible] to hold protest meetings and [illegible] educate public opinion about the dangers inherent in the plan to make the State an [illegible] Republic within the Indian Republic. Protest resolution expressing [illegible] of the people in this move should be passed at such meetings and their copies forwarded to the Government of India and the President of the Constituent Assembly and the Chief Minister of the State.

As the President and many of the members of the Praja Parishad [illegible] vested with full powers of the [illegible] with the responsibility to lead the people till the emergency lasts. His decisions shall be deemed as the decisions of the committee. He is also authorised to nominate a successor if and as felt necessary.

[illegible signature]

Vice President

ALL JAMMU & KASHMIR PRAJA PARISHAD

From:

Bal Raj Madhok,
Organising Secretary,
Jammu & Kashmir Praja Parishad
(C/o Paramount Press, Dariaganj, Delhi).

To

Shri G.S. Bajpai,
Secretary General,
External Affairs Ministry,
Government of India, NEW DELHI.

Dear Sir,

I beg to submit as 'aide [illegible]' the gist of the points that I made out during my talk with you on the [illegible].50 as also those which I could not touch due to shortage of time, regarding [illegible] view point of the Praja Parishad, the most representative organisation of [illegible] held Jammu Province of the Jammu & Kashmir State, about the Kashmir problem.

1. The Praja Parishad would [illegible] the Government of India to not to [illegible] a plebiscite in Kashmir [illegible] time. But since the Government of India stands committed to it, [illegible] impolitic and undemocratic to allow the predominantly Muslim [illegible] of Kashmir to decide the future of the Dogras of Jammu or Ladakhis [illegible] they have nothing in common whatsoever by holding the ple[illegible] taking the whole State as a unit. The choi[ce] of the people of Jammu and Ladakh [illegible] part of India is clear and unequivocal. Therefore no plebiscite [illegible]. If it must be held at all it should be confined to Kashmir valley alone.

2. Praja Parishad is as much opposed to the independence of the State as to its accession to Pakistan. It is therefore perturbed by the subtle moves of Sh. Abdullah and his communist supporters to secure independence for the entire India held part of the State. Let the Government of India and Sheikh Abdullah do whatever they think proper with Kashmir valley. But nothing should be done to break the natural, historical, political, economic and cultural ties of the people of Jammu (from Pathankot [illegible] Banihal) and Ladakh with India.

3. Care should be taken to keep Bhadarwah (Hindu majority) and Kishtwar (slight Muslim majority now due to immigration of Kashmiri Muslims), the two richest and strategically most important parts of Jammu with Jammu and Bharat. This is important because Sheikh Abdullah's Government has been trying in a very subtle way since its very in[illegible] to [illegible] off from the Hindu majority districts of Udhampur and thus destroy the territorial link between Jammu and Ladak[h]. They have been constituted by [illegible] into a new district of Doda whose Muslim population has swelled recently [illegible] Muslim immigrants from Kashmir valle[y] from across the Banihal [illegible] that link Jammu with Kashmir valley.

4. In deciding the future of the State or taking any other decisive step concerning it the representatives [illegible] Praja Parishad should also be consulted. The Government of India, I would like to assure you, can always depend upon Praj[a] Parishad for anything for the good of India and the State.

I would like to post you with some more facts and therefore would request you to give sometime [illegible] some other day at your earliest convenience.

Yours faithfully,

(Bal Raj Madhok)

Dated.
the 27th May 1950.

नव भारत दिल्ली में डा॰ मुखर्जी का भाषण

काश्मीर के भारत में विलय पर श्री नेहरू ने बाधा दी

—डा॰ मुकर्जी

(कार्यालय प्रतिनिधि द्वारा)

[illegible]

निजाम को हटाने की मांग

[illegible]

लाठियों-गोलियों से जम्मू-आंदोलन को दबाया नहीं जा सकता

डा॰ श्यामाप्रसाद मुखर्जी द्वारा नेहरू व अब्दुल्ला सरकार को चेतावनी

(हमारे कार्यालय प्रतिनिधि द्वारा)

[illegible]

नवभारत टाइम्स

दिल्ली, शुक्रवार माघ कृष्णा २ सम्वत् २००९

जम्मू प्रजा-परिषद का सत्याग्रह

जांच मंडल भेजने का निश्चय

नेताजी की मृत्यु के बारे में जांच की मांग

Hindustan Standard
Delhi
24.4.52

SRI PREM NATH DOGRA, President of the Praja Parishad, Jammu and Kashmir, (with garlands) was given a reception on his arrival in Delhi at the Railway Station on Wednesday morning.

Jammu Praja Parishad Chief In Delhi

Address At Public Meeting

NEW DELHI, APRIL 23—Sri Prem Nath Dogra, President of the Jammu Praja Parishad, told a public meeting here today that the Parishad would continue to agitate for the full application of the Indian Constitution to the State of Jammu and Kashmir.

"We also want to enjoy the freedom of Press and platform which the Constitution of India guarantees to all its citizens and of which the people of the State are deprived. We want the jurisdiction of the Supreme Court of India to be extended to the State so that liberty of the individual is guaranteed and enforced in the State also," he said.

Sri Dogra refuted the charge that the Parishad was a communal organisation and said its main aim was to educate the people of Jammu, who were politically more backward than the people of Kashmir.

Referring to the recent student agitation in Jammu, he said as a citizen he surely sympathised with the school children, but as President of the Parishad he scrupulously avoided being entangled in the affair.—P.T.I.

Sheikh Abdullah And Communalism

Sir,—Since Prime Minister of Kashmir Sheikh Abdullah's statement of April 11, our Prime Minister Sri Nehru has said that he did not like the tone of the speech and we read with pleasure your excellent editorial "[illegible]" in your issue of April 15-16.

Sheikh Abdullah wanted to clarify his statement and even his latest has not satisfactorily done so. Where was the justification for the most uncalled for speech? One should remember that the Indian boys sacrificed themselves for and are still defending that land and India is yet spending crores for it.—Yours, etc., [illegible] PRASAD [illegible], Advocate, Calcutta.

"Hindustan Times" D/3-5-52

KASHMIR'S TIES WITH INDIA

Controversy Regretted

SRINAGAR, May 1.—Addressing a May Day meeting in Srinagar last night, the Deputy Prime Minister of Kashmir, Bakshi Ghulam Mohamed, said the people of the State could never be separated from the rest of India. He said there was no greater friend of India than Sheikh Abdullah.

Communalists and extremists, Bakshi Ghulam Mohamed said, were trying to sow seeds of dissension, but this should never be countenanced. He said certain elements in India were doing a disservice to India and Kashmir by imputing statements and views to Sheikh Abdullah that were not his. In doing so, Bakshi Ghulam Mohamed said, they were not only hurting the sentiments of millions of Indians, but also the sentiments of Sheikh Abdullah's followers in Jammu and Kashmir.

Kashmir's special position, he said, had been conceded not only in the Instrument of Accession, but also in India's Constitution. There was no room for confusion or controversy about this.

U.N. MEDIATION

Referring to the U.N. mediation efforts in Kashmir, Bakshi Ghulam Mohamed said Kashmiris were not in the least perturbed over how interested world Powers proposed to tackle the Kashmir problem. They knew their destiny was in their own hands. As far as Dr Graham was concerned, Kashmiris did not mind his visiting this country once again, if he chose to. But he made it clear their fundamentals stand on the question of accession would remain unaltered.

Bakshi Ghulam Mohammad dwelt at length on Indo-Kashmir relationship and said: "I wish to make it clear that dreams of those communal elements who demand the application of the entire Indian Constitution to Kashmir will never materialise. Kashmir has acceded to India only in respect of three subjects, namely, Defence, Communications and Foreign Affairs. We are free to shape our destiny, as far as the other subjects are concerned."

"The Indian Press has known Sheikh Abdullah for more than 20 years as a real and sincere friend of the Indian people. Why should any one turn round suddenly and impute motives to him," he asked.

He said: "Let me make it clear that nothing can break the bonds of kinship between Kashmir and India."

He also referred to the land reforms in Kashmir and said Kashmir had already given a lead to India in this respect. "What Kashmir has done today other Indian States will do tomorrow."

Bakshi Ghulam Mohammed appealed to the Indian Press and leaders "to respect the sentiments of Sheikh Abdullah and write and speak about Kashmir after due deliberation and in the best interests of India and Kashmir."—U.P.I.

"Tribune" D/3-5-52

Accession To India Irrevocable, Says B. Ghulam Mohd.

(From Our Own Correspondent)

SRINAGAR, May 2.— Bakshi Ghulam Mohammad, Kashmir's Deputy Premier, said here last night that nothing could separate Kashmir from India. Addressing a May Day rally, he said: "If the present unfortunate controversy over Kashmir's position had done anything it has only brought us closer to India than ever before. All interested attempts to draw Sheikh Abdullah away from India, the land of Gandhiji and Pandit Nehru are bound to fail. There is no greater friend of the Indian people than Sheikh Abdullah."

He went on to say: "Kashmir has acceded to India only in defence, foreign affairs and communications, and so far as the rest of subjects are concerned, it is free to decide her destiny in whatever way she pleases. No one can doubt or question Kashmir's freedom to decide her internal affairs. Some interested elements in India and Jammu are wrong if they think that they can force Kashmir to accede to India in subjects other than the three subjects in which she has already acceded. Kashmir's special position has been clearly laid down in the Instrument of Accession. There is no reason why some quarters should raise a controversy at this stage."

He asserted it was wrong on the part of anybody to think that they "can bring down Sheikh Abdullah. We will never permit our leader to be brought down. We will always stand by him."

He said that Kashmir had transferred land to tillers without paying any compensation to landlords and claimed that land would be transferred to tillers all over India and "Kashmir lead would be followed."

U.P.I. adds: Referring to U.N. mediation efforts he said Kashmiris were not perturbed over how interested world powers tackled the Kashmir problem. They knew their destiny was in their own hands. Kashmiris, he said, did not mind if Dr. Graham visited the State again, but he should know that fundamental stand on the question of accession would remain unaltered.

...द का आंदोलन जमींदारों का आंदोलन है'

...कार लोगों की शिकायतें दूर करे

WITH BASIC PRINCIPLES

Bajpai Re-affirms India's Stand

GENEVA, February ...

Tribune Ambala 4 Feb.

Police Open Fire On Parishad Mob: 4 Killed

نہرو اور جموں کا ستیہ گرہ

प्रजा परिषद के जलूस पर पुनः अश्रु गैस का प्रयोग

टाडा में प्रजापरिषद [illegible] पुलिस को अश्रु गैस

कश्मीर सरकार जनसंघ से मान्यता देने को तैयार नहीं

SECTION 144 IN NEW DELHI

DEMONSTRATION ON JAMMU FIRING

By A Staff Reporter

[illegible]

Police Disperse Procession In New Delhi

JAN SANGH PROTEST AGAINST FIRING IN JAMMU VILLAGE

THE police on Sunday dispersed a procession which was organised by the Jan Sangh in New Delhi as a protest against the police firing at Jourian in Jammu and Kashmir State.

The procession, consisting of over 1,000 persons, started from the Regal Park in the afternoon but was stopped near [illegible] House by police officers who announced the District Magistrate's order under Section 144, Criminal Procedure Code, banning processions in the municipal limits of New Delhi.

Nearly 200 of the processionists, however, managed to reach [illegible] in accordance with their plan to hold a black-flag demonstration in front of Kashmir Government offices. They were informed by the Additional District Magistrate, Mr. H. S. Dhillon, who headed a force of over 300 policemen that the order applied to meetings as well as processions. Mr. [illegible] Chander Sharma, thereupon, told his followers to disperse as "our leaders have not yet decided to break the law." Despite his advice, however, a section of the crowd continued to shout slogans. Quiet was, however, restored by the leaders of the demonstrators who accompanied by a police escort made their way back.

The ban on meetings and processions within the municipal limits of New Delhi, Mr. Dhillon said, would be in force for 15 days.

Later in the evening, a number of public meetings were organised by the Jan Sangh in Old Delhi where speakers severely condemned the Kashmir Government's action in resorting to firing on Praja Parishad [illegible] and criticised the District Magistrate for stopping the Jan Sangh procession.

The Secretary of the Delhi [illegible] Jan Sangh, Mr. [illegible] Lal Gupta, said in a statement [illegible]

PROTEST HARTAL IN JAMMU

From Our Correspondent

JAMMU, Feb 1.—[illegible]

7. Page.

THE UNIVERSAL PRESS SERVICE,
MADRAS-2, INDIA.

Clipping No. ....

Name .... Bombay Chronicle

Publ. .... Bombay

Date 29/7/52 Page 2 Column No. 5/6

Kashmir Must Accept Full Integration

MOOKERJEE'S POSER TO ABDULLAH

NEW DELHI, July 28. (UPI).

DR. Shyama Prasad Mookerjee, President of the Bharatiya Jan Sangh, said here this evening that if Sheikh Abdullah regarded himself as an Indian first and then a Kashmiri and then a Muslim, he should have no hesitation in accepting full integration of Kashmir with India.

Addressing a largely attended public meeting in the Gandhi Grounds Dr. Mookerjee declared that the main point about Kashmir was not regarding the Maharaja's future or even the flag, but that since Kashmir was an integral part of the Indian Union, it should agree, at no distant time, to be integrated with India just like any other Part 'B' State. If one or two local matters require special treatment, this can be separately examined in an atmosphere of goodwill and mutual understanding he said.

The Jan Sangh leader, in a 60-minute speech, reviewed the Kashmir problem, East Bengal situation, food policy of the Government of India and the Preventive Detention Act.

FUTURE OF THE RULER

Referring to Kashmir, Dr. Mookerjee said that in fact the Maharajah's rule had largely come to an end and he is nothing but a mere constitutional head with no special responsibility. Whether the rulership will continue or not is not peculiar to Kashmir and it has to be decided in respect of the whole of India by none else but the Indian Parliament, Dr. Mookerjee observed. What they wanted was a uniform system for the selection of the Governor or Raj Pramukh of every state within the Indian Union including Kashmir.

Dr. Mookerji was not prepared to treat the flag question as a minor issue. The adoption of a separate flag for Kashmir alone was a symbol not of loyalty to India but one of cleavage and disruption, he said. Sheikh Abdullah and his supporters, he said, made no efforts in replying to the vital principles involved in these matters.

NO PARTITION

He expressed surprise over the fact that the Kashmir Premier had charged his critics with a desire to partition Jammu and Kashmir. All that had been suggested was that if Sheikh Abdulla and his supporters remained stubborn, then a possible solution might be to allow Jammu and Ladakh to integrate fully with India and the Kashmir Valley to have a limited integration.

Referring to the "growing deterioration" in the East Bengal situation, Dr. Mookerjee expressed the fear that if the situation did not improve a disastrous calamity would befall India. He was simply amused to find that the Pakistan Minister for Minorities had referred to the unabated exodus of non-Muslims from East Bengal as a natural event in this part of the year.

AGGRESSION

The essential fact, he said, had to be borne in mind that Pakistan was determined not to keep the Hindus in East Bengal except the poorest classes who would remain as serfs and would soon become converts. What was happening was in the nature of aggression by Pakistan on India.

Parishad Workers Meet In Jungle

Decide To Agitate More Effectively

(From Our Own Correspondent)

JAMMU, Dec. 28.—An important two-day meeting of about 40 Parishad workers was held this week under the chairmanship of Shri Durgadass Varma, [illegible] Parishad movement, who has been declared by the Government as absconder. It was said in a Parishad press release that the meeting took place in a jungle near [illegible] about 14 miles from Jammu and was also attended by Shri [illegible] Mahanta, a member of the Parishad Working Committee, who has been touring India ever since the Parishad movement began. He acquainted the meeting with outside reactions.

A press release added: "It was decided to run the movement more effectively [illegible] and some other important decisions were also made. The meeting also considered how to meet Government violence and wrong propaganda."

"The participants from all over Jammu province expressed that people in their respective regions were prepared to make any sacrifices for the agitation," concluded the Parishad press release.

Another press release from the Parishad alleged harassment of the people by police and militia at Chhamb after the incident of late December there in which one man was alleged to have been killed in police firing. It made similar allegations about the behaviour of the police at Nowshera. According to the press release a large number of places have been raided at both these towns in search of Parishad workers. It also said, [illegible] persons offered themselves for arrest at Basohli on December 25.

The authorities at first refused to arrest them but on great insistence by satyagrahis they were all arrested.

PARISHAD AGITATION

[illegible]

DRASTIC CHANGES

[illegible]

DR. MOOKERJEE WANTS INDIA TO WITHDRAW KASHMIR CASE FROM U.N.

By EXPRESS Staff Reporter

DR. S. P. MOOKERJEE on Friday demanded withdrawal of the Kashmir complaint from the United Nations.

The Jan Sangh leader, who was addressing a Press conference in Delhi, reiterated his plea for a round table conference between the representatives of Kashmir Government and Praja Parishad to solve the present dispute.

He also demanded that the Kashmir Constituent Assembly should pass a resolution "finally and irrevocably" acceding to India.

Dr. Mookerji said that the East Bengal situation was fast deteriorating and referred to the Basic Principles Committee report of the Pakistan Constituent Assembly which he said "demonstrated the true character of Pakistan."

He added that the report showed that "people belonging to the minority community in Pakistan will not be allowed to live there as citizens enjoying equal rights."

NO AID TO PARISHAD

Dr. Mookerji denied that his party had sent any financial or other aid to the Praja Parishad agitation though he said it fully sympathised with their movement.

Dr. Mookerji revealed that Sheikh Abdullah in his talks with him had said that he was willing to accede fully to India but Prime Minister Nehru did not allow it.

Dr. Mookerji criticised the Delhi authorities for using tear gas on a "peaceful procession" organised by the Jan Sangh in Delhi on New Year's Eve in observance of Jammu Day.

Later, at a public meeting which was addressed by the Jan Sangh president, a resolution was passed demanding "judicial inquiry" into the matter.

20 SATYAGRAHIS ARRESTED

Jammu Agitation

From Our Own Correspondent

JAMMU, January 2: About 20 Parishad volunteers were taken into custody last evening for taking out an unauthorised procession in Jammu city.

[illegible]

SITUATION IN JAMMU

Sangh To Send Observers

[illegible]

[illegible]

Page. 51

Dr. Mookerjee Against Any Plebiscite In Jammu & Kashmir

Hindusthan Standard

Verdict By State Consembly Demanded

3 Jan.

By A Staff Correspondent

Addressing a Press conference in Delhi on Friday, Dr. Syama Prasad Mookerjee, President, Bhartiya Jan Sangh, expressed himself against holding of a plebiscite in Jammu and Kashmir to decide the State's future relation with India.

THE Constituent Assembly of Jammu and Kashmir, he demanded, should immediately pass a resolution on the State's irrevocable accession to India and thus set at rest any doubts in the mind of the people of Jammu about their future.

Dr. Mookerjee disclosed that during his last visit to Kashmir the Premier of that State had told him that he was prepared to pass a resolution to this effect in the Constituent Assembly but the Prime Minister, Sri Jawaharlal Nehru was opposed to it.

Stressing the need for a peaceful and amicable settlement of the Jammu question, he said that if for any reason Sheikh Abdullah felt that he could not carry the people of Kashmir valley with him at the moment, there was no reason why the people of Jammu and Ladakh should not be given the opportunity to accept in toto the provisions of the Indian Constitution.

Dr. Mookerjee repudiated that the movement in Jammu had been instigated by the Jan Sangh and maintained that it was spontaneous and the responsibility for starting it rested with the accredited representatives of that State.

Referring to the East Bengal situation, he said that the continuance of the present policy of weakness, cowardice and appeasement would intensify popular bitterness and would create a situation for which the entire responsibility would be of the Government.

He condemned the lathi-charge and use of tear gas on a group of demonstrators in Delhi on December 31 last and said that this indicated how a peaceful situation could be turned into something serious by the mistakes of local authorities.

Dr. Mookerjee said that the two resolutions on which the Kanpur session of the Bharatiya Jan Sangh had laid special stress were on Kashmir and East Bengal. In regard to both of these the Government of India had a special responsibility. The Jan Sangh had urged that both these matters should be settled as early as possible.

ڈاکٹر مکرجی کا بھاشن

INTEGRATE JAMMU AND LADAKH WITH INDIA

Dr. Mookerjee's Plea

ADDRESS TO JAN SANGH CONFERENCE

KANPUR, Dec. 29.

"JAMMU and Ladakh must be fully integrated with India and if Sheikh Abdullah is adamant, Kashmir valley may be recognised as a separate state within the Indian Union" said Dr. S. P. Mookerjee, delivering his presidential address to the first all-India session of the Jan Sangh here to-day.

India Needs Psychological Shake-Up

JAN SANGH'S WORK

PARISHAD PROCESSION THRICE TEAR-GASSED

Traffic Being Closely Guarded

Movement To Counteract Parishad Agitation

میں دیکھتا چلا گیا

जम्मू-लद्दाख का भारत के साथ विलय हो

कानपुर में डा० मुखर्जी की घोषणा

जम्मू-लद्दाख पृथक हो

Jammu Agitation 'Ill Advised', Says Deputy Premier

From Our Correspondent

Major Events

1947

August

14 British India partitioned and a new theocratic state of Pakistan created.

15 At the stroke of the midnight hour, India attained freedom.

19 Lord Mountbatten visited Srinagar.

October

15 Justice Mehar Chand Mahajan took over as the Prime Minister of Jammu & Kashmir.

22 Armed tribesmen, supported by the Pakistani army, entered the state territory at several points.

24 Tribal invaders advanced towards Baramulla and Srinagar; state forces' chief, Brigadier Rajinder Singh killed; the only power station at Mohra destroyed by the raiders, plunging the Valley into darkness; the Maharaja sent his Deputy Prime Minister to Delhi with letters seeking assistance.

26 Maharaja Hari Singh signed the Instrument of Accession to India.

27 Governor General Lord Mountbatten accepted the Instrument of Accession; the first batch of Indian troops, 1st Sikh Regiment landed at Srinagar Airport.

30 Maharaja Hari Singh appointed Sheikh Mohammad Abdullah as the Head of the Emergency Administration.

November

17 Birthday of the Praja Parishad.

December

1 Maharaja Hari Singh inaugurated Jammu Radio Station.

1948

January

1 India approached the United Nations Security Council for preventing Pakistan from participating or assisting the invasion of the state.

February

5 Addressing the Security Council, Sheikh Mohammad Abdullah said aggression, not accession, as Prime Minister.

March

5 The Maharaja announced an interim government with Sheikh Mohammad Abdullah as Prime Minister.

June

1 Government Transport Undertaking, the first public sector undertaking, was born.

July

1 Radio Kashmir, Srinagar, inaugurated; Gurez liberated.

4 Brigadier Usman killed while fighting the Pakisatni raiders and troops at Jhangar area of Rajouri district.

11 Tribal attack on Leh repulsed.

November

1 Indian troops crossed 11,578 feet-high Zojila with tanks.

2 Jammu & Kashmir University established.

1949

January

1 Ceasefire took effect from last midnight.

5 The UNCIP passed resolution on holding of plebiscite with certain conditions, including vacation of aggression on a part of J&K, by Pakistan.

April

28 Maharaja Hari Singh left Jammu for Delhi.

June

6 Three persons were nominated by the interim government to represent the state in Parliament to enact the Indian Constitution. They were Sheikh Mohammad Abdullah, Mirza Syeed Massodi, Moti Ram Baigra.

16 Sheikh Mohammad Abdullah, Maulana Masoodi, Mirza Afzal Beg and Moti Ram Baigra took seats in Union Constituent Assembly, Delhi.

20 Maharaja Hari Singh signed a proclamation in Delhi, making Yuvraj Karan Singh as the regent.

October

17 Article 370 of the Union Constitution adopted.

1952

January

15 Students protest against the hoisting of National Conference flag by Sheikh Abdullah, resulting in students' agitation.

February

8 Big demonstration by students outside the then Civil Secretariat in Mubarak Mandi, resulting in police firing and 72-hour curfew in Jammu city. Pt. Prem Nath Dogra and some others arrested.

May

5 First regular Budget for 1952-53 presented to Constituent-cum-Legislative Assembly showing a deficit of Rs. 141.75 lakhs.

June

19 President of India, Dr. Rajendra Prasad visited Jammu and PP delegation by Pt. Prem Dogra submitted a memorandum protesting against the separatist moves of Sheikh-led government.

July

24 Prime Minister Nehru announced the special position for J&K under Delhi agreement; Parliament told Kashmir's accession to India is complete in law and in fact.

28 Sheikh Abdullah declared at Lal Chowk that Kashmir is part and parcel of India.

November

14 The ruling dynasty of Maharajas came to an end.

15 106-year old hereditary rule abolished. Constituent Assembly elected Yuvraj Karan Singh as Sadar-i-Riyasat.

17 Karan Singh took over as Sadar-i-Riyasat.

26 Pt. Prem Nath Dogra along with other *satyagrahis* arrested and agitation launched for removal of barriers between this state and rest of India.

1953

May

11 Dr. S.P. Mookerjee entered the state without permit and was taken to Srinagar in a jeep.

June

23 Dr. Mookerjee died during his detention, shrouded in mystery.

July

7 The PP/BJS agitation was withdrawn on the appeal of Prime Minister Jawaharlal Nehru.

August

8 Sheikh Mohammad Abdullah was deposed and arrested. The same night, Bakshi Ghulam Mohammad took over as Prime Minister of the state.

9 Sadar-i-Riyasat, Yuvraj Karan Singh dismissed the state government; Sheikh Mohammad Abdullah arrested. Bakshi Ghulam Mohammad sworn in as Prime Minister.

1954

February

6 Constituent Assembly ratified accession of the state to India.

May

14 Constitution (application to J&K) order issued by the President under Article 370, extending the Union Constitution to the state with exceptions and modifications.

17 Srinagar linked with Delhi by teleprinter.

December

31 Public Service Recruitment Board established.

1955

January

5 Work on the Banihal Tunnel began.

December

10 Soviet leaders Bulganin and Khruschev arrived in Srinagar and declared that Kashmir question as one of the states of India has been settled by the people of Kashmir.

1956

March

16 China's Chou En-lai said that the people of Kashmir have already expressed their will regarding accession to India.

October

19 The government decided to set up a medical college in Srinagar.

November

17 State Constituent Assembly adopted the constitution, inter alia, declaring state as inseparable part of India.

20 Former British Prime Minister Attlee says, "Kashmir has definitely opted for union with India."

December

22 Vice President, Dr. Radhakrishnan declared open the Jawahar Tunnel.

1957

January

26 State Constitution came into force.

September

2 State Public Service Commission set up in place of the Recruitment Board.

1958

May

1 Jurisdiction of the Comptroller and Auditor General of India extended to J&K.

1959

January

26 J&K High Court brought at par with other High Courts in India.

1960

September

23 Regional Engineering College opened in Srinagar.

November

1 Union Election Commission for the first time conducted an Assembly by-election in the Zadibal constituency.

5 New Civil Secrctariat building at Jammu inaugurated.

1961

April

26 Maharaja Hari Singh passed away in Bombay at the age of 64.

1962

April

27 Soviet delegates to Security Council said 'question of Kashmir as integral part of India has been decided by the people of Kashmir.'

October

20 China launched an attack on Ladakh.

November

21 China declared unilateral ceasefire after occupying 14,500 sq. miles in Ladakh.

1963

March

1 Pakistan illegally transferred 200 sq. miles of state territory, under its illegal control, to China under a boundary agreement.

October

2 Prime Minister, Bakshi Ghulam Mohammad resigned under the Kamraj Plan.

1964

December

3 Decision to extend Articles 356 and 357 of the Union Constitution to J&K announced.

1965

January

19 Communist Party of India set up its state unit in Jammu.

26 National Conference converted into J&K Pradesh Congress Committee with Syed Mir Qasim as its president.

March

30 State constitution amended; Sadar-i-Riyasat and Prime Minister renamed as Governor and Chief Minister, respectively.

August

5 Pakistan pushed armed guerrillas into Kashmir.

September

2 UN Secretary General informed the Security Council that violations began with armed men crossing ceasefire line from the Pakistan side.

3 Security Council demands immediate ceasefire and withdrawal of forces.

4 Indian troops crossed the boundary in the Lahore sector.

5 Indian troops entered Sialkot sector; Security Council the again urged withdrawal of troops to pre-August 5 positions.

11 Ceasefire came into force.

1967

November

6 Ganjendragadkar Commission set up to inquire into the complaints of regional discrimination.

18 Srinagar linked with Delhi by direct dialling system of telephone.

1968

December

3 Ganjendragadkar Commission Report presented to the Chief Minister.

19 Maulvi Mohammad Farooq became the Mirwaiz of Kashmir.

1969

August

9 Panchayat elections held in Kashmir for the first time.

September

5 Separate university for Jammu created.

18 Chief Minister lays the foundation stone of Town Hall in Jammu.

1970

May

1 Government announced 8 per cent reservation for Scheduled Castes, 42 per cent for Backward Classes including 2 per cent for Ladakh in the Services.

9 Foundation stone of Srinagar Doordarshan Kendra laid.

1971

August

24 Article 226 of the Indian Constitution extended to the state.

December

3 Pakistan attacked India; National Emergency declared.

6 India recognised Bangladesh; Pak air force attacked Jammu.

16 Unconditional surrender by Pakistani forces in Bangladesh; India declared unilateral ceasefire on the western front.

1972

February

10 Sheikh Mohammad Abdullah said, "Our quarrel with Government of India is not about accession but about quantum of autonomy."

20 Pt. Prem Nath Dogra passed away due to cancer in Jammu.

July

15 Bakshi Ghulam Mohammad passed away of cardiac arrest.

October

2 Jammu back on the railway map after 25 years.

1973

November

10 Sheikh Mohammad Abdullah reiterated Kashmir's accession to India as final.

1975

February

25 Sheikh Mohammad Abdullah took over as Chief Minister with three Cabinet ministers, M.A. Beg, D.D. Thakur, Sonam Narboo.

July

5 Plebiscite Front dissolved.

March

13 Parliament approved the Indira-Sheikh accord.

June

29 Emergency declared in J&K in line with rest of the country.

1984

April

26 Jagmohan took over as Governor of J&K.

1989

September

14 State BJP vice-president, Tika Lal Taploo gunned down by militants.

December

13 Five militants freed in exchange of Rubaiya Sayeed's release.

1990

January

19 Jagmohan re-appointed as Governor; Dr. Farooq Abdullah resigned in protest; Governor's rule imposed and State Assembly kept in suspended animation.

May

25 Governor Jagmohan resigns.

1992

January

26 BJP president, Murli Manohar Joshi unfurled the tricolour at Lal Chowk.

1994

March

13 Governor Rao inaugurated the Akhnoor Bridge.

September

3 Governor Rao inaugurated the new High Court complex at Janipora, Jammu.

1995

July

20 Nineteen persons killed, 60 injured in Purani Mandi (Jammu) bomb blast.

After Release from the Paraja *Sataygraha* September, 1949

1st row (right to left) Surinder Nathji Ubbott, Ranjit Singhji, Ex zaildar, Vidya Parkashji Padda, M.A., L.L.B., Vakil, Kathua
Standing row: Chaggar Singhji B.A., Baldev Singhji B.A., L.L.B., Vakil, Tasmergarh

Swamiraj and Kripa Ram Kotwal

Dayakrishan Kotwal, Swamiraj and Kripa Ram Kotwal

□

List of *Kamalpushp*

S. No.	Name	Place
1	Mulkh Raj Pargal	JMU
2	Ruder Mani Sangra (Hira Nagar)	At Delhi
3	Durga Dass Verma	JMU
4	Th. Baldev Singh	Hira Nagar
5	Pt. Prem Nath Dogra	JMU
6	Rishi Kumar Koushal	Reasi
7	Lala Roop Chand Nanda	Reasi
8	Manmohan Gupta	Kishtwar
9	Bhikham Chand Magotra	UDH
10	Pt. Rohlu Ram	AKH
11	Mohan Lal Gupta	JMU
12	Shyam Lal Sharma	JMU
13	Prof. Chaman Lal Gupta	JMU
14	Sat Paul Gupta	JMU
15	Th. Ghansara Singh	Birpur
16	Vaid Veshnu Dutt	JMU
17	Yash Pal Puri	JMU
18	Khusi Ram Padha	Basholi
19	Darshna Devi	Hira Nagar
20	Atma Ram Sharma	AKH
21	Dev Raj Gupta	JMU
22	Darshna Gupta	JMU
23	Jawala Parkash Gupta	Hira Nagar

24	Kuldeep Raj Gupta	Rajouri
25	Parkasho Devi	JMU
26	Nain Chand	Jammu Bhore Camp
27	Pt. Krishan Dutt Basotra	Nagrota Gujroo
28	Gian Chand Sharma	JMU
29	Rup Lal Rohmetra	JMU
30	Shiv Lal	Bishna
31	Sant Mehar Singh	JMU
32	Bansi Lal Dogra	AKH
33	Vadiya Chajju Ram	Gharota
34	Ch. Chager Singh	Kathua
35	Amar Nath Gupta	JMU
36	Surinder Aggarwal	JMU
37	Surjeet Kumar Gupta	JMU
38	Th. Seh Dev Singh	AKH
39	Suraj Parkash Kapoor	JMU
40	Bhagwat Saroop	At Delhi
41	Prof. Shakti Sharma	JMU
42	Madhav Lal Nanda	Reasi
43	Bimla Dogra	Sunderbani
44	Gopal Sachar	JMU
45	Dhani Ram Gupta	JMU
46	Daya Krishan Kotwal	Bhadrawa
47	Mahant Baba Durga Dass	Sunderbani
48	Master Sohan Lal Sharma	JMU
49	Shiv Kumar Gupta	JMU
50	Hans Raj Gupta	AKH
51	Tilak Raj Kaila	Now at Dehradun
52	Vinod Kumari Sharma	JMU
53	Om Parkash Wazir	Kathua
54	Tilak Raj Pandoh	JMU

55	Hem Raj Pujari	Katra
56	Badri Nath	Katra
57	Ved Parkash Chauhan	JMU
58	Dheru Ram	Gharota
59	Bishan Dass	Bishnah
60	Nand Lal Bhagat	Mira Sahib
61	Rajinder Singh	AKH
62	Kashi Ram Nai	Gharota
63	Mahant Charajidass	Gharota
64	Dr. Babu Ram Gupta	JMU
65	Sita Ram Gharota	AKH
66	Mangu Ram Verma	Gharota
67	Subder Basant Singh	Gharota
68	Dr. Ved Parkash Gupta	Nowshera
69	Swami Raj Katal	Doda
70	Pt. Sita Ram Sepolia Seri Pandta	Gharota
71	Pt. Sita Ram Doomi	Gharota
72	Shiv Ram Gupta	JMU
73	Ishewar Dass	Gharota
74	Bhagwati Devi	UDH
75	Chunni Lal Sharma	UDH
76	Durga Devi	UDh
77	Vishwa Nath Khajuria	UDH
78	Shanti Devi	UDH
79	Rajinder Lal Gupta	UDH
80	Rama Nand Baria	UDH
81	Papa Dina Nath Gupta	UDH
82	Padda Singh	Gharota
83	Ramesh Sabarwal	JMU
84	Pt. Uma Dutt	Ram Kote
85	Th. Brij Lal	Doda

86	Dharam Veer	JMU
87	Hari Ram Vaid	UDH
88	Hari Bhagat Gudda	UDH
89	Ishar Dass Kalsotra	UDH
90	Dr. Om Parkash Mengi	JMU
91	Susheela Mengi	JMU
92	Sheela Chauhan	JMU
93	Krishan Lal Gupta	JMU
94	Om Parkash Gupta	JMU
95	Ch. Waryan Singh, Samilpur	Bishna
96	Paras Ram Pachialo	UDH
97	Gouri Shanker Prohit	UDH
98	Krishan Lal Zargar	UDH
99	Anil Parihar and Ajeet Parihar	Kishtwar
100	Satish Kumar Bhandari	Doda
101	Devi Ditta Bucha	UDH
102	Som Nath Sharma	Kishtwar
103	Dharamveer Sethi	JMU
104	Chander Kant Sharma	Kishtwar
105	Bhagwan Dass	JMU
106	Satish Mahajan	JMU
107	Ruchir Kumar	Doda
108	Th. Santosh	Doda
109	Kesho Ram	JMU
110	Sant Ram Arora	JMU
111	Ram Lal Arora	JMU
112	Hari Wazir	JMU
113	Mahesh Chander	Basholi
114	Baldev Raj	Gajansoo
115	Sanji Ram Gupta	JMU
116	Jag Mohan Khanna	JMU

117	Pt. Omkar Nath Kak	JMU
118	Tika Lal Taploo	At Delhi
119	Adv. Vidya Parkash Padha	Kathua
120	Th. Dhayan Singh	Billawar
121	Subash Gupta	JMU
122	Narsingh Dass Sharma	JMU
123	Banarasi Dass Gupta	JMU
124	Adv. Onkar Seth	JMU
125	Hans Raj Dogra	JMU
126	Master Jerman Singh, Mandi Andrar	Gura Salathia
127	Shiv Kumar Sharma	JMU
128	Khajur Singh Mandi Garota	Gura Salathia
129	Diwan Chand	JMU
130	Master Dhian Singh	Gura Salathia
131	Anchal Singh, Mandi Rajgarh	Gura Salathia
132	Kripa Ram Kotwal	Bhadrawa
133	Pt. Prem Nath Bhat	JMU
134	Swaran Singh, Mandi Rajgarh	Gura Salathia
135	Trilok Nath	Kishtwar
136	Lala Dina Nath Gandotra	UDH
137	Prabhu Dayal Verma	Gharota
138	Babu Ram Gupta	Gharota
139	Sodagar Mal Gupta	JMU
140	Rajinder Paul Chadha	JMU
141	Bimal Kumar Jain	JMU
142	Yash Bhasin	JMU
143	Sat Pal Grover	JMU
144	Dina Nath Sharma	JMU
145	Joginder Pal Gupta	JMU
146	Surjeet Singh Jamwal	Bhadrawa
147	Madhav Lal Manhas	Doda

148	Om Parkash Sangra	At Delhi
149	Adv. Swami Raj Kotwal	Doda
150	Chandu Lal Chouhan	Doda
151	Bhumi Parkash	Doda
152	Hans Raj, Ram Nagar	UDH
153	Faqir Chand Razdan	Doda
154	Ved Parkash Bajaj	JMU
155	Rȧm Rakha Mal Urf (Koda Shah)	JMU
156	Krishan Lal Bhagi	Bishna
157	Durga Dass Sam	Samba
158	Raghunath Singh Sambyal	Samba
159	Des Raj Salotra	Hira Nagar
160	Nanak Singh Charak	Bishna
161	Krishni Devi	JMU
162	Pt. Durga Dass Dogra	R.S. Pura
163	Pt. Mansa Ram	Ram Kote
164	Prof. Kul Bhushan Mohtra	JMU
165	Ram Saroop Gupta	JMU
166	Lala Shiv Charan Gupta	UDH
167	Mulkh Raj Sharma	JMU
168	Suhag Rani	JMU
169	Chander Parkashi	Kishtwar
170	Mast Nath Yogi	Bhadrawa